The Best of
Freezer Cooking

The Best of
Freezer Cooking

Joan Hood

Hamlyn
London · New York
Sydney · Toronto

ACKNOWLEDGEMENTS

The author is indebted to Audrey Hundy and Vivien Donald for information on wines and spirits in the Drinks chapter, much of which first appeared in *Home & Freezer Digest*. Also to home economists Caroline Ellwood, Sylvie Ireland, Heather Lambert, Margot Mason, Rosemary Wadey for their work in preparing recipes for colour photography. For the photographs themselves, acknowledgements are due as follows:

Photographs on pages 10/11, 14/15, 34/5, 58/9, 66/7, 70/1, 78/9, 90/1, 96/7, 104, 136, 140/1, 144/5, 152/3, 156/7, 164/5, 176/7, 178/9, 180/1, 184/5, 186/7, 198/9, 230/1, 234/5, 238/9, 242/3 Rex Bamber; on pages 260/267 Bob Belton; on pages 22/3, 83, 124 David Davies; on pages 81, 172/3 John Harris; on pages 210/1, 246/7 Tim Hazel; on pages 174/5, 214/5 Howard Kemp; on pages 26/7, 38/9, 42/3, 46/7, 50/1, 62/3, 74/5, 84/5, 86/7, 88, 92/3, 100/1, 108/9, 112/3, 116/7, 120/1, 128/9, 132/3, 148/9, 160/1, 168/9, 182/3, 190/1, 194/5, 202/3, 206/7, 218/9, 222/3, 226/7 David Levin; on pages 30/1, 54/5 Paul Williams.

Published by
The Hamlyn Publishing Group Limited
London . New York . Sydney . Toronto
Astronaut House, Feltham, Middlesex, England
© Copyright British European Associated Publishers Limited 1979
ISBN 0 600 34595 5

Printed in Italy.

CONTENTS

Joan Hood
FREEZER COOK

If you talk to Joan Hood about cookery you'll find that just one word will light up her eyes and spark her enthusiasm.

Flavour.

She will happily discuss flavour, every imaginable flavour, in long and loving detail. How coriander is 'spicy orange' that underlines and complements the sweetness of carrot in a soup. How rhubarb and ginger can be teamed rather than blended to take on new subtlety in a flan. How a marinade of wine and herbs will make a rich and aromatic stew of beef . . .

It's a delight to hear her. Because, to Joan,

flavour is poetry, is science, is art – and is what cookery is all about.

Is she, then, one of those dedicated zealots who think that all would-be cooks should delight in spending hours at the stove? Hardly. She's a busy mother of three teenagers; she runs a large country house and garden; and she combines her journalistic career with that of supervising – by remote control! – a traditional English 'tea room' in the depths of Gloucestershire. She and her husband love to entertain at home, yet she can rarely manage to cook 'on the day'. So the freezer has been part of her life 'since the children were small'.

Properly used, the freezer can, she declares, be the best-of-all aids to a cook who wants to serve the best, and only the best – 'especially when you have to budget your time as well as your housekeeping!'

In this book, Joan's selection of recipes demonstrates her love of good ingredients and fine flavour combined with a practical approach to the cooking and freezing. You'll find many of Joan's recipes are quite short – because, she says, 'I see no reason to complicate what should be an easy and enjoyable activity.'

Each recipe also demonstrates Joan's firm belief that, to justify inclusion in a book such as this, it must not only freeze, but freeze *beautifully.*

'After all', she says, 'you *can* freeze almost everything. But the good freezer cook gradually learns the things that freeze best of all.'

Joan Hood should know. It is she who researched, for *Home & Freezer Digest,* the Will-It-Freeze Dictionary of Foods – a little book that has rapidly become a work of reference for very many first-time freezer owners.

Regular readers of *Home & Freezer Digest* will continue to read Joan's 'Freezer Cook' menus every month. Like the recipes here, they are all thoroughly freezer tested and full of the author's own favourite 'magic ingredient' – flavour.

JILL CHURCHILL, EDITOR OF HOME & FREEZER DIGEST

How to use this book

1. **Look for the 'snowflake'** ❄ sign within every recipe. *This marks the point at which you can freeze it away.* Full 'TO FREEZE' instructions are given below each recipe (look for the *larger* snowflake) followed by 'TO USE' notes that tell how to proceed when taking the dish from the freezer for thawing/reheating/finishing. If you wish to make and serve a recipe without freezing it first – simply ignore the snowflake symbols and follow the recipe.

2. **To make up a menu,** see the suggestions that start on page 273. Each is chosen to give a good blend of flavour, texture, colour and nutritional value. There are, of course, hundreds more permutations within the book. You will find, too, that many of our 'cakes and bakes' are also suitable as puddings; and that many 'starters' would also serve as light luncheon or buffet dishes. On page 250 a chapter on Drinks gives thorough guidance on what might be served both before and during a meal to best complement the food. *Check each recipe for its number of servings:* this always appears at the end of the method. You can then 'double up', if necessary, when catering for a larger number.

3. **For extra expertise,** study our 'chef's techniques' pictures that start on page 260. This chapter is full of 'how to' information on some of the trickier points of food preparation. Elsewhere throughout the book you will find that we have taken care to use 'demonstration pictures' whenever we have felt they would be helpful.

4. **For the best results after freezing** study the chapter on freezer packaging, page 268. Note, too, that we give a recommended 'freezer life' (eg 'use within 3 months') at the end of the 'TO FREEZE' section of each recipe. If you exceed this freezer life, though, your recipe will *not* constitute a health hazard. Our recommendations are intended solely to guide you to enjoying each dish while flavour, texture, colour are still at their best.

USEFUL FACTS AND FIGURES

Spoon measures

BRITISH	AMERICAN	AUSTRALIAN
1 teaspoon	1 teaspoon	1 teaspoon
1 tablespoon	1 tablespoon	1 tablespoon
2 tablespoons	3 tablespoons	2 tablespoons
$3\frac{1}{2}$ tablespoons	4 tablespoons	3 tablespoons
4 tablespoons	5 tablespoons	$3\frac{1}{2}$ tablespoons

An Imperial/American guide to solid and liquid measures

Solid measures

IMPERIAL	AMERICAN
1 lb butter or margarine	2 cups
1 lb flour	4 cups
1 lb granulated or caster sugar	2 cups
1 lb icing sugar	3 cups
8 oz rice	1 cup

Liquid measures

IMPERIAL	AMERICAN
$\frac{1}{4}$ pint	$\frac{2}{3}$ cup
$\frac{1}{2}$ pint	$1\frac{1}{4}$ cups
$\frac{3}{4}$ pint	2 cups
1 pint	$2\frac{1}{2}$ cups
$1\frac{1}{2}$ pints	$3\frac{3}{4}$ cups
2 pints	5 cups ($2\frac{1}{2}$ pints)

NOTE : WHEN MAKING ANY OF THE RECIPES IN THIS BOOK, FOLLOW
ONLY ONE SET OF MEASURES AS THEY ARE NOT INTERCHANGEABLE

NOTES

Spoon measures All spoon measures given
in this book are level unless otherwise stated.

Flour/sugar Plain/all-purpose flour and
granulated sugar are used unless otherwise
stated.

Can, carton and package sizes The Imperial
weight/volume appears on cans, cartons and
packages, together with the exact (usually to
the nearest whole number) metric equivalent.
This practice has been followed throughout
this book wherever it is applicable.

The table below gives recommended equivalents
Oven temperatures

	°C	°F	Gas Mark
Very cool	110 130	225 250	$\frac{1}{4}$ $\frac{1}{2}$
Cool or slow	140 150	275 300	1 2
Warm	170	325	3
Moderate	180	350	4
Moderately hot	190	375	5
Fairly hot	200	400	6
Hot	220	425	7
Very hot	230 240	450 475	8 9

American and Australian Users
American users should remember that the Imperial pint, used in Britain and Australia, is 20 fl oz, and does not equal the American pint, which is 16 fl oz. Therefore the 8-oz measuring cup used in America for both weight and volume equals an American $\frac{1}{2}$ pint only.

Australian users should remember that their metric measures are now used in conjunction with the standard 250 ml measuring cup.
Both American and Australian users should note that their tablespoons differ from each other and from the British tablespoon (see table above for comparisons).

Watercress and Chicken Soup

A delicate and nourishing soup.
Cooked chicken can be used but if you have a rather
mild stock cooking the chicken portion in it will
boost the flavour

4 oz (100 g) raw chicken
2 pints (1·1 litre) chicken stock
2 oz (50 g) watercress
2 spring onions or 1 small leek
salt and pepper

Use a small chicken portion, preferably breast meat, for this soup. Put it into a pan with the chicken stock and simmer gently until the meat is cooked – about 15 minutes. Remove the chicken meat and cut it into small cubes or shred it, discarding skin and bones.

Return the chicken meat to the stock, together with the watercress, roughly chopped, and the onions or leek, peeled or trimmed and cut into thin rings. Season with salt and pepper and simmer the soup gently for 5 minutes. ❄Serve with melba toast. Serves 4.

❄ TO FREEZE. Cool the soup rapidly, then pour into a rigid container, allowing about ½ in. (1cm) head – space for expansion, seal, label and freeze. Use within 2 months.

TO USE. Thaw the soup overnight in the fridge. Turn into a pan, reheat gently, check the seasoning and complete as from ❄ in the recipe above.

Sweetcorn Soup

The crisp salty garnish
contrasts well with the
sweet creaminess of this
corn soup

1 small onion
1 medium-sized potato
1oz (25g) butter
12oz (350g) sweetcorn kernels,
fresh or frozen
¾ pint (425ml) chicken stock
salt and pepper
TO FINISH:
¼ pint (150ml) creamy milk
2-3 rashers streaky bacon

Peel and finely chop the onion. Peel and cut the potato into small dice.

Melt the butter in a pan, then add the chopped onion and diced potato. Turn over in the butter and let them cook without colouring for a minute or two. Add the corn kernels, stirring them into the buttery juices, then pour over the stock which should just cover the vegetables. Season with salt and pepper, cover, and cook until tender – about 20 minutes. Rub the mixture through a sieve or purée in a blender. ❄ Tip into a clean pan and reheat, adding the creamy milk to thin and enrich the soup. Check the seasoning, remembering that the bacon garnish will be salty.

Derind the bacon, then fry or grill until the rashers are crisp; break into small pieces and sprinkle over the soup just before serving. Serves 4.

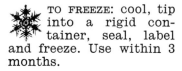 TO FREEZE: cool, tip into a rigid container, seal, label and freeze. Use within 3 months.

TO USE: complete as from ❄ in recipe.

Plum Soup

Fruit soups are most popular in central Europe – in this country we are only beginning to discover what an interesting and pleasant change they can make from other soups

Halve and stone the plums and put them into a pan with the water, sugar and cinnamon. Cook over a gentle heat until the plums are soft and collapsed. Rub them through a sieve and return the purée to the heat. Check to see if it needs a little more sugar though it should be on the sharp side.

Mix the cornflour to a paste with a little cold water. Add this to the sieved plums, stirring all the time until the mixture thickens. Remove from the heat and pour into a basin to cool. ❄ When cold set in fridge to chill well before serving.

Pour the soup into individual bowls and, if liked, top each with a swirl of soured cream. Serves 4.

1lb (450g) red plums
¾ pint (425ml) water
½ teasp. (2.5ml) powdered cinnamon
3oz (75g) sugar
1 tablesp. (15ml) cornflour

❄ TO FREEZE: when cold pour the soup into a rigid container, allowing about ½in. (1cm) headspace for expansion, seal, label and freeze .Use within 2 months.

TO USE: thaw soup overnight in the fridge. Complete as from ❄ in recipe.

Green Pea Soup

The French way to cook tender young peas is to braise them with lettuce and onions. We've used the same method here but with additional stock to make a summer soup of exquisite flavour and sweetness

4 spring onions or 1 small onion
4 lettuce leaves
2 oz (50g) butter
1 lb (450g) fresh shelled or frozen peas
½ teasp. (2.5ml) sugar
salt
1 pint (550ml) water
TO FINISH:
1 oz (25g) butter

Peel and chop the onions. Wash the lettuce leaves. Melt the 2 oz (50g) butter in a saucepan, add the onion and cook gently until soft but not coloured, then add the lettuce, cut into shreds, and the peas. Turn them in the butter until coated, then sprinkle over the sugar and a little salt.

Pour on the water, bring to the boil, reduce the heat, cover the pan and cook gently until the peas are tender. Rub through a sieve or purée in a blender. ❄ Return the soup to the pan and reheat; check the seasoning. Cut the 1 oz (25g) butter into small pieces and add to the hot soup just before serving. Hand melba toast (see right) separately. Serves 4.

❄ TO FREEZE: cool the soup, pour it into a rigid container, leaving about ½ in. (1cm) headspace for expansion, seal, label and freeze. Use within 3 months.

TO USE: put the frozen soup into a pan and complete as from ❄ in recipe.

Toast bread: remove crusts, cut each slice in half horizontally

Lightly rub off loose crumbs from slices

Toast white bread side, till slices curl slightly and brown

Mushroom Broth

'Broth' usually refers to a thin, clear soup obtained by cooking meat or vegetables in water or stock. This one, with its delicate flavour of mushrooms, would make a perfect soup for slimmers

1 stick celery
1 small onion
1 oz (25g) butter
8 oz (225g) mushrooms
1½ pints (825ml) beef stock
salt and pepper

Wash and trim the celery, then cut it into tiny dice. Peel and chop the onion into tiny dice. Melt the butter in a pan and add the diced vegetables; cook over a gentle heat until they are softened but not coloured.

Wipe the mushrooms with a damp piece of muslin (see below) to remove any stray earth. This is all the cleaning cultivated mushrooms should need. Chop them and add to the pan, and cook a further 3 minutes, stirring from time to time. Pour over the stock, bring to the boil, cover the pan and simmer for 30 minutes. Season with salt and pepper. ✳ Serves 6.

✳ TO FREEZE: cool the broth and when cold, pour into a rigid container, leaving ½in. (1cm) headspace for expansion, seal, label and freeze. Use within 2 months.

TO USE: tip the broth into a pan and heat through gently, stirring from time to time, to prevent it catching on the bottom of the pan.

Broccoli Soup

A delicious soup that's quick and easy to make. The broccoli should be cooked very lightly so as to preserve its bright colour and flavour. Serve it with a bowl of grated Parmesan cheese handed round separately

Peel and finely chop the onion. Melt the butter in a pan large enough to take the vegetables and stock. Soften the onion in the butter.

Rinse the fresh broccoli and break into pieces. Add to the pan and turn over in the buttery juices. If using frozen broccoli, let it thaw in the butter, turning it from time to time. Pour on the stock and season lightly. Bring to the boil, cover with a lid, lower the heat and cook gently until tender, about 15 minutes – a little less for the frozen broccoli. Put through a sieve or purée in a blender. ❄Thin down with a little top of the milk or single cream. Check the seasoning and serve piping hot sprinkled with grated Parmesan. Serves 4.

1 small onion
1 oz (25g) butter
1 lb (550g) broccoli, fresh or frozen
1 pint (600ml) chicken stock
salt and pepper
TO FINISH:
grated Parmesan cheese
top of milk or single cream

❄ TO FREEZE: cool, then pack the soup into a rigid container, leaving about ½ in. (1 cm) headspace, seal, label and freeze. Use within 2 months.

TO USE: reheat the soup gently from frozen, stirring from time to time. Complete as from ❄ in recipe.

Summer Soup

A light soup using early summer vegetables – peas, lettuce, carrots, dwarf beans – all briefly cooked in chicken stock to retain their flavour, texture and colour

2 carrots
3 or 4 spring onions or 1 small onion
1 oz (25g) butter
½ teasp. (2.5ml) sugar
2 or 3 lettuce leaves
2 pints (1.1 litre) veal, chicken or vegetable stock
few french beans
handful of shelled peas
salt and pepper
TO FINISH:
finely chopped chives or chervil

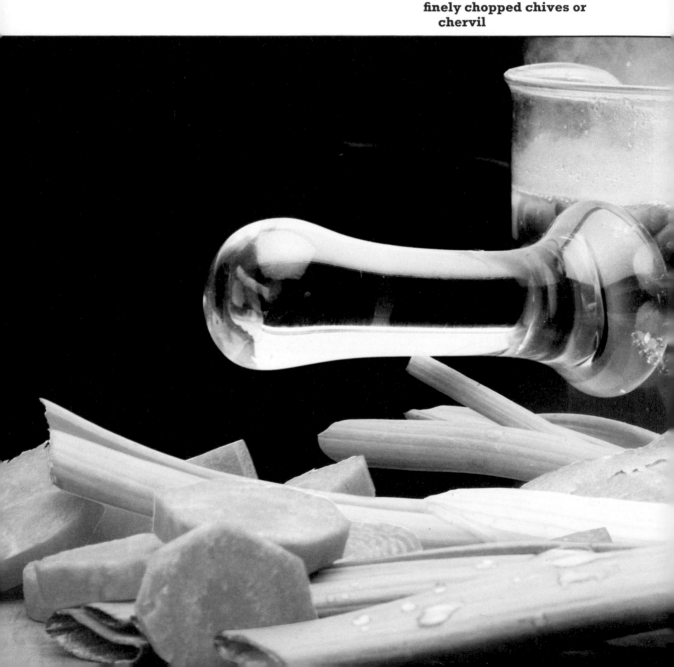

Peel and slice or chop the carrots and onions the same size. Melt the butter in a pan, add the sugar, then the carrots and onions and cook gently for a few minutes until the vegetables are glazed but not browned.

Shred the lettuce leaves and add to the pan. Pour over the stock, bring to the boil, lower the heat, cover the pan and simmer for 10 minutes. Add a few French beans, broken into short lengths, and a handful of shelled peas and cook a further 5-10 minutes depending on the age of the vegetables. They should still retain a slight crunchiness. ❄ Check the seasoning and sprinkle with chopped chives or chervil. Serves 4-6.

❄ TO FREEZE: cool the soup, pour into a rigid container, leaving about ½ in. (1 cm) headspace for expansion, seal, label and freeze. Use within 3 months.

TO USE: turn the soup into a pan and reheat; don't cook it longer than necessary or the vegetables will soften too much. Complete as from ❄ in recipe.

Vichyssoise

A leek soup with mild yet distinctive flavour – at its best when served chilled. Freeze when leeks are in season, ready to serve as a summer soup garnished with cream and chopped chives

1lb (450g) leeks
1 onion
12oz (350g) potatoes
2oz (50g) butter
2 pints (1.1litre) chicken stock
salt and pepper
TO FINISH:
¼ pint (150ml) single cream or top of milk

Cut off the roots and trim the tops of the leeks, leaving on a little of the green. Slit them down from the top about 1 in. (2.5cm) and up end them in a jug or pan of cold water. Left like this for about 30 minutes any grit or dirt settled between the leafy layers will float out. Cut the leeks into chunks after soaking. Peel and chop the onion, peel and dice the potatoes.

Melt the butter in a pan, add the vegetables and turn them in the butter until well coated but not browned. Add the stock, salt and pepper, bring to the boil, then lower the heat and simmer gently until the vegetables are tender – about 30 minutes. Remove the pan from the heat, rub the soup through a sieve or purée in a blender. ❋ Add the single cream or top of the milk, check the seasoning and serve. Or serve chilled, sprinkled with chopped chives. If you've no chives available, use the green tops of spring onions. Serves 6.

❋ TO FREEZE: cool, then pour the soup into a rigid container, leaving about ½ in. (1cm) headspace for expansion, seal, label and freeze. Use within 3 months.

TO USE: tip the soup into a pan and reheat, stirring from time to time. Or thaw until chilled and complete as from ❋ in recipe.

Cucumber and Yogurt Soup

The delicate flavour of the cucumber is sharpened by the addition of natural yogurt stirred in just before serving

Melt the butter in a pan. Peel and finely chop the onion and add it to the butter; cook gently until soft but not coloured. Peel the cucumber and cut into small dice. Add to the pan and cook for 1 minute in the buttery juices. Pour on the stock, season with salt and pepper, cover and cook until the cucumber is tender. Rub the mixture through a sieve or purée in a blender. Check the seasoning and return the purée to the pan. Heat gently.

Blend the cornflour with a little cold water, then stir into the soup. Bring to the boil, stirring, until it thickens slightly. Cook a further 2 minutes, then pour into a basin and leave to cool. When cold put the soup in the fridge to chill.

❋ Stir the mint into the yogurt and just before serving blend it into the soup. Check the seasoning and serve. Serves 4.

❋ TO FREEZE: when cold pour the soup into a rigid container, leaving about $\frac{1}{2}$in. (1cm) headspace for expansion, seal, label and freeze. Use within 3 months.

TO USE: thaw the soup overnight in fridge. Complete as from ❋ in recipe.

1oz (25g) butter
1 small onion
1 large cucumber
$\frac{3}{4}$ pint (425ml) chicken stock
salt and pepper
1 tablesp. (15ml) cornflour
TO FINISH:
2 teasp. (10ml) chopped fresh mint
$\frac{1}{4}$ pint (150ml) natural yogurt

Carrot and Coriander Soup

Eye-catching to look at, this smooth, creamy soup is lightly spiced with crushed coriander seeds; and their faintly orange scent is accentuated by the addition of fresh orange juice

1 lb (450g) carrots
1 medium onion
1½oz (40g) butter
salt and pepper
1 teasp. (5ml) sugar
1 tablesp. (15ml) crushed
coriander seeds
1½ pints (825 ml) stock
½ orange, juice only

TO FINISH:
creamy milk
chopped parsley
croûtons

Peel and slice the carrots. Peel and chop the onion. Melt the butter in a pan and stir in the carrots and onion. Cook gently for 2 or 3 minutes or until the onion is beginning to soften. Season with a little salt and pepper and the sugar. Add the coriander seeds, which can be crushed with a pestle and mortar or ground in a peppermill.

Pour in the stock, bring to the boil, cover, lower the heat and simmer about 15 minutes or until the carrots are tender. Rub the soup through a sieve. Then add the orange juice to the purée.

❋Thin it down with creamy milk and continue heating until piping hot. Sprinkle with chopped parsley and serve with croûtons. Serves 4.

❋ TO FREEZE. Cool the soup. Pour it into rigid containers, seal, label and freeze. Use within 2 months.

TO USE. Tip the soup into a pan and heat gently, stirring from time to time. Complete as from ❋ in recipe.

Chilled Vegetable Soup

A well flavoured soup that's quick and simple to make. If you'd rather serve it hot, garnish with croûtons – tiny cubes of fried bread – instead of the whipped cream

1 small onion
3 sticks celery
8oz (225g) potatoes
8oz (225g) fresh shelled or
frozen peas
1¼ pints (700ml) chicken stock
salt and pepper
TO FINISH:
whipped cream
few chopped chives

Peel and chop the onion. Wash the celery and cut into rough chunks. Peel and cut up the potatoes. Put all the prepared vegetables into a pan together with the peas and pour on the stock. Season lightly with salt and pepper and cook over a gentle heat until the vegetables are tender.

Blend or rub through a sieve to a purée. If using a blender sieve the purée afterwards to remove any stringy pieces of celery that may be left. Set the soup aside to cool. ❄ Check the seasoning and adjust if necessary, cover the soup and chill in the refrigerator. Serve cold garnished with whipped cream to which a few chopped chives have been added. Serves 6.

❄ TO FREEZE: when cold, pour the soup into a rigid container, leaving ½in. (1cm) headspace for expansion, cover, seal, label and freeze. Use within 3 months.

TO USE: thaw soup overnight in the fridge, then complete as from ❄ in recipe.

Sorrel Soup

Sorrel is a perennial herb found growing wild in many places though it can be cultivated quite easily in the garden. It has a pronounced acid taste which gives the soup its distinctive flavour

Wash the sorrel well and pull the leaves off the thick central stalk in the same way as you do for spinach. Peel and cut up the potatoes. Peel and finely chop the onion.

Melt the butter in a pan, add the onion and cook gently until it is beginning to soften. Add the sorrel, stirring now and again until it has collapsed, softened and changed colour. Then add the potatoes, the stock and season with salt and pepper. Bring to the boil, lower the heat and cook gently until the vegetables are soft. Purée in a blender or rub through a sieve. ❄

Return the soup to a clean pan and reheat. Check the seasoning and stir in a little cream if liked. Serves 4.

4oz (100g) sorrel
8oz (225g) potatoes
1 onion
2oz (50g) butter
1 pint (550ml) chicken stock
salt and pepper
cream, optional

❄ TO FREEZE: cool the soup and pour into a rigid container, leaving ½in. (1cm) headspace for expansion, cover, seal, label and freeze. Use within 3 months.

TO USE: thaw the soup overnight or reheat from frozen. Complete as from ❄ in recipe.

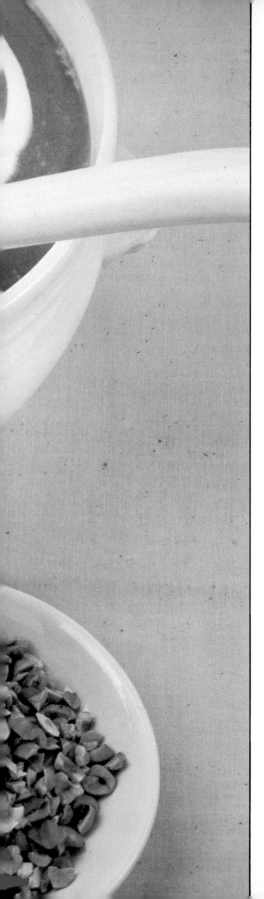

Sprout and Hazelnut Soup

Roasted and chopped hazelnuts add extra flavour and texture contrast to this creamy soup of puréed brussels sprouts

2 lb (900g) brussels sprouts
2oz (50g) butter
1 large onion
1¼ pints (700ml) stock
salt and pepper

TO FINISH:
2oz (50g) hazelnuts
½ pint (300ml) creamy milk
a little double cream

Remove any yellow outer leaves from the sprouts and trim the stalks. Chop the sprouts roughly.

Melt the butter in a pan, peel and finely chop the onion, then add to the pan and cook gently until softened but not coloured. Add the sprouts and turn them in the butter until well coated. Pour on the stock and season with salt and pepper. Bring to the boil, cover, lower the heat and simmer gently for 15 minutes or until the sprouts are tender. Sieve or purée the mixture in a blender.

❋Brown the hazelnuts by roasting in the oven (350 deg. F, 180 deg. C, Gas No. 4) for about 10 minutes. Rub off the skins in a clean cloth and roughly chop the nuts.

Return the soup to the pan. Stir in the milk and heat through until piping hot. Check the seasoning. Turn into a soup tureen, swirl a little cream through it and sprinkle with some of the chopped nuts. The rest of the nuts can be put in a dish and handed separately.

❋ TO FREEZE. Cool and pack the purée in a rigid container, leaving ¼in. (1cm) headspace for expansion. Seal, label and freeze. Use within 3 months.

TO USE. Thaw at room temperature for 2 hours. Complete as from ❋ in recipe.

Curried Parsnip Soup

The parsnips are cooked with curry powder to give a mildly spiced and sweet soup. Try serving it with toasted coconut as a change from croutons

1 medium-sized onion
2oz (50g) butter
1lb (450g) parsnips
1 medium-sized potato
1 teasp. (5ml) curry powder
1 pint (550ml) chicken stock
salt and pepper
TO FINISH:
$\frac{1}{4}$-$\frac{1}{2}$ pint (150-300ml) single cream or creamy milk
toasted coconut

Peel and chop the onion. Melt the butter in a pan, add the onion and cook gently until starting to soften.

Peel the parsnips and the potato and cut them up roughly. Put them into the pan, turning them over in the buttery juices. Sprinkle in the curry powder and stir it into the vegetable mixture. Pour over the stock and season with a little salt and pepper.

Bring to the boil, cover the pan, lower the heat and cook until the vegetables are tender – about 20–30 minutes. Purée in a blender or rub through a sieve. Set the soup aside to cool. ❇ Stir in the cream or creamy milk to thin the soup to the desired consistency. Cover and chill in the refrigerator. Check the seasoning and serve cold sprinkled with a little toasted coconut. Serves 6.

TO FREEZE: when cold pour the soup into a rigid container, leaving $\frac{1}{2}$in. (1cm) headspace for expansion, cover, seal, label and freeze. Use within 1 month.

TO USE: thaw the soup overnight in the fridge, then complete as from ❇ in recipe.

Almond Soup

This soup can be made with freshly skinned and ground almonds if you prefer, though bought ground almonds simplify the making of it. It can be served hot but is even more delicious cold

Put the ground almonds into a saucepan over a gentle heat and, stirring and turning them gently, cook until golden-brown. Take care not to let them burn. Turn into a basin.

Rinse out and dry the pan, put in the butter and melt over a gentle heat. Stir in the flour and cook for 1 minute, then blend in the stock, stirring to make a thin sauce. Stir in the almonds, together with a pinch of sugar and a little salt. Stirring all the time, bring the mixture just to the boil. Check the seasoning, pour into a basin and leave to cool. ❄

Stir in the cream, chill in the fridge, then serve the soup sprinkled with a little grated lemon rind. Serves 6.

5oz (125g) ground almonds
½oz (15g) butter
½oz (15g) flour
1¼ pints (700ml) chicken stock
pinch sugar
salt
TO FINISH:
¼ pint (150ml) single cream
little grated lemon rind

❄ TO FREEZE: when cold pour the soup into a a rigid container, leaving ½in. (1cm) headspace for expansion, cover, seal, label and freeze. Use within 3 months.

TO USE: thaw the soup overnight in fridge, then complete as from ❄ in recipe.

6oz (150g) smoked mackerel
fillets
½ lemon, juice only
6oz (150g) shortcrust pastry
(see page 170)
2 eggs
¼ pint (150ml) single cream or
top milk
freshly ground black pepper

Remove the skin from the mackerel, as well as any remaining bones, and cut the fillets into strips. Sprinkle with lemon juice and leave for 30 minutes.

Roll out the pastry and line an 8-in. (20-cm) flan case with it. Bake blind (400 deg. F, 200 deg. C, Gas no. 6) for 15 minutes (see page 260). Remove foil and beans, or whatever you have used to bake the case "blind", and return the pastry to the oven for a further 5 minutes.

Arrange the mackerel over the base of the flan. Beat together the eggs and cream and season with pepper. Pour over the mackerel. Bake (350 deg. F, 180 deg. C, Gas No. 4) for 25 minutes. ❄ Serves 6.

Smoked Mackerel Quiche

Quiche is a savoury custard flan which originated in the French province of Lorraine. Traditionally made from bread dough, it is now more usually found with a shortcrust pastry base. The main ingredient of the filling gives the quiche its name as in this Smoked Mackerel Quiche

TO FREEZE. When cold open freeze quiche, then pack into a polythene bag, seal, label and return to the freezer. Use within 1 month.

TO USE. Reheat the quiche from frozen (350 deg. F, 180 deg. C, Gas No. 4) for 15 minutes and serve warm, or thaw at room temperature for 2 hours and serve cold.

Spinach and Cottage Cheese Flan

Wholemeal flour gives
the pastry for this flan a
deliciously nutty flavour

1lb (450g) fresh spinach or 8oz
(225g) frozen spinach
4oz (100g) cottage cheese
2 eggs
¼ pint (150ml) single cream or
top of milk
4 tablesp. (60ml) grated
Parmesan cheese
salt and pepper
PASTRY:
6oz (150g) wheatmeal flour
1 teasp. (5ml) baking powder
pinch salt
1½oz (40g) lard
1½oz (40g) margarine
water

First make the pastry. Sieve the flour, baking powder and salt into a basin and tip any bran left in the sieve on to the flour. Rub the fat into the flour until the mixture resembles fine breadcrumbs. Bind with cold water – about 2 tablespoons (30ml) should be sufficient – and lightly knead to a firm dough. Form into a ball, wrap in foil or a polythene bag and chill for 1 hour if possible before rolling out.

Roll out the pastry and line into a loose-bottomed 8-in. (20-cm) diameter flan tin. Bake blind at 375 deg. F, 190 deg. C, Gas no. 5 (line uncooked pastry case with foil or greaseproof paper, weight down with dried beans, pasta or crusts, and bake as given in recipe for about 15 minutes; remove lining and return flan to the oven for a further 5 minutes until it is just coloured and dry).

While the pastry is baking, cook the spinach, drain, pressing it well to remove surplus water. Turn it into a basin and stir in the cottage cheese. Beat the eggs and cream together just sufficiently to mix them, stir in the Parmesan and add this to the spinach mixture. Season with salt and pepper and spoon the filling into the flan case.

Bake the flan in a preheated oven (350 deg. F, 180 deg. C, Gas no. 4) for 30 minutes or until the filling is lightly set. ❄ Remove the flan ring but leave the flan on the flan base and serve on a plate. Serves 4–6.

❄ TO FREEZE: cool the flan, then open freeze, cover it with foil or slip it into a polythene bag, seal, label and return to the freezer. Use within 2 months.

TO USE: remove the wrappings and reheat the flan from frozen (375 deg. F, 190 deg. C, Gas no. 5) for 35 minutes. Complete as from ❄ in recipe.

Leeks à la Grecque

Strictly speaking, à la grecque dishes should be of Greek origin but this is rarely the case. The term refers to a method, used in France, of serving vegetables cooked in wine and oil with herbs and seasonings. As with our recipe for leeks, they are served cold in the cooking liquor

Cut the root ends and most of the green tops off the leeks. Wash the stems in plenty of cold water to remove all the grit.

Put the olive oil, wine, water and seasonings into a pan, bring to the boil, lower the heat and simmer for 2 minutes.

Cut the leeks into 3-in. (7.5-cm) lengths, add to the pan and simmer gently for 5 minutes. Skin, seed and chop the tomatoes and add to the pan. Cook a further 5 minutes or until just tender.

✳Serve as part of a mixed hors d'œuvre or as a first course with French bread. Serves 4.

8 medium-sized leeks
4 tablesp. (60ml) olive oil
6 tablesp. (90ml) white wine
3 tablesp. (45ml) water
1 teasp. (5ml) coriander seeds
1 bay leaf
few parsely stalks
2 tomatoes
salt and pepper

✳ TO FREEZE: cool the leeks rapidly, then pack them into a rigid container, allowing about $\frac{1}{2}$in. (1cm) head-space for expansion, seal, label and freeze. Use within 1 month.

TO USE: thaw the leeks overnight in the fridge. Complete as from ✳ in recipe above.

Individual Onion Flans

Tasty, easy-to-make flans
that are ideal for a first
course or lunch snack. The
Danish blue cheese, with its
pronounced sharp flavour, is
particularly good with the
sweet onion filling

Divide the pastry into four and roll each piece into a round slightly larger than the flan tins. Line the pastry into the flan tins and bake the cases blind (400 deg F, 200 deg C, Gas No. 6) – see page 260 – for 15 minutes.

Peel and slice the onions. Heat the oil in a pan and cook the onions gently until softened but not coloured.

Whisk together the egg, cream or milk and seasoning: go lightly on the salt if the cheese is salty. Sprinkle the base of the flans with the cheese, cut into small pieces or crumbled. Spread over the softened onion, then pour on the seasoned cream. Bake (350 deg F, 180 deg C, Gas No. 4) for 35 minutes or until the flans are set and lightly browned. ✳ Serve hot or cold. Serves 4.

✳ TO FREEZE. Cool flans, then either freeze in the tins or open freeze until hard, tip out of the flan tins and pack into polythene bags or rigid containers, seal, label and return to the freezer. Use within 2 months.

TO USE. Remove wrappings and reheat the flans from frozen (350 deg F, 180 deg C, Gas No. 4) for about 15 minutes or thaw them at room temperature for 2 hours and serve cold.

6 oz (150 g) shortcrust pastry (see page 170)
8 oz (225 g) onions
2 tablesp. (30 ml) oil
1 egg
¼ pint (150 ml) single cream or top of milk
salt and pepper
1½ oz (40 g) Danish blue cheese

made in four 4½ in. (11.5cm) dia flan tins

Chicken Layer Pâté

This liver pâté has a layer of chicken meat running through it. Rich and filling, serve it sliced with a salad for lunch or supper or in smaller portions with toast as a first course

½ pint (300ml) milk
1 small onion
6 peppercorns
1 bay leaf
1 clove garlic
4 oz (100g) streaky bacon
1 lb (450g) chicken livers
2 oz (50g) butter
1 teasp. (5ml) anchovy essence
salt and pepper
1 tablesp. (15ml) flour
10 oz (275g) raw chicken meat

Pour the milk into a small pan, add the onion, peeled and halved, peppercorns, and bay leaf. Bring to the boil, remove the pan from the heat and leave to infuse for 15 minutes.

Remove the papery coating from the garlic clove. Cut the rind off the bacon. Chop the chicken livers roughly, removing any green parts as they would make the mixture bitter. Sauté the livers in a good 1 oz (25g) butter or simmer them for 1 minute in a little salted water, to firm them. Mince the bacon, livers and garlic. Add the anchovy essence and seasoning to taste.

Melt the remaining butter in a pan, stir in the flour to make a roux and cook gently for 1 minute. Gradually stir in the strained milk and cook until thickened and boiling.

Add this to the liver mixture, blending it in thoroughly. Put half the liver mixture into a greased 2-lb (900-g) loaf tin or round earthenware dish. Arrange strips of chicken over it and finish with the rest of the liver mixture.

Cover the tin or dish with foil and place in a roasting pan containing 1 in. (2.5cm) hot water. Cook in preheated oven (325 deg. F, 170 deg. C, Gas no. 3) for about 2½ hours. Remove the foil, cover the pâté with greaseproof paper and a plate. Weight and leave overnight in a cool place to firm. ❊ Serve with French bread, toast, or a salad. Serves 8-10.

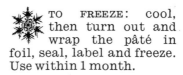 TO FREEZE: cool, then turn out and wrap the pâté in foil, seal, label and freeze. Use within 1 month.

TO USE: thaw the pâté overnight in the fridge. Remove the wrappings before serving as in recipe.

Mackerel with Breton Sauce

The creamy Breton sauce
makes a change from
mayonnaise and is simpler
to make. Use any fresh
herbs you have to hand:
parsley, fennel or chives

Gut the fish, cut off the heads and bone out. Wash and dry them. Roll up from head to tail and put in a large ovenproof dish.

Peel and thinly slice the carrot and onion, then mix with the rest of the ingredients (excluding those for the sauce) together and pour over the fish. Cover and cook (275 deg. F, 140 deg. C, Gas no. 1) for 1½ hours. Leave the fish to cool and marinate in the liquid. ✳

To make the sauce: beat together the egg yolks, mustard and vinegar. Gradually add the melted butter, whisking all the time (see below). The sauce should be of the consistency of mayonnaise. Season with salt and pepper and stir in the parsley. Serve the mackerel from their dish and hand the sauce separately. Serves 8.

✳ TO FREEZE: drain the fish and pack them in a rigid container, seal, label and freeze. Use within 1 month.

TO USE: thaw overnight in fridge, put on serving dish. Complete as from ✳ in recipe.

8 small mackerel
1 carrot
1 onion
¼ pint (150ml) wine vinegar
¼ pint (150ml) water
juice 1 lemon
6 peppercorns
2 bay leaves
few parsley stalks
1 teasp. (5ml) salt
SAUCE:
2 egg yolks
1 tablesp. (15ml) French mustard
1 tablesp. (15ml) tarragon vinegar
3oz (75g) butter, melted
salt and pepper
1 tablesp. (15ml) chopped parsley

Hummus

This is a delicious dip known throughout the Arab world. It is made from a purée of chick peas mixed with tahina – a sesame seed paste obtainable at delicatessen and health food shops. Serve it with Pitta Bread (see recipe on page 262)

4 oz (100g) chick peas
4 tablesp. (60ml) lemon juice
6 tablesp. (90ml) water (optional)
2 cloves garlic
7 tablesp. (105ml) tahina paste
1½ teasp. (7.5ml) salt
TO FINISH:
olive oil
paprika
chopped parsley

Soak the chick peas overnight in water to cover (see right). Drain, put them in a saucepan, cover with cold water, bring to the boil and cook gently until tender. This can take up to 2 hours depending on the quality and age of the chick peas. Test after 1-1½ hours, topping up the pan with more water if necessary. When cooked, drain the chick peas but reserve the liquor.

If you have a blender, the next stage is simple. Put the lemon juice and either the 6 tablespoons (90ml) water or the equivalent of the reserved cooking liquor into the blender, add the chick peas and peeled cloves of garlic and blend until smooth. Add the tahina paste and salt and blend again. The mixture should be like a creamy mayonnaise. If it's too thick, add a little more water. Taste and adjust the seasoning, adding more lemon juice and salt if you think it necessary.

If you haven't a blender, sieve the chick peas, peel and crush the garlic with salt and mix it into the chick peas with the rest of the ingredients, beating well, and tasting and adjusting seasoning as you go. ❋ Spoon the hummus into one or two shallow bowls. Dribble a little olive oil mixed with paprika over the top, sprinkle with chopped parsley if liked. Serve as a dip with Pitta bread (see recipe on page 262). Serves 4–6.

❋ TO FREEZE: spoon the hummus into a rigid container, cover with foil, seal, label and freeze. Use within 1 month.

TO USE: thaw the hummus overnight in the fridge. Complete as from ❋ in recipe.

Chick peas need lots of soaking before cooking to help soften them. So stand them in a bowl of cold water overnight

Smoked Haddock Shells

We give a choice of fillings
– one with tomato and
cheese in the sauce, the
other with fennel, an
aniseed-flavoured herb
that combines beautifully
with the smoky fish. When
the herb is not in season
use the feathery leaves and
a little of the root of
Florence fennel instead

8oz (225g) smoked haddock
milk
SAUCE:
1oz (25g) butter
1oz (25g) flour
1 tablesp. (15ml) freshly
chopped or 2 teasp. (10ml)
dried fennel or 1 tomato, plus
1 tablesp. (15ml) grated
Parmesan
salt and pepper
TOPPING:
1lb (450g) potatoes
1oz (25g) butter
a little milk

Place the haddock in a pan and just cover with milk. Simmer gently for about 10 minutes or until the fish is cooked. Remove the fish and reserve the milk.

To make the sauce, melt the butter in a pan, mix in the flour and cook for 1 minute. Blend in the reserved cooking liquor made up to ½ pint (300 ml) if necessary with extra milk. Bring to the boil, stirring, and simmer for 5 minutes. If making a fennel sauce add the fennel at this stage and omit the tomato and cheese. Season. Skin and flake the haddock, removing any bones, and add to the sauce. If making a tomato and cheese sauce, skin the tomato, halve, remove the seeds and cut the pulp into small pieces. Mix into the fish and sauce, then spoon the mixture into 4 clean scallop shells or individual flameproof mousse dishes.

Peel and cook the potatoes in boiling salted water until soft, then drain and mash them. Add the butter and a little milk and beat well to a smooth purée. Pipe a border of potato round the haddock.

If serving the tomato and cheese sauce, sprinkle Parmesan over the fish and tomato mixture now.

❉Brush the potato border with a little melted butter and put under the grill to brown. Serves 4.

❉ TO FREEZE: leave the fish shells until cold. Open freeze and when hard, wrap in foil, seal, label and return to the freezer. Use within 1 month.

TO USE: remove wrappings and reheat fish shells from frozen (350 deg. F, 180 deg. C, Gas no. 4) for 30 minutes. Complete from ❉ in recipe, browning in the oven not under the grill.

Stuffed Aubergine

The aubergines are cooked, then hollowed out and filled with a savoury mixture of ham, tomatoes, onions and aubergine pulp. Cheese and breadcrumbs are sprinkled over them for the final baking

Cut the unpeeled aubergines in half lengthwise. Run the point of the knife round the edge between the skin and the flesh, score across the surface. Sprinkle the cut surface with salt and leave for 30 minutes to drain.

Heat 2 tablespoons (30ml) oil in a large frying pan. Pat aubergines dry, squeezing them gently to extract any liquid. Cook them over a low heat until soft, about 8 minutes on each side. Drain the aubergines and when cool enough to handle scoop out the pulp with a spoon, leaving the skins intact. Chop the pulp.

Heat the remaining tablespoon (15ml) oil in a pan. Peel and chop the onion and cook gently in the oil until soft. Peel and chop the tomatoes and add these, the chopped aubergines and the ham, cut into small dice, to the pan. Cook for about 10 minutes, stirring from time to time. Stir in the breadcrumbs. Season with salt and pepper.

Put the aubergine skins into a foil container, and spoon the mixture into them. ❈ Sprinkle them with the breadcrumbs and grated cheese, mixed together, and dot with the butter. Place in the oven (350 deg. F, 180 deg. C, Gas No. 4) to heat through for 30 minutes. Serves 4.

2 medium-sized aubergines
3 tablesp. (45ml) oil
1 medium-sized onion
4 tomatoes
2oz (50g) ham
1 tablesp. (15ml) fresh white breadcrumbs
salt and pepper
TO FINISH:
stale breadcrumbs
grated cheese
1oz (25g) butter

❈ TO FREEZE. Cool the stuffed aubergines. Cover the dish with foil, seal, label and freeze. Use within 2 months.

TO USE. Remove the foil covering. Complete as from ❈ in recipe.

Country Pâté

This is a simple country pâté which can be varied by using different herbs and seasonings. If you like a really smooth pâté, sieve or blend the mixture; for a coarser texture chop the meat finely

1 lb (450g) pig's liver
1 lb (450g) belly pork
1 onion
1 clove garlic (optional)
salt and pepper
2 eggs
6oz (150g) streaky bacon
2 tablesp. (30ml) sherry
½ bay leaf

Mince together the liver, pork, peeled onion and the garlic, if used; don't forget to remove its papery coating. Season with salt and pepper and beat in the eggs.

Trim the rinds off the bacon, remove any little bones and stretch the rashers by stroking them out with the back of a knife.

Line a 7½- x 4- x 2-in. (18.5- x 10- x 5-cm) loaf tin or earthenware terrine with the bacon rashers, leaving enough to turn over the top. Spoon in the pâté mixture and pour over the sherry. Put the bay leaf on top and fold over the ends of the rashers. Cover the loaf tin or terrine with foil. Stand the dish in a roasting pan of hot water and

bake (325 deg. F, 170 deg. C, Gas No. 3) for 1½ hours. (Add more hot water if necessary to keep the pan topped up.) Leave covered until cold. ❄ Turn out the pâté and serve sliced, with French bread or toast. Serves 6.

❄ TO FREEZE. Turn out and wrap the pâté in foil, seal, label and freeze, or leave in container and cover with a clean piece of foil, seal, label and freeze. Use within 2 months.

TO USE. Thaw the pâté overnight in the fridge and complete as from ❄ in recipe.

Trim the rinds off the streaky bacon rashers and snip out any little bones. Hold one end of rasher, and with the back of a knife, stroke it out to stretch it

Tomato and Cheese Tart

Tomato and cheese – a rather ordinary filling for a sandwich – takes on an exotic Mediterranean flavour when packed into a pastry case and sprinkled with basil and oil

8oz (225g) tomatoes
salt
6oz (150g) shortcrust pastry
4oz (100g) mature Cheddar cheese
freshly ground black pepper
½ teasp. (2.5ml) dried basil
oil

Skin the tomatoes, if liked, then slice them thickly, salt lightly and leave to drain for 30 minutes.

Roll out pastry and line into an 8-in. (20-cm) or 4×4½in. (4×12cm) diameter loose-bottomed flan tin(s).

Bake blind at 375 deg. F, 190 deg. C, Gas no. 5 (line uncooked pastry case(s) with foil or grease-proof paper, weight down with dried beans, pasta or crusts, and bake as given in recipe for about 15 minutes. Remove the lining and return the flan(s) to the oven for a further 5 minutes until just coloured and dry). Cool.

Slice the cheese and layer it over the bottom of the pastry case(s). Arrange the sliced tomatoes over the cheese. Season with freshly ground black pepper and sprinkle with basil. Dribble a little oil over the top and bake (375 deg. F, 190 deg. C, Gas no. 5) for 25 minutes for the large tart, 15 minutes for the small tarts. ❄ Serves 4.

TO FREEZE: cool, then either freeze tart(s) in the tin(s), slipped into a polythene bag, or open freeze until hard, tip tart(s) out of tin(s) and pack into a polythene bag or rigid container, seal, label and return to freezer. Use within 2 months.

TO USE: remove wrappings and reheat tart from frozen (350 deg. F, 180 deg. C, Gas no. 4) for 20 minutes for the large tart, or 10 minutes for the small ones.

Stuffed Peppers

These spicy rice-filled peppers not only make a gorgeous first course but can be used as a stuffing for a joint: there's a recipe for pepper-stuffed pork on page 103

Cut the tops off the peppers, remove the core and seeds and rinse well. Blanch in pan of boiling water for 2 minutes, then drain.

Pour the rice into a large pan of boiling salted water and cook about 8 minutes or until just tender.

Peel and chop the onion, fry lightly in the oil until softening, add the peeled and chopped tomato and seasonings. Cover and simmer for 10 minutes.

Drain the rice, add the currants and parsley to the onion mixture, then stir this into the rice. Pile this mixture into the peppers. ❄ Stand in an ovenproof dish and sprinkle with stock. Cover loosely with foil and bake (300 deg. F, 150 deg. C, Gas no. 2) for 1 hour. Serves 4.

8 small green peppers
4oz (100g) long grain rice
1 medium-sized onion
1 tablesp. (15ml) oil
1 large tomato
½ teasp. (2.5ml) powdered coriander
¼ teasp. (2.5ml) dried basil
1oz (25g) currants
1 tablesp. (15ml) chopped parsley
4 tablesp. (60ml) stock

❄ TO FREEZE: cool, pack in large rigid container, seal, label and freeze. Use within 2 months.

TO USE: thaw overnight in fridge. Continue as from ❄ in recipe.

Fish Pâtés

All quick and easy to prepare, smoky Kipper . . . devilled Sardine . . . soft, dip-like Taramasalata . . . each would make an attractive first course for a dinner party. They're good, too, spread on canapés to serve with drinks

DEVILLED SARDINE PATE

2 cans sardines
2 oz (50g) butter
1 teasp. (5ml) French mustard
12 capers
black pepper
salt

Drain the sardines, remove the backbones and mash the fish to a smooth paste. Melt the butter and work this into the sardine paste together with the French mustard, salt and black pepper to taste. Fold in the capers ❋ and spoon the pâté into a dish or individual pots. Serve with French bread or toast. Serves 4.

KIPPER PATE

8 oz (225g) kipper fillets
6 fl. oz (180ml) double cream
1 tablesp. (15ml) lemon juice
black pepper
2 tablesp. (30ml) melted butter

Boil in the bag kipper fillets are good for this pâté. Cook as instructed on the pack, then purée the flesh in a blender or rub through a sieve. Stir in the cream, season with lemon juice and black pepper. Stir in the melted butter. Taste and adjust the seasoning if necessary. ❋ Spoon the pâté into a dish or individual pots. Serve as for Devilled Sardine Pâté. Serves 4.

❋ TO FREEZE: spoon the pâté into a rigid container, cover, seal, label and freeze. Use within 1 month.

TO USE: thaw the pâté overnight in the fridge. Complete as from ❋ in recipe.

Take your pick of the pâtés: Devilled Sardine (top left), Taramasalata (top right) and Kipper

TARAMASALATA

4 oz (100g) smoked cod's roe
3 tablesp. (45ml) fresh, white
breadcrumbs
1 tablesp. (15ml) cold water
3 tablesp. (45ml) olive oil
1½ tablesp. (22.5ml) lemon juice
black pepper
2 teasp. (10ml) chopped chives

Skin the roe and pound or blend it to a paste. Soak the breadcrumbs in the water for 2 or 3 minutes then add them, with the water, to the roe and continue to pound or blend until smooth. Work in the oil and lemon juice until the mixture is creamy. Season with freshly ground black pepper and stir in the chopped chives. ✳ Spoon the pâté into a dish or individual pots. Serve as for Devilled Sardine Pâté. Serves 4.

Melon and Grapes in Port

This would make a light, refreshing start to a meal that has a substantial main course. For a more pronounced flavour of port add it just before serving rather than freezing it in the syrup

½ pint (300ml) water
4oz (100g) sugar
4 tablesp. (60ml) port
1 small melon to yield about 12oz (350g) prepared fruit
8oz (225g) grapes

Measure the water into a pan and add the sugar. Heat gently until the sugar has dissolved, stirring from time to time, and bring to the boil; boil for 2 minutes. Set aside to cool. Add the port.

Peel, cut and remove seeds from the melon. Cut the flesh into cubes or, using a potato baller, shape into balls. Halve and deseed the grapes; peel if liked. You could use the tiny seedless ones when in season. Mix the fruits together and pour over the port syrup. ✳ Spoon into individual glass dishes to serve. Serves 4.

✳ TO FREEZE: pack the fruit and syrup into a rigid container, leaving about ½in. (1cm) headspace for expansion, seal, label and freeze. Use within 3 months.

TO USE: thaw the fruit overnight, covered, in the fridge and complete as from ✳ in recipe.

Gnocchi

An Italian savoury dish made with semolina, milk and cheese. The mixture can be rolled into cork shapes, cut into rounds or, as here, in squares. It could make a light lunch served with tomato sauce and a green salad

Beat the egg and set aside.

Pour milk in a pan, season with salt and pepper and bring just to the boil. Tip in the semolina and, stirring all the time, cook until the mixture thickens and leaves the sides of the pan cleanly. Remove from the heat, stir in the 2oz (50g) grated cheese and the beaten egg. Taste and add extra seasoning if necessary.

Turn the mixture into a greased shallow tin 9×9in. (23×23cm) square and spread to an even thickness all over. Leave until cold. Cut into 1½-in. (3.5-cm) squares. ❄ Arrange in a shallow ovenproof dish, flake the butter and dot it all over the gnocchi. Heat in the preheated oven (375 deg. F, 190 deg. C, Gas no. 5) for 15 minutes. A few minutes before removing from the oven, and serving, sprinkle with the remaining 1oz (25g) of grated cheese. Serves 4.

1 egg
1 pint (550ml) milk
salt and pepper
6oz (150g) semolina
2oz (50g) grated Parmesan cheese
TO FINISH:
2oz (50g) butter
1oz (25g) grated Parmesan cheese

❄ TO FREEZE: put the pieces of gnocchi into a foil dish, cover, seal, label and freeze. Use within 3 months.

TO USE: thaw the gnocchi overnight in the fridge and continue as from ❄ in recipe.

Pisto

A Spanish version of the French ratatouille, this is a colourful mixture of sweet peppers, tomatoes, onions and courgettes. They're cooked gently together until tender but still retaining their shape

2 tablesp. (30ml) oil
8oz (225g) onions
1 lb (450g) red or green peppers
1 lb (450g) courgettes
1 lb (450g) tomatoes
salt and pepper

TO FINISH:
1 tablesp. (15ml) chopped parsley

Heat the oil in a heavy-based pan. Peel and slice the onions and cook them gently over a low heat until beginning to soften, about 15 minutes.

Wash the peppers, halve them and remove the core and seeds. Cut them into slices and add to the onions. Add the courgettes, sliced or quartered; there's no need to peel them if they're young and small.

Skin, seed and chop the tomatoes and add these to the pan. Cover and continue to cook a further 15 minutes or until the vegetables are soft but not mushy. If there's a lot of liquid towards the end of the cooking time remove the lid and boil briskly so that it evaporates.

Season with salt and pepper. ❄ Sprinkle with chopped parsley and serve hot or cold. Serves 4.

❄ TO FREEZE. When cold. pack the pisto into a rigid container, seal, label and freeze. Use within 3 months.

TO USE. Tip the pisto into a heavy-based pan and re-heat gently, stirring from time to time; check the seasoning. Or thaw for 3-4 hours at room temperature. Complete as from ❄ in recipe.

Rillettes

Versions of this potted pork are to be found all over France. The meat most often used is belly of pork and it must be cooked very gently so that the meat doesn't brown and harden. After cooking it is drained and shredded (rather than pounded to a paste), seasoned and then covered with the strained fat

1½lb (675kg) belly pork
1 clove garlic
1 sprig thyme or marjoram, or 1 bouquet garni (see page 101)
salt and pepper
2½floz (75ml) water

Peel and chop the garlic. Remove the rind and bones from the meat, then cut into small strips or cubes. Put into an ovenproof dish with the garlic, herbs, salt, pepper and water. Cover and cook in the preheated oven (275 deg. F, 140 deg. C, Gas no. 1) for about 4 hours or until the pork pieces are very soft.

Place a sieve over a bowl and pour the meat and fat into the sieve. Remove the herbs or bouquet garni, then gently press the meat so that as much fat as possible drips through. Leave the fat to set.

Chop or shred the meat. Check the seasoning and add more if necessary, so the meat is well flavoured. Pack into foil or rigid containers. Cover with the fat, from the cooking, melted to a pouring consistency (don't include the meaty juices at the bottom of the fat when you remove it from the bowl). Leave to set. ✳ Serve with toast or crusty French bread. Serves 4.

✳ TO FREEZE: cover rillettes, seal, label and freeze. Use within 1 month.

TO USE: thaw rillettes overnight in the fridge, then complete as from ✳ in recipe.

Courgettes Ragoût

Cooked gently with onion and tomatoes, then served hot or cold, courgettes this way are a delicious starter or an interesting accompaniment to meat

Peel and slice the onion. Heat the oil in a pan and gently cook the onion until soft but not coloured.

Top and tail the courgettes and cut into ½-in. (1-cm) thick slices. Skin and chop the fresh tomatoes or drain and chop the canned ones.

Add the courgettes to the pan, then tomatoes. Season with salt and pepper and cook gently for about 15 minutes or until the vegetables are just tender. ❋ Check the seasoning and serve as a first course or as a vegetable with meat. The ragoût can also be served cold. Serves 4.

1 medium-sized onion
2 tablesp. (30ml) oil
1lb (450g) courgettes
8oz (225g) fresh, or 1 x 14oz (396g) can, tomatoes
salt and pepper

❋ TO FREEZE: cool the ragoût, pack in a rigid container, seal, label and freeze. Use within 3 months.

TO USE: tip the ragoût into a pan and reheat gently, stirring from time to time. Or thaw overnight in fridge and serve cold. Complete as from ❋ in recipe.

Ham and Tongue Mousse

Beaten egg whites are folded through this cold mousse to give it a soufflé texture. The mixture is then poured into a collared dish to come above the rim, so that when set the mousse appears to have risen as a hot soufflé would

Prepare a 1¼-pint (700-ml) soufflé dish by tying a collar of double thickness foil about 2 in. (5 cm) deep round the top. Chop ham, then pound to a purée – an electric blender will do this in seconds. Cut the tongue into small dice and mix the two meats together. Season with pepper.

Put the stock into a small basin. Sprinkle over the gelatine, then stand the basin in a pan of hot water to dissolve. Cool, then gently mix the gelatine into the ham. Whip the cream and fold this in. Whip the egg whites until firm and standing in peaks, then fold them gently but thoroughly through the ham mixture. Turn the mixture into the prepared soufflé dish and leave to set. ❄ Then carefully remove the collar, and garnish the mousse with slices of cucumber. Serves 8.

1lb (450g) cooked ham
6oz (150g) cooked ox tongue
pepper
¼ pint (150ml) stock
½oz (15g) powdered gelatine
½ pint (300ml) double cream
3 egg whites

TO FINISH:
slices of cucumber

❄ TO FREEZE. Open freeze, leaving the collar in position and when hard, slip the mousse into a polythene bag, seal, label and freeze. Use within 1 month.

TO USE. Thaw the mousse overnight in the fridge. Complete as from ❄ in recipe.

Prepare the soufflé dish by fastening a band of double thickness foil with string round the outside to come about 2 in. (5 cm) above the top of the dish. Freeze the mousse with the collar in position. Before serving, remove the foil band by easing it off with a knife

Pissaladière

Traditionally this dish from the Provençal region of France is made on a yeast dough base. Here a crisp pastry case makes a lighter variation. The filling remains the same : onions and tomatoes latticed with anchovy fillets and decorated with black olives

1lb (450g) onions
3 tablesp. (45ml) oil
6oz (150g) shortcrust pastry (see page 170)
1 x 8oz (225g) can tomatoes or 4 small fresh tomatoes
salt and pepper
1 x 1¾oz (50g) can anchovy fillets
few black olives

Peel and thinly slice the onions. Heat the oil in a pan. Add the onions and cook over a gentle heat until soft and translucent – about 20 minutes.

Roll out the pastry and use to line a 7-in. (17.5-cm) diameter flan tin. Prick the base and bake blind at 375 deg. F, 190 deg. C, Gas no. 5 (line uncooked pastry case with foil or grease-proof paper, weight down with dried beans, pasta or crusts, and bake as given in recipe for 10-15 minutes. Remove the lining and return the flan case to the oven for a further 5 minutes until just coloured and dry). See step-by-step photo strip on page 260.

Drain and chop the canned, or skin and chop the fresh, tomatoes. Add to the cooked onion mixture, season with salt – go carefully with this as the anchovies are salty – and pepper and cook for 2 minutes, stirring the tomatoes into the onions. Spoon the filling into the case. Arrange the anchovy fillets in a lattice pattern (see page 160) over the top and decorate with halved and stoned olives. ✻

Bake the flan in preheated oven (375 deg. F, 190 deg. C, Gas no. 5) for about 20 minutes. Serve warm. Serves 4.

✻ TO FREEZE: cool flan, then open freeze until hard. Slip it into a polythene bag, seal, label and return to the freezer. Use within 1 month.

TO USE: uncover the flan and while still frozen, complete as from ✻ in recipe, allowing an additional 10 minutes cooking time.

Individual Cheese Soufflés

The crunchy walnut surround is a good texture contrast to the creamy soufflé. If you don't like walnuts or find the job fiddly, just garnish each soufflé with a slice of pimento-stuffed olive

Tie a paper or foil collar to extend 1in. (2.5cm) above the rim of 8 individual soufflé dishes.

Make up the aspic, according to the instructions on the packet, and add the wine vinegar and seasoning. When cool and just beginning to set beat until frothy and mix in the cheese. Fold in the mayonnaise. Lightly whip the cream and fold this into the mixture. Whip the egg whites until they stand up in peaks and fold them through the mixture.

Spoon into the soufflé dishes, filling them to the top of the collars, and put aside in a cold place to set. ✳ When firm carefully remove the collars, then coat the sides of the soufflés with the finely chopped walnuts. Serves 8.

✳ TO FREEZE: when set open freeze the soufflés until hard, then pack into a rigid container, seal, label and freeze. Use within 2 months.

TO USE: thaw the soufflés in fridge overnight. Complete as from ✳ in recipe.

7½fl oz (220ml) aspic jelly
1 teasp. (5ml) wine vinegar
½ teasp. (2.5ml) salt
½ teasp. (2.5ml) cayenne pepper
6oz (150g) finely grated mature
   Cheddar cheese
2½fl oz (75ml) real mayonnaise
12½fl oz (375ml) double cream
3 egg whites
TO FINISH:
finely chopped walnuts

Asparagus Flan

Used in this way a small quantity of asparagus will serve six. For crisp, well-cooked pastry use a flan tin, preferably one with a removable base, rather than one made of porcelain or china, as metal is a better conductor of heat

8 oz (225g) asparagus, fresh or frozen
8 oz (225g) shortcrust pastry (see page 170)
1 small onion
1 oz (25g) butter
3 eggs
7½ fl oz (225ml) single cream
salt and pepper

Cook the frozen asparagus or if using fresh scrape the asparagus stems with a sharp knife, cutting away any tough 'woody' bits, wash and cook asparagus in boiling water, or steam till tender. Reserve about 10 spears; chop the rest.

Roll out the pastry and line into a loose-bottomed 10-in. (25-cm) diameter flan tin. Prick the base lightly with a fork. Bake blind at 400 deg. F, 200 deg. C, Gas no. 6 (line the pastry case with foil, weight down with dried beans or pasta and bake as given in recipe for 15 minutes; remove the foil lining and return the flan to the oven for a further 5 minutes). Remove the flan and turn

the oven down to 350 deg. F, 180 deg. C, Gas no. 4.

Peel and finely chop the onion and sauté it gently in the butter until soft. Break the eggs into a basin and beat lightly with a fork. Stir in cream, onion, chopped asparagus and season.

Pour the asparagus mixture into the flan case, return the flan to the oven and bake for about 35 minutes or until the custard is set. About 5 minutes before the end of the cooking time arrange the reserved asparagus spears on top of the flan. Serves 6-8.

TO FREEZE: cool the flan, open freeze, then cover with foil, seal, label and return to freezer. Use in 2 months.

TO USE: remove wrappings, then either heat the flan from frozen (375 deg. F, 190 deg. C, Gas no. 5) for 30 minutes or thaw at room temperature for 4 hours and serve cold.

Potted Pigeon

This potted meat can be used as a pâté with toast or French bread or as a sandwich filling. Other meats can be treated in the same way. Remember to season them well. If you've no mace to hand use grated nutmeg instead

8oz (225g) cooked pigeon
4-6oz (100-150g) melted butter
½ teasp. (2.5ml) powdered mace
1 tablesp. (15ml) port, optional
salt and freshly ground pepper

Remove all bones and skin from the pigeon, then mince the flesh and work in the melted butter – start with 4oz (100g) only or put both meat and butter in a liquidizer and mix until well blended. Pigeon can be rather dry but, if it has been cooked in liquid, then it may be sufficiently moist with this amount of butter. If not, add the extra amount.

Season the mixture with the mace, port if using, a little salt and a few grindings of pepper. Taste and adjust the seasoning if necessary. Pack the mixture into small pots. Cover with foil and chill. ❄ Serve with hot toast. Serves 4.

❄ TO FREEZE: seal the pots, label and freeze. Use within 1 month.

TO USE: thaw the pots overnight in the fridge. Remove wrappings and complete as from ❄ in recipe.

Duck and Liver Terrine

Lightly cooked duck is sliced and layered into a dish with a well seasoned liver mixture, then gently steamed to make a rich and luxurious dish. As with all terrines it is eaten cold, cut into slices. The words terrine and pâté have become interchangeable, though strictly speaking a pâté should be baked in a pastry crust and a terrine in a pottery dish

1 frozen duckling, approximately 4lb (1¾kg), thawed
salt
2 shallots or 1 small onion
8oz (225g) calf's or lamb's liver
4oz (125g) bacon
2 tablesp. dripping and juices from duckling
freshly ground black pepper
pinch powdered mace
pinch dried sage

Pat the duckling dry inside and out with absorbent kitchen paper. Prick the skin all over with a fork and sprinkle with salt. Peel and chop the shallots or onions.

Preheat the oven (350 deg. F, 180 deg. C, Gas no. 4). Place the duckling on a grill rack (trivet) in a shallow roasting tin, breast uppermost, and roast on the centre shelf of the preheated oven, allowing 20 minutes per lb (450g).

Cut the liver into small pieces, trim and chop the bacon. Heat the duckling dripping and juices in a pan, add the liver, bacon and shallots or onion and fry gently for 3–4 minutes, stirring until lightly browned. Season with salt, pepper, mace and sage. Put through a mincer or work in a blender. Carve the lightly-cooked duckling into thin slices. Spread a layer of prepared liver mixture over base of a loaf tin, then add a layer of duckling. Continue in layers, finishing with the liver mixture.

Cover the top with a lid or foil and steam for 2 hours. Allow to cool, then chill in fridge. ❄ Slice and garnish with tomatoes and gherkins and serve with toast. Serves 8.

❄ TO FREEZE: when cold, cover the terrine with clean foil, seal, label and freeze. Use within 2 months.

TO USE: thaw the terrine in the fridge overnight. Complete as from ❄ in recipe.

Corn and Cod Pie

Sweetcorn and tomatoes give colour and texture to this tasty fish pie. Serve it with tomato and mushroom kebabs

1 lb (450g) cod fillet, fresh or frozen
milk
water
1½ lb (675g) potatoes
2 oz (50g) butter
5 oz (125g) frozen sweetcorn
2 tomatoes
SAUCE:
1 oz (25g) butter
1 oz (25g) flour
¾ pint (425ml) liquid from poaching fish
salt and pepper

Poach the cod in sufficient milk and water to cover. While it's cooking, peel and boil the potatoes. Strain the cod and set aside the poaching liquid for the sauce. Strain the potatoes, put the pan back on a gentle heat to dry them off, shaking the pan so they don't stick. Rub them through a sieve or Mouli. Stir in a knob of butter and a little hot milk and beat well.

Melt the butter for the sauce in a saucepan, stir in the flour to make a roux and cook for 1 minute without colouring. Blend in the poaching liquid, made up with extra milk if necessary. Cook until the sauce is smooth and thickened, then season to taste. Cook the sweetcorn in boiling water for 5 minutes. Drain and add to the sauce. Stir in the fish. Skin, deseed and chop the tomatoes and add these to the fish mixture. Turn into a 2-pint (1.1-litre) flameproof dish.

Fill the creamed potatoes into a piping bag (an easy way to fill a piping bag is shown on page 266), fitted with a rose nozzle, and pipe creamed potato round the edge of the dish. ❄ Place under a hot grill to brown the potatoes and serve at once with tomato halves and button mushrooms, grilled on kebab sticks or fried. Serve 4.

❄ TO FREEZE: when completely cool, open freeze the pie, cover with foil, seal, label and return to the freezer. Use within 2 months.

TO USE: remove the wrappings and cook the pie from frozen in a moderately hot oven (375 deg. F, 190 deg. C, Gas no. 5) for about 1 hour. Complete as from ❄ in recipe.

Salmon Kulebyaki

This version of the traditional Russian fish pie uses puff pastry rather than the usual yeast dough. It's good hot with melted butter, but even better cold with soured cream and a salad

12oz (350g) fresh salmon
salt and pepper
1 bay leaf
3oz (75g) long grain rice
2oz (50g) butter
lemon juice
1 small onion
4oz (100g) button mushrooms
2 hard-boiled eggs
1 x 13oz (368g) packet frozen or homemade puff pastry (see recipe on page 264)
1 egg
TO FINISH:
2oz (50g) butter or ½ pint (300ml) soured cream

Poach salmon in water just to cover, seasoned with salt, pepper and the bay leaf, until cooked – about 10 minutes. Remove the salmon and set aside to cool. Remove the bay leaf, make up the fish liquor to 1½ pints (825ml) with water, bring to the boil and cook the rice in it for about 10 minutes. Drain the rice and stir in the flaked salmon and 1 oz (25g) butter. Season with salt and pepper and lemon juice. Set aside.

Peel and finely chop the onion, wipe and slice the mushrooms. Melt the other 1 oz (25g) butter in a pan and soften the onion in it. Add the mushrooms and fry for 3 minutes. Remove the pan from heat and stir in chopped hard-boiled eggs. Season with salt and pepper to taste. Set aside.

Roll out the pastry to a rectangle about 14 x 10 in. (35 x 25cm). Trim the edges. Put half the rice mixture down the centre of the pastry, Spoon the mushroom mixture on top. Cover with the rest of the rice mixture.

Brush the pastry edges with beaten egg. Fold each side of the pastry over the filling to meet in the centre, seal and pinch the edges together. Turn the slice over carefully so that the sealed edge is underneath. Cut leaves or other shapes from the pastry trimmings, brush with beaten egg and use to decorate the slice. ❋ Place it on a wetted baking sheet. Brush the top with beaten egg, and make 3 or 4 slits in the top. Bake in preheated oven (425 deg. F, 220 deg. C, Gas no. 7) for about 40 minutes or until puffed and golden.

Either melt butter and pour through the slits in the top of the slice or serve with soured cream handed separately. Serves 4.

❋ TO FREEZE: open freeze the slice and when hard, wrap completely in foil, and return to the freezer. Use within 1 month.

TO USE: thaw the slice for 3 - 4 hours at room temperature. Remove the foil and complete as from ❋ in recipe.

Seafood Vol-au-vent

A sumptuous dish of mixed shellfish folded into a sauce aurore: a creamy sauce flavoured and coloured with tomato purée. Crisp, buttery layers of puff pastry make the light-as-air pastry case

If you have made your own puff pastry, roll it and then cut out the vol-au-vent shape (see page 264). ❋ Brush with beaten egg.

Bake vol-au-vent case in preheated oven (450 deg. F, 230 deg. C, Gas no. 8) for 25 minutes. Remove any uncooked pastry in the case and return the vol-au-vent to the oven to dry out for about 5 minutes. If using frozen pastry, shape and bake it on the day you are serving the vol-au-vent.

To make the sauce, beat the egg yolk and cream in a basin. Melt the butter in a pan, add the flour and stir the two together to make a roux, cooking for 2 minutes without letting it colour. Heat the milk in a separate pan until hot. Remove the roux from the heat, pour the hot milk on to it, beating well with a spoon or wire whisk. Season with salt and pepper. Return the pan to the heat and bring slowly to the boil, stirring all the time. Pour a little of the sauce on to the egg yolks and cream, beat well and then pour on to the rest of the sauce, beating all the time. Return the pan to the heat and bring slowly to simmering point, stirring. Check the seasoning, beat in the tomato purée, using sufficient to turn the sauce a delicate pink. Cover the sauce with wetted greaseproof paper so that a skin doesn't form. Keep warm.

Poach the white fish in a little salted water, remove and add the slightly thawed shellfish; simmer gently for 5-10 minutes. Wipe the mushrooms and sauté in a little butter. Flake the white fish into the sauce, drain the shellfish and add them to the sauce with the mushrooms; check the seasoning. ❋ ❋ Pile seafood mixture into the vol-au-vent case and serve. Serves 4.

❋ TO FREEZE: if using homemade pastry, open freeze the uncooked vol-au-vent on a piece of card or other firm base, wrap in foil when hard, seal, label and return to the freezer. Use within 6 months. Spoon the cooled sauce into a rigid container, leaving ½ in. (1cm) headspace for expansion, seal, label and freeze. Use within 2 months.

1lb (450g) homemade puff pastry (see recipe on page 264) or 2 x 13oz (368g) packets frozen puff pastry

FILLING:
6-8oz (150-225g) frozen fillets of white fish (halibut, haddock, cod, etc.)
8oz (225g) frozen shellfish (prawns or scallops or mussels or cockles or a mixture of any of these)
4oz (100g) mushrooms
butter

SAUCE:
1 egg yolk
¼ pint (150ml) single cream
1½oz (40g) butter
1½oz (40g) flour
¾ pint (425ml) milk
salt and pepper
2 teasp. (10ml) tomato purée

TO USE: thaw the sauce overnight in the fridge, put into the top of a double boiler or in a basin over a pan of boiling water and heat, stirring from time to time, for about 30 minutes. Bake the homemade pastry case from frozen in a preheated oven as in recipe above but allow an extra 5-10 minutes baking time. Or thaw frozen pastry, roll out, shape and bake as in recipe. Complete as from ❋ and ❋ ❋ in recipe.

To prepare fresh cooked crab, first twist off the legs and remove the big claws

Crack the claws, using a heavy weight or nutcrackers

Remove body section from the back shell by pushing up and outwards with your thumbs

Crab Mousse

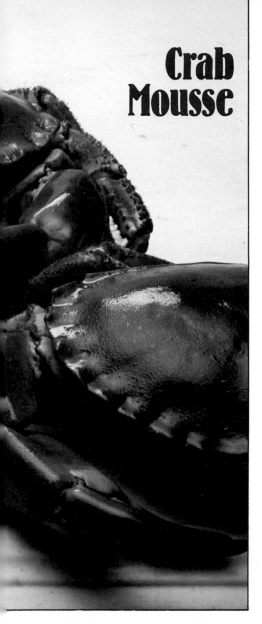

There's plenty of flavour in the brown meat so use it as well as the white for this mousse. It can be served with brown bread and butter as a first course or with salad and new potatoes as a main course

2 tablesp. (30ml) lemon juice
1 tablesp. (15ml) water
½ oz (15g) gelatine
¼ pint (150ml) mayonnaise
10 oz (275g) prepared crab meat, fresh (see below) or frozen
¼ teasp. (1.25ml) paprika
salt
2 tablesp. (30ml) double cream

TO GARNISH:
cucumber slices
tomato quarters

Put the lemon juice and water into a small basin, and sprinkle the gelatine over the top. Stand the basin in a pan of water and heat gently until the gelatine has dissolved completely.

Spoon the mayonnaise into a basin, stir in the gelatine liquid and the crab meat. Season with paprika and a little salt. Lightly whip the cream, a fork will do the job adequately for this small amount. Fold it into the crab mixture and turn into a 1-pint (550-ml) mould.❋Place in the fridge to set. When firm, turn out the mousse on to a serving dish and garnish with cucumber or tomato. Serve with brown bread and butter. Serves 4-6.

❋TO FREEZE: cover the container (do not use a glass mould which could shatter during freezing) with foil, seal, label and freeze. Use within 1 month.

TO USE: thaw the mousse overnight in fridge. Complete as from ❋ in recipe.

With a skewer lever out the stomach bag attached to the shell in the head

Using your fingers, pull away the white fleshy 'dead man's fingers' from the body section

Extract white meat from claws and legs and mix with brown body meat in a bowl

Goujons of Plaice

Crisp, golden strips of plaice served with a piquant sauce or dip make a simple yet attractive start to a meal. Or they make quick tasty tit-bits to hand round hot with drinks at a party

1½ lb (675g) plaice fillets
flour
salt and pepper
2 eggs
fine white breadcrumbs

Cut the plaice into narrow ribbon-like strips about 3 x ½ in. (7.5 x 1cm).

Have ready three shallow dishes. In one put flour seasoned with salt and freshly ground black pepper. In another the eggs, beaten together, and in the third fresh white breadcrumbs,

Dip the plaice strips in the flour, then in the egg and finally toss them in the breadcrumbs until evenly coated.

Lift each strip up, give it a twist and put it into a frying basket in hot deep fat (375 deg. F, 180 deg. C) for about 3 minutes or until golden-brown and crisp. Drain the strips on absorbent paper.

❋Serve with Sauce Tartare or Paprika Dip. Serves 4-6.

TO FREEZE. Cool the strips, spread them on a baking tray and open freeze. When hard, pack them into a rigid container or polythene bag, seal, label and return to the freezer. Use within 1 month.

TO USE. Spread the frozen goujons on a baking tray and reheat (375 deg. F, 190 deg. C, Gas No. 5) for 25 minutes or until heated through. Complete as from ❋ in recipe.

SAUCE TARTARE: add chopped chives to mayonnaise.

PAPRIKA DIP: blend together ¼ pint (150 ml) soured cream, 1 button onion, peeled and finely chopped, 2 teasp. (10 ml) lemon juice, salt and ½ teasp. (2.5 ml) paprika pepper.

Prawn Creole

Based on the traditional American creole sauce of onions, tomatoes and peppers, this full flavoured version would be good with white fish too

Heat the oil in a pan. Peel and chop the onion finely; trim, wash and dice the celery. Deseed the pepper and chop finely. Remove the papery coating from the garlic and crush. Tip all into the pan and fry gently for 5 minutes.

Peel and deseed the fresh tomatoes and chop, or drain canned ones (reserving the juice if using) and chop them. Add to the pan with the stock or tomato juice, salt and pepper and bay leaf. Cover and cook for 20 minutes.

❋ Thaw the prawns, drain them and pat dry. Add to the sauce and heat through. Serve with rice and a green salad. Serves 4.

TO FREEZE: pack the sauce into a rigid container, seal, label and freeze. Use within 1 month.

TO USE: tip the sauce into a large pan and reheat gently. Complete as from ❋ in recipe.

1 tablesp. (15ml) oil
1 small onion
1 stick celery
1 small green pepper
1 clove garlic
1lb (450g) fresh or 1 x 14oz (396g) can tomatoes
½ pint (300ml) stock or tomato juice, or the drained juice from canned tomatoes, made up to ½ pint (300ml) with water, if necessary
salt and pepper
1 bay leaf
1lb (450g) frozen prawns

Plaice with Mushrooms and Prawns

8 plaice fillets, about 4 oz (100g) each
3 oz (75g) mushrooms
¾ oz (22g) butter
2 oz (50g) shelled prawns
¾ oz (22g) plain flour
4 tablesp. (60ml) single cream
salt and pepper

Plaice stuffed with mushrooms and garnished with prawns and new potatoes make a light dish for summer entertaining. Serve with baby carrots or a green salad

FOR POACHING:
1 carrot
1 onion
1 bay leaf
7½ fl oz (225ml) dry white wine
¼ pint (150ml) water

SAUCE:
½ oz (15g) butter
½ oz (15g) flour
¼ pint (150ml) creamy milk

TO FINISH:
1 heaped tablesp. (15ml) fresh
   white breadcrumbs
2 teasp. (10ml) grated Parmesan
   cheese
whole prawns
baby new potatoes
chopped parsley

Skin, wash and dry the plaice fillets. Wipe and finely chop the mushrooms. Melt the butter in a pan, add the mushrooms and cook for 2 minutes, roughly chop the shelled prawns and add to the pan. Sprinkle in the flour and cook for 1 minute. Add the cream, bring to the boil and cook until thickened; season.

Lay the fillets, skinned side up, on a board; season with salt and pepper. Divide the mushroom mixture between the fillets and roll up.

Peel and slice the carrot and onion, put them in an ovenproof dish with the bay leaf and season with salt and pepper. Arrange the rolled fillets on top. Pour over the wine and about ¼ pint (150ml) water. Cover with buttered greaseproof paper and cook in the oven (375 deg. F, 190 deg. C, Gas no. 5) for 15 minutes.

Remove the dish from the oven, drain the fillets and arrange them round the outer edge of a flameproof serving dish. Keep warm. Strain the poaching liquor into a pan, boil until it is reduced to about ¼ pint (150ml) and reserve.

Melt the butter for the sauce in a pan, stir in the flour and cook for 1 minute. Gradually stir in the reserved liquor and the milk. Cook gently until the sauce thickens. Check the seasoning and pour the sauce over the fish. ✳

Mix the breadcrumbs with the cheese and sprinkle on top of the fish, put the dish under a hot grill to brown. Garnish with whole prawns, and heap baby new potatoes in the centre; sprinkle with parsley. Serves 4.

✳ TO FREEZE: pack the fillets into a rigid container and coat with the sauce. Cool, cover, seal, label and freeze. Use within 1 month.

TO USE: thaw the fish overnight in the fridge. Arrange in an ovenproof serving dish and complete recipe, reheating in the oven (375 deg. F, 190 deg. C, Gas no. 5), not under the grill, for 25 minutes.

Plaice Florentine

A classic dish this, in which
the fish is gently poached
in wine then set on a bed
of spinach and topped with
a creamy cheese sauce

8 plaice fillets
¼ pint (150ml) dry white wine
salt and pepper
1lb (450g) fresh or 8oz (225g)
frozen spinach
SAUCE:
1oz (25g) butter
1oz (25g) flour
about ¼ pint (150ml) creamy
milk
2oz (50g) grated Cheddar
cheese

Skin the plaice fillets, roll them up and arrange in a shallow pan. Pour over the wine and season with salt and pepper. Cover and cook over a gentle heat for about 10 minutes or until just tender. Lift out the fish and keep warm; strain the liquor and reserve.

Cook fresh spinach in boiling salted water for about 4 minutes or thaw frozen spinach and re-heat in a pan, about 2 minutes. Drain thoroughly and season with salt and pepper.

Put the spinach in the base of a buttered oven-proof dish. Arrange the fish on top.

To make the sauce: melt the butter in a sauce-pan, stir in the flour and cook for about 1 minute. Gradually stir in the reserved liquor, made up to ½ pint (300ml) with milk, and heat until the sauce thickens. Remove the pan from the heat and stir in the cheese. Adjust the seasoning, then spoon the sauce over the fish.

❋ Serve with new potatoes and buttered carrots. Serves 4.

❋ TO FREEZE: cool the fish dish quickly, cover, seal, label and freeze. Use within 1 month.

TO USE: thaw 8 hours in fridge. Reheat (400 deg. F, 200 deg. C, Gas no. 6) for about 25 minutes. Continue as from ❋ in recipe.

Scalloped Fish

It's not essential to bake
these in scallop shells but
when turned out their
shape and fluted decoration
looks most attractive

Poach the haddock in sufficient milk and water
to cover for about 10 minutes. If using scallops
poach these at the same time. Drain and reserve
½ pint (300ml) of the cooking liquid for the sauce.

Clean and slice the mushrooms. Melt the butter
in a small pan and sauté the mushrooms for 1
minute.

To make the sauce, melt the butter in a pan,
stir in the flour and cook this roux a minute.
Blend in the reserved liquid made up with extra
milk if necessary. Cook until the sauce is smooth
and thickened. Season to taste with salt and
pepper. Flake the fish and stir into the sauce,
together with the scallops or prawns and the
mushrooms. Cool.

Roll out the pastry and use to line 6 scallop
shells. As a rough guide to the size and shape
cut round an upturned shell. If you can't get
hold of scallop shells, this amount of mixture will
fill 6 × 4½-in. (11-cm) diameter foil dishes. Divide
the filling between the shells or dishes.

Roll out the remaining pastry and cut out lids.
Dampen the edges, place over the filling and seal.

❋Brush with beaten egg and bake in preheated
oven (375 deg. F, 190 deg. C, Gas no. 5) for about
25 minutes or until the pastry is set and golden.
Remove from shells for serving and turn upside
down to show the shell ridging on the pastry.
Serves 6.

8oz (200g) haddock fillet
4oz (100g) scallops or peeled
  prawns
2oz (50g) button mushrooms
1oz (25g) butter
12oz (350g) shortcrust pastry
  (see page 170)
SAUCE:
½oz (15g) butter
½oz (15g) flour
½ pint (300ml) liquid used for
  poaching the fish
salt and pepper

❋TO FREEZE: open
freeze the shells and
when hard cover
with foil, seal, label and
return to freezer. Use
within 1 month.

TO USE: remove the covers
and complete as from ❋
in recipe, allowing an
extra 10 minutes cooking
time.

Trout with Orange

A sharp fresh sauce of oranges and lemon is particularly good with the delicately flavoured flesh of the trout

4 trout (6-8 oz (150-200g) each)
1 small onion
1 oz (25g) butter
2 oz (50g) mushrooms
2 tablesp. (30ml) chopped
fresh parsley
6 tablesp. (90ml) white
breadcrumbs
1 egg
seasoned flour
2 oz (50g) butter for frying trout
SAUCE:
2 oranges, juice only
½ lemon, juice only
TO FINISH:
1 orange
1 oz (25g) butter
caster sugar

Remove the heads from the trout and vandyke the tails. Split, gut and bone them (see page 266). Set aside any roes.

To make the stuffing: peel and chop a small onion and fry it gently in 1 oz (25g) butter to soften; add the mushrooms, cleaned and chopped, and cook for 1 minute. Cut the reserved roes, if any, into small pieces and add to the pan, cook for 1 minute to firm them. Remove the pan from the heat and stir in the parsley and breadcrumbs. Bind with a beaten egg and use to stuff trout. Secure with small skewers or cocktail sticks.

Roll the stuffed fish in flour seasoned with salt

Fry orange slices for 1 minute in butter, turn, sprinkle with sugar and cook briskly till juices are a sticky caramel

and pepper. Melt the remaining butter in a frying pan, put the fish in and cook until golden-brown for 3-5 minutes on each side. Remove them ❋ and place on a serving dish; keep warm.

Put the squeezed juice of the oranges and half lemon into the pan, stirring it round, bring to the boil and boil for a minute or two to reduce the liquid and concentrate the flavour.   ❋ ❋ Slice orange and fry 1 minute in the butter; sprinkle with a little caster sugar and continue cooking until it caramelizes (see left).   Dish up the trout, pour over the sauce and put a slice of orange on each fish. Serves 4.

❋ TO FREEZE: place the trout in a foil tray and cool. When cold, cover, seal, label and freeze. Pour the sauce separately into a small rigid container, seal, label and freeze. Use both within 1 month.

TO USE: thaw the fish and sauce overnight in the fridge. Pour the sauce over the fish and reheat (325 deg. F, 170 deg. C, Gas no. 3) for about 20 minutes. Complete as from ❋ and ❋ ❋ in recipe.

Smoked Fish Pie

Spinach and smoked fish
are layered with lasagne
and tomatoes, then topped
with a cheese sauce to
make a colourful, filling
and tasty fish pie

1¼lb (550g) smoked haddock
2 x 8oz (225g) packets frozen
spinach
1 x 14oz (396g) can tomatoes
2oz (50g) butter
3oz (75g) flour
1 pint (550ml) milk
salt and pepper
6oz (150g) grated mature
Cheddar cheese
4-6oz (100-150g) Barilla lasagne

Poach the haddock in water, just to cover, for about 10 minutes. Remove haddock and set aside to cool, then flake it into a basin.

Place the frozen spinach in a pan over a gentle heat and leave to thaw, stirring from time to time.

Drain the tomatoes and chop them up roughly.

Melt the butter in a pan, stir in the flour and cook for a minute. Gradually stir in the milk and cook until the sauce is smooth and thick. Season with salt and pepper. Measure a ¼ pint (150ml) of the sauce and stir it into the haddock. Add 5oz (125g) grated cheese to the rest of the sauce, stirring it in until it has melted, then check the seasoning.

Arrange a layer of lasagne in a dish measuring about 9½×9½×2in. (24×24×5cm). Cover this with the tomatoes, season lightly with salt and pepper. Spread the haddock on top, then the spinach, well drained. Add another layer of lasagne and top with the cheese sauce. Sprinkle with the remaining grated cheese. ❋ Bake in preheated oven (375 deg. F, 190 deg. C, Gas no. 5) for about 30 minutes or until bubbling hot and golden. Serves 4-6.

TO FREEZE: when cold cover the pie, seal, label and freeze. Use within 1 month.

TO USE: thaw the pie overnight in the fridge. Remove the cover and complete as from ❋ in recipe, allowing an extra 15 minutes cooking time.

Savoury Baked Fish

The spicy tomato sauce – add a crushed clove of garlic as well if you like – goes well with the blandness of the fish. You could double the quantity of sauce and freeze half separately to serve with chops or steaks

Heat the oil in a pan. Peel and finely chop the onion, then add to the pan and cook gently until soft but not coloured. Add the tomatoes, including their juice, and break them down a little with a spoon. Remove any leaves and rust marks from the stick of celery, wash and chop it finely and add to the pan, together with the capers and basil. Season lightly with salt and pepper and simmer for about 5 minutes. ❄

Arrange the portions of frozen fish in a buttered shallow ovenproof dish and pour over the sauce. Cover and cook (375 deg. F, 190 deg. C, Gas no. 5) for about 25 minutes. Check the seasoning and serve. Serves 4.

2 tablesp. (30ml) oil
1 medium-sized onion
1 x 8oz (225g) can tomatoes
1 stick celery
1 tablesp. (15ml) drained capers
½ teasp. (2.5ml) dried basil
salt and pepper
4 frozen haddock or other firm white fish portions

❄ TO FREEZE: cool the sauce and pack in a rigid container, leaving about ½in. (1cm) headspace, seal, label and freeze. Use within 1 month.

TO USE: thaw the sauce in the fridge overnight. Remove the fish portions from the freezer and complete as from ❄ in recipe.

MEAT

Apricot Stuffed Lamb

Apricots and walnuts are combined to make an interesting and tasty stuffing for a boned shoulder of lamb

4lb (1.80kg) shoulder of lamb, boned (see page 260)
1oz (25g) dripping
1 onion
1 carrot
1 bay leaf
½ pint (300ml) stock

STUFFING:
2oz (50g) fresh breadcrumbs
pinch thyme
1oz (25g) chopped walnuts
1 small onion
oil
1 x 7oz (175g) can apricots or 4oz dried apricots, soaked overnight in cold water
salt and pepper
1 egg

Prepare the stuffing first. Place the breadcrumbs, thyme and walnuts in a basin. Sauté the onion gently in a little oil until soft but not coloured. Add to the breadcrumbs. Drain and roughly chop the apricots and stir them into the stuffing mixture. Season with salt and pepper and bind with a little beaten egg to make a moist stuffing.

Set the oven (350 deg. F, 180 deg. C, Gas No. 4). Season the lamb with salt and pepper and spoon the stuffing into it. Tie the joint into a long shape.

Heat the dripping in a flameproof casserole and brown the meat all over. Add the peeled and sliced onion and carrot and bay leaf. Pour over the stock. Bring to the boil, cover and cook in the oven for 1½ hours. ❋Take the joint from the casserole, place on a serving dish and remove the string. Sieve the sauce and pour over the lamb. Serves 6.

❋ TO FREEZE. Transfer the joint to a plate and cool quickly. When the joint is cold, wrap in foil, seal, label and freeze. Remove the bay leaf, sieve the sauce and when cold, pour it into a rigid container, leaving ½in. (1cm) headspace for expansion, seal, label and freeze. Use within 2 months.

TO USE. Thaw the joint in the fridge for 24 hours. Thaw the sauce overnight. Remove the string from the joint, place it in a casserole, pour over the sauce and cook (350 deg. F, 180 deg. C, Gas No. 4) for 1 hour. Place the lamb on a serving dish and pour over the gravy.

Burgundy Beef Stew

There are many versions of this beef and wine dish from France. In some the meat is cooked as a joint, in others cubed. We cube ours so it's quicker to thaw, easier to portion. But whichever way it's cut, long slow cooking produces a rich aromatic stew. Serve it with the traditional Burgundy garnish of button mushrooms and glazed onions

2lb (900g) topside, chuck or stewing beef
salt and pepper
1 large onion
sprig of thyme
1 bay leaf
2 sprigs parsley
2 tablesp. (30ml) oil
½ bottle red wine
2oz (50g) beef dripping
4oz (100g) salt pork or streaky bacon, in the piece
2 carrots
2 shallots
1oz (25g) flour
1 pint (550ml) beef stock
1 bouquet garni
1 clove garlic

TO FINISH:
6oz (150g) button onions
4oz (100g) button mushrooms
2oz (50g) butter
1 teasp. (5ml) sugar
chopped parsley

Cut meat into 1½-in. (3.5-cm) cubes, trimming off any fat and gristle. Put the pieces in a dish, season with salt and pepper and cover with the large onion, peeled and sliced, the herbs, oil and red wine. Leave to marinade for 4 hours.

Melt the beef dripping in a large frying pan. Cut the salt pork or bacon into little strips and fry them until crisp and brown. Transfer them to a 4-pint (2.3-litre) casserole. Brown the carrots, peeled and diced, and shallots, peeled and sliced, and add them to the bacon. Drain and dry the pieces of meat – they won't brown if they're damp – strain the marinade and reserve. Sauté the pieces of meat, a few at a time, in the remaining fat until brown all over, then add them to the casserole.

Stir the flour into the pan juices. Add the strained marinade and stock, stirring to make a smooth sauce. Bring to the boil, pour over the meat. Add the bouquet garni, clove of garlic, peeled, and season to taste. Cover and simmer on top of the stove or in the oven (325 deg. F, 170 deg. C, Gas No. 3) for 3 hours or until meat is tender.

While the meat is cooking prepare the garnish. Peel the onions and blanch in boiling water for 7 minutes. Drain and place them in a pan with 1oz (25g) butter and the sugar. Cook gently, covered, shaking the pan from time to time until the onions are tender and well glazed. Cook the mushrooms in the other 1oz (25g) butter. When the meat is cooked, remove the bouquet garni and garlic. ❋ Garnish with the mushrooms and glazed onions. Check the seasoning. Sprinkle with chopped parsley and serve with boiled or creamed potatoes and a green salad. Serves 6.

❋ TO FREEZE. Cool the stew and remove any surplus fat. Pack into a rigid container. Seal, label and freeze. Pack cooled onions and mushrooms together in another container, seal, label and freeze. Use within 2 months.

TO USE. Thaw the meat overnight in the fridge. Reheat it in a casserole in the oven (325 deg. F, 170 deg. C, Gas No. 3) for about 1 hour. Toss the mushrooms and onions in a little butter to thaw and reheat. Complete as from ❋ in recipe.

To glaze button onions, first blanch and drain them well; then put in a pan with butter and sugar

Cook the onions gently until tender and browned, and well coated with a sticky, rich glaze

Rosemary Lamb Cobbler

Rosemary gives a delicious fragrance to this lamb casserole. It's cooked with the meat and added to the cobbler topping. As rosemary leaves are thin and spiky, make sure you cut them up finely so they are palatable

1½ lb (675g) stewing lamb, off the bone
1 large onion
2 carrots
1 stick celery
1 tablesp. (15ml) flour
salt and pepper
2 tablesp. (30ml) oil
¾ pint (425ml) stock
1 tablesp. (15ml) tomato purée
½ teasp. (2.5ml) dried or freshly chopped rosemary

COBBLER:
8 oz (225g) self-raising flour
pinch salt
2 oz (50g) margarine
½ teasp. (2.5ml) dried or
1 tablesp. (15ml) fresh rosemary
about 6 tablesp. (90ml) milk

Cut the lamb into cubes. Peel and chop the onion. Peel and dice the carrots. Chop the celery. Season the flour with salt and pepper and toss the meat in it.

Heat the oil in a pan and cook the onions and carrots over a low heat until the onions are beginning to soften. Using a slotted spoon, transfer the vegetables to a casserole. Add the meat to the juices in the pan, raise the heat and brown on all sides. Transfer to the casserole.

Pour the stock into the remaining juices in the pan and, stirring, bring to the boil. Strain over the meat and vegetables. Stir in the tomato purée and the dried or chopped rosemary. Cover and cook (350 deg. F, 180 deg. C, Gas No. 4) for 1 hour.

Make the cobbler by sieving the flour and salt together into a bowl. Rub in the margarine, add the dried or chopped rosemary and mix to a soft dough with the milk. Roll out on a floured surface to about ¾-in. (1.5-cm) thickness and cut into rounds. Place them on a greased baking tray, brush with milk and bake (425 deg. F, 220 deg. C. Gas No. 7) for 15 minutes. Remove from the oven.

❇ Arrange the scones over the lamb, return to the oven for about 5 minutes and serve. Serves 4.

❇ TO FREEZE. When cool, pack the stew into a rigid container, seal, label and freeze. Use within 2 months. Pack the cooled scones into a polythene bag, seal, label and freeze. Use within 2 months.

TO USE. Thaw the stew in the fridge overnight and reheat in a casserole (375 deg. F, 190 deg. C, Gas No. 5) for 35 minutes. Complete as from ❇ in recipe but return the casserole to the oven for a further 15 minutes to thaw and heat the frozen cobbler.

Lamb Reform

1½ lb (675g) best end of lamb boned (see page 260)
butter
SAUCE:
1 small onion
1 tablesp. (15ml) oil
2 oz (50g) mushrooms
1 tablesp. (15ml) flour
1 x 10½ oz (298g) can consommé, condensed
1 tablesp. (15ml) sherry
1 teasp. (5ml) redcurrant jelly
salt and pepper
TO FINISH:
2 oz (50g) lean ham
1 hard-boiled egg white
3 cocktail gherkins

Bone and roll the lamb, tie and cut into noisettes (see page 264).

To make the sauce, peel and finely chop the onion and sauté in the oil until soft but not browned. Add the wiped and thinly-sliced mushrooms and cook for 1 minute. Stir in the flour and cook a further minute, then blend in the consommé, sherry and redcurrant jelly and cook, stirring, for 5 minutes. Correct the seasoning with salt and pepper if necessary. ❄

Meanwhile, melt a little butter in a grill pan or frying pan and grill the noisettes for 5-8 minutes on each side or fry them for about 10 minutes on each side. ❄ ❄

Cut the ham, egg white and gherkins into strips, add to the sauce, heat for about 1 minute, then pour over the noisettes and serve. Serves 4.

❄ TO FREEZE: pack the noisettes in a single layer in a rigid container or stack with pieces of freezer paper or foil between each one (see right). Wrap in foil and freeze. Use within 6 months. Pour the sauce into a rigid container, leaving ½ in. (1cm) headspace for expansion, seal, label and freeze. Use within 2 months.

TO USE: thaw the noisettes of lamb overnight in the fridge, then remove the wrappings. Grill or fry them as from ❄ in recipe. Or you can cook them frozen, in which case grill them for about 10 minutes on each side or fry them for 15 minutes on each side. Turn the sauce into a pan and heat gently from frozen, stirring from time to time, until hot. Complete as from ❄ ❄ in recipe.

Separate noisettes with foil or freezer paper, form into a roll and wrap in foil to freeze

Freeze the noisettes (see how to prepare them on page 264) and cook them while reheating the sauce. The Reform sauce has been a traditional accompaniment to lamb cutlets since it was created by Alexis Soyer, famous French chef of the Reform Club in London in Victorian days

Halve pepper crosswise.
Using a sharp knife, cut out
centre core and all seeds

Beef Goulash

Conceived as gulyas, a fiery stew from Hungary, then adopted and mellowed by Austria as gulasch, this rich meat stew is now internationally famous. Paprika, its essential ingredient, gives it its characteristic red colour and flavour, while its garnish of peppers adds spice and texture

1 lb (450g) onions
1 oz (25g) lard
1 tablesp. (15ml) paprika
pinch caraway seeds
1½ lb (675g) stewing beef
1 tablesp. (15ml) tomato purée
2 tablesp. (30ml) water
salt
1 green pepper
TO FINISH:
paprika
¼ pint (150ml) soured cream or yogurt

Peel and thinly slice the onions. Melt the lard in a deep frying pan, tip in the onions and cook them gently until they are transluscent but not coloured. Work in paprika and caraway seeds.

Cut the meat into cubes, removing any fat or gristle. Add the meat to the pan, stirring well. Add tomato purée, water and season with salt.

Halve, core, and deseed the pepper (see left); the little seeds can be very hot so make sure you remove them all. Cut it into slices and arrange these on top of the beef. Cover the pan tightly and simmer the meat mixture gently for about 2 hours or until the meat is tender. Should the liquid dry up, add a little more water – just enough to prevent the meat and vegetable sticking. ✳Check the seasoning and at the last moment blend in a little extra paprika mixed with 1 tablespoon (15ml) water to lift the colour. If liked, stir in a spoonful or two of soured cream or yogurt. Serves 4.

✳ TO FREEZE: when cold pack the goulash in a rigid container, leaving about ½ in. (1cm) headspace for expansion, seal, label and freeze. Use within 2 months.

TO USE: thaw the goulash overnight in the fridge, turn into a pan and reheat for about 20 minutes or until really hot. Complete as from ✳ in recipe.

Ham and Parsley Mould

A cool and tempting dish for a hot summer's day: chunks of ham are set in a wine-flavoured jelly liberally laced with parsley

Soak the gammon or ham overnight if you think it might be salty. Put it in a large pan with the stock, wine and bouquet garni and cook, covered, for 40 minutes or until tender. Remove the rind and cut the meat into large chunks. Drain, reserve cooking liquid – there should be about 1 pint (550ml) – and discard the bouquet garni.

Rinse a 2-pint (1.1-litre) basin in cold water. Coat the inside evenly with all but 3 tablespoons (45ml) of the parsley (see below) and add the chunks of ham.

Put the gelatine in a bowl and mix with 2 tablespoons (30ml) cold water; stand the bowl over a pan of hot water until the gelatine has dissolved completely. Add to the strained stock with the vinegar and leave to stand in a cool place until it begins to set.

Stir the remaining parsley into the setting stock and pour over the ham. Leave to set over-night in a cool place. ❄Turn out the ham, slice and serve with salad. Serves 4.

1 lb (450g) gammon or ham joint
½ pint (300ml) chicken stock
½ pint (300ml) dry white wine
1 bouquet garni
1 oz (25g) chopped parsley
¾ oz (22g) powdered gelatine
2 tablesp. (30ml) cold water
1 tablesp. (15ml) tarragon
   vinegar

❄ TO FREEZE: cover the ham with foil, seal, label and freeze. Use within 1 month.

TO USE: thaw the ham overnight in the fridge. Complete as from ❄ in recipe.

Turn wetted basin on its side; rotate to coat inside evenly with parsley

Veal Roll with Spinach

2-3 lb (900g-1.35kg) breast of veal
salt and pepper
1 tablesp. (15ml) lemon juice
1 lb (450g) fresh spinach or
8 oz (225g) frozen spinach, thawed
1 small onion
4 oz (100g) mushrooms
3 oz (75g) butter
8 oz (225g) sausagemeat
1 teasp. (5ml) mixed herbs
1 tablesp. (15ml) flour
2 tablesp. (30ml) oil

Bone the veal, or get your butcher to do it for you when you buy it. Flatten out the meat, season with salt and pepper and sprinkle with lemon juice.

If using fresh spinach, strip off the stalks and wash the leaves well in plenty of water. Put them into a pan with a little salt. There's no need to add water, there'll be enough clinging to the leaves. Cook for 5-10 minutes, shaking the pan from time to time, drain and set aside.

Peel and finely chop the onion. Wipe and chop the mushrooms. Melt 1 oz (25g) of the butter in a

Spinach and sausagemeat stuffing add colour and flavour to the veal. Sliced and served cold it makes a splendid dish for a buffet party

pan, add the onion and sauté gently until soft. Add the mushrooms and cook for 1 minute, stirring. Stir in the sausagemeat, broken up, and the herbs, and season with salt and pepper.

Lay the stuffing down the centre of the veal. Top with the cooked fresh or thawed and drained frozen spinach. Roll up the veal neatly and either sew with thread or tie with string to secure. Dust with flour.

Heat the remaining 2 oz (50g) butter in a flame-proof dish with the oil, add the veal and brown all over. Transfer the dish to the oven (350 deg. F, 180 deg. C, Gas no. 4) and cook, covered, for 1 hour. Reduce the heat to 300 deg. F, 150 deg. C, Gas no. 2) for a further 45 minutes, basting occasionally. Remove the thread or string. ❋ When cold, slice the roll and serve. Serves 6.

❋ TO FREEZE: cool the meat, wrap in foil, seal, label and freeze. Use within 2 months.

TO USE: thaw the meat overnight in the fridge. Remove wrappings and complete as from ❋ in recipe.

Lamb in Dill Sauce

Dill is a sharply aromatic herb widely used in Scandinavian cooking but rather neglected in Britain. In this recipe, Swedish in origin, dill gives pungency to the rich sauce coating the lamb

3-3½ lb (1.35-1.50kg) shoulder of lamb
1 large carrot
1 medium onion
2 sticks celery
salt and pepper
2 teasp. (10ml) cornflour
1 teasp. (5ml) vinegar
pinch sugar
1 tablesp. (15ml) cream
2 egg yolks
1 tablesp. (15ml) fresh chopped
    dill or 2 teasp. (10ml) dried dill

Bone out the shoulder or get your butcher to do it for you. Cut the joint into fairly large chunks, trimming off some of the fat.

Peel the carrot and cut into sticks; peel onion, trim and wash the celery and cut into chunks.

Put the chunks of meat and vegetables into a large pan. Season with salt and pepper and barely cover with water. Bring to the boil, lower the heat, cover the pan and simmer gently for 1 hour. Transfer the meat and vegetables to a dish. Skim the fat from the juices. ✳

Blend the cornflour to a smooth paste with a little cold water. Add this to the juices and stir well. Blend the vinegar and sugar together and add to the pan. Beat together the cream and egg yolks. Blend into the sauce and heat all together gently without allowing it to boil. Stir in the fresh or dried dill and return the meat and vegetables to the sauce. Heat through. Serves 4.

✳ TO FREEZE: pour the skimmed juices over the meat and pack in a rigid container; cool, seal, label and freeze. Use within 2 months.

TO USE: thaw the lamb overnight in the fridge. Turn into a pan and reheat gently for about 20 minutes. Strain the juices off the meat into a clean pan and complete as from ✳ in recipe.

Pork Fricassée

A fricassée can be made with poultry, veal, lamb or pork. The meat is cut in small pieces and cooked in stock, and the sauce is finally thickened with egg yolk and cream

1½ lb (675 g) lean pork
1 medium-sized onion
1 carrot
1 bouquet garni
¾ pint (425 ml) stock
4 oz (100 g) button mushrooms
2 oz (50 g) butter
1 oz (25 g) flour
1 egg yolk
2 tablesp. (30 ml) cream
2 tablesp. (30 ml) sherry
salt and pepper
few cooked peas, optional

Cut the meat into cubes and put into a pan with the peeled and halved onion, peeled carrot, bouquet garni and stock. Bring to the boil, lower the heat and simmer, covered, until the meat is tender – about 1 hour. Remove the onion, carrot and bouquet garni. Strain off the liquor to use for the sauce.

Wipe and trim the mushrooms and sauté in 1 oz (25 g) of the butter.

Melt the remaining 1 oz (25 g) butter in a clean pan, stir in the flour and cook gently for 1 minute. Gradually stir in the reserved liquor. Bring to the boil, stirring all the time and cook gently for 2–3 minutes. In a basin blend the egg yolk with the cream, then stir in a spoonful of the hot sauce. Add this egg mixture to the sauce in the pan. Stir in the sherry, meat and mushrooms, and check the seasoning. ✳Heat gently, stirring, until really hot but do not let it boil or it will curdle. Stir in a few cooked peas if liked. Serves 4.

✳ TO FREEZE. Cool the fricassée rapidly, then pack into a rigid container, seal, label and freeze. Use within 2 months.

TO USE. Thaw the fricassée overnight in the fridge. Tip it into a pan and reheat gently, stirring, until really hot. Complete as from ✳ in recipe above.

Lamb Cutlets en Croûte

Lovely way to serve lamb for a party. Each cutlet is topped with finely chopped ham and mushrooms, then wrapped in strips of puff pastry

Peel and chop the onion finely, wipe and chop the mushrooms. Shred the ham finely.

Melt the butter in a pan, add the onion and fry gently until soft but not coloured – about 2 minutes. Add the mushrooms to the pan and fry for a further 3 minutes. Stir in the tomato purée, ham and parsley. Season with salt and pepper. Leave to cool.

Roll out the pastry on a lightly-floured board to a rectangle 20×8in. (50×20cm). Cut into 8 strips, each measuring 20×1in. (50×2.5cm).

Spread a little of the cooled filling on each of the cutlets. Damp the pastry strips and wrap one around each cutlet, starting from the narrow end, overlapping the pastry as you wind it. Leave a little bit of the bone exposed.

Stand the cutlets on a baking sheet and brush with beaten egg. Bake in preheated oven (425 deg. F, 220 deg. C, Gas no. 7) for about 20 minutes. ❄
Top the bones with a cutlet frill and serve hot with new potatoes and vegetables. Serves 4.

❄ TO FREEZE: cool the cutlets, wrap, seal, label and freeze. Use within 2 months.

TO USE: thaw cutlets for 6 hours at room temperature, then reheat in preheated oven (350 deg. F, 180 deg. C, Gas no. 4) for about 20 minutes, and complete as from ❄ in recipe or serve cold if preferred.

1 small onion
6oz (150g) mushrooms
2oz (50g) cooked ham
1oz (25g) butter
2 teasp. (10ml) tomato purée
1 tablesp. (15ml) chopped parsley
salt and pepper
12oz (350g) puff pastry
1½lb (675g) best end of neck of lamb, divided into cutlets
beaten egg

Stuffed Beef Rolls with Mushroom Sauce

1 lb (450g) topside, cut into 4
slices
mustard
seasoned flour
dripping
1 medium onion
1 stick celery
2 carrots
½-¾ pint (300-425ml) beef stock
1 bouquet garni
1 oz (25g) butter
4 oz (100g) mushrooms
1 tablesp. (15ml) sherry
STUFFING:
6 oz (150g) pork sausagemeat
½ small onion
½ oz (15g) butter
2 oz (50g) fresh white
breadcrumbs
1 teasp. (5ml) mixed herbs
salt and pepper

Put the slices of topside, one at a time, between two sheets of greaseproof paper – wet the paper to prevent the meat sticking – and bang out with meat mallet or rolling pin (see below). Cut each slice into two.

Put sausagemeat into a basin. Peel and chop the onion, melt ½ oz (15g) butter in a pan, add the onion and sauté for 1 minute. Stir this into the sausagemeat with crumbs, herbs and seasoning.

Spread each slice of beef with a little prepared mustard, pile on a portion of the stuffing, roll up, tie with fine string or thread. When all are made, roll in seasoned flour.

Melt a little dripping in a pan and brown the rolls on all sides. Remove them from the pan and

Lay slice of beef between two sheets of greaseproof, dampened to prevent it sticking, and beat with rolling pin to flatten

Make a prime cut of meat go further. Roll thin slices of lean beef round a herby sausagemeat stuffing and serve with a thickened mushroom sauce

add the onion, celery and carrot, all peeled and sliced, and fry gently until the onions begin to soften; replace beef rolls on top of vegetables.

Add enough stock just to cover the meat, tuck in the bouquet garni, cover with the lid and simmer gently for 1–1½ hours or until tender. Towards the end of the cooking time, melt the remaining butter in a pan, add the cleaned mushrooms and sauté them for 1 minute.

❋Lift out the beef rolls, and remove the thread. Place them on a dish and keep warm.

Strain the sauce (will be about ¾ pint (425ml) on to the mushrooms, stir in the sherry, bring to the boil, adjust the seasoning and pour over the beef rolls. Serves 4.

 TO FREEZE: place the beef rolls in a rigid container and cool. Cool the finished sauce separately and when cold pour over the beef. Cover with lid or foil, seal, label and freeze. Use in 2 months.

TO USE: thaw the beef rolls sufficiently to remove from the container, then place the beef rolls and their sauce in a thick saucepan and heat gently until hot (about 25 minutes). Serve at once.

Gammon with Pineapple and Green Pepper Sauce

The pairing of gammon and pineapple is well known. But for a variation on that popular theme add diced green pepper to give extra piquancy to the sauce. If the gammon is salty, soak it in cold water for an hour or two to draw out surplus salt before using

2oz (50g) butter
1 clove garlic
4 x 6oz (150g) gammon steaks
1 green pepper
1 x 15½oz (439g) can pineapple slices
1 tablesp. (15ml) cornflour
salt and pepper
TO FINISH:
1 tablesp. (15ml) demerara sugar

❄ TO FREEZE: place the gammon steaks in a large foil container and leave to cool. When the sauce is cold, pour over the gammon, cover with foil, seal, label and freeze. Use within 1 month.

TO USE: thaw the gammon overnight in the fridge, loosen the foil covering the container but leave it over the dish and reheat (375 deg. F, 190 deg. C, Gas no. 5) for 25 minutes. Remove the foil. Complete as from ❄ and ❄❄ in recipe.

Gently heat the butter in a sauté or deep frying pan. Remove the papery coating from the garlic clove, split it in two and add to the pan. Allow to cook for 1 minute, taking care that the garlic doesn't burn. Remove the garlic and add the gammon steaks. (If the steaks have fat on them, nick it with a knife in several places to stop the steaks curling and twisting during cooking.) Cook the steaks for about 2 minutes (those with fat will need a few minutes longer) on each side. Transfer them ❄ to an ovenproof dish.

Halve the pepper, remove all the little seeds, cut the flesh into dice and add them to the juices in the pan. Drain the pineapple slices and add the juice – about 7 fl. oz (200ml) – to the pan. Simmer 5-10 minutes or until the pepper is just tender.

Mix the cornflour with a little cold water to a paste. Add it to the pan and cook, stirring, until the sauce thickens. Check the seasoning. Set aside 4 slices of pineapple, roughly chop the rest and add to the pan. Pour the sauce over the gammon steaks. ❄❄ Place steaks in the oven (375 deg. F, 190 deg. C, Gas no. 5) for 20 minutes.

Put the reserved pineapple slices in the grill pan, sprinkle with the demerara sugar and place under a hot grill until the sugar caramelizes and browns. Arrange the caramelized slices on the gammon and serve at once. Serves 4.

Stuffed Pork in Sour Cream Sauce

The slightly sharp, creamy sauce is made by stirring soured cream into the pan juices that remain after cooking the chops

Get your butcher to bone out the pork. Cut it into 6 slices about 1-in. (2.5-cm) thick. Make a pocket in each slice by slitting horizontally through the lean. Fill with this stuffing:

Peel and chop the onion finely. Wipe and chop the mushrooms into small pieces. Heat 1 tablespoon (15ml) oil and sauté the onion until beginning to soften. Add the mushrooms and cook for 1 minute. Remove the pan from the heat. Chop the ham finely and add to the pan together with the parsley and breadcrumbs, season with salt and pepper and mix well. Beat the egg lightly and stir into the stuffing; and sew up with thread or secure with a cocktail stick.

Heat the rest of the oil in a frying pan and brown the meat on both sides. Transfer the meat to a roasting tin and pour over the first $\frac{1}{4}$ pint (150ml) beef stock. Any leftover stuffing can be dotted round the slices of meat. Bake (350 deg. F, 180 deg. C, Gas no. 4) for 45 minutes. ❋ Transfer the meat to a serving dish and keep warm.

Melt the butter in a saucepan. Stir in the flour and cook for 1 minute. Gradually stir in the rest of the stock and juices remaining in the roasting tin, skimmed of excess fat, and cook until thickened. Stir in the soured cream and reheat gently. Check the seasoning and pour over the meat or serve the sauce separately. Serves 6.

3 lb (1.35kg) loin of pork
1 small onion
2 oz (50g) mushrooms
3 tablesp. (45ml) oil
2 oz (50g) ham
1 tablesp. (15ml) chopped parsley
1 tablesp. (15ml) fresh white breadcrumbs
salt and pepper
1 egg
$\frac{1}{4}$ pint (150ml) beef stock
TO FINISH:
1 oz (25g) butter
1 oz (25g) flour
$\frac{1}{2}$ pint (300ml) beef stock
$\frac{1}{4}$ pint (150ml) soured cream

❋ TO FREEZE: transfer the meat to a rigid container. Pour over pan juices. Cool, seal, label, freeze. Use in 2 months.

TO USE: thaw the meat overnight in the fridge. Transfer to a roasting tin, place in oven (375 deg. F, 190 deg. C, Gas no. 5) and reheat for 30 minutes. Complete as from ❋ in recipe.

Daube of Lamb

Chunks of lamb are marinaded in wine, oil, herbs and vegetables, then slowly simmered until tender. And because a daube is all the better for reheating, it's an ideal freezer dish. As for the name, daube, it comes from daubière – an earthenware dish in which meat was cooked

Cut the lamb into chunks and place in a bowl. Pour over the wine, 2 tablespoons (30ml) oil and the peeled and roughly-chunked onions and carrots. Season with salt and pepper and a pinch of thyme. Cover and leave the meat to marinade at least 3 hours, stirring from time to time.

Cut the pork into tiny cubes or strips and fry

in a little oil until golden. Put them into a casserole. Remove the pieces of meat from the marinade and drain them. Toss them in flour seasoned with salt and pepper and fry them, a few at a time, turning them to brown on all sides.

Put the chunks of lamb into the casserole, then add the carrots and onions from the marinade, and the mushrooms, wiped and sliced. Pour over the marinade. Add enough stock just to cover the contents of the pot. Tuck in a bouquet garni of the bay leaf, orange and parsley, tied together (see below). Cover tightly (put a piece of foil over the dish under the lid if it doesn't fit well) and cook (325 deg. F, 170 deg. C, Gas no. 3) for about 2 hours or until the meat is tender. ❄ Remove the bouquet garni. Serves 6.

3-4 lb (1.30-1.80kg) shoulder of lamb, boned (see page 260)
½ bottle red wine (about ¾ pint-425ml)
2-3 tablesp. (30-45ml) oil
2 onions
2 carrots
salt and pepper
thyme
4 oz (100g) belly pork
seasoned flour
4 oz (100g) mushrooms
¾ pint (425ml) beef stock
1 bay leaf
piece orange peel
3 or 4 sprigs parsley

❄ TO FREEZE: cool, and when cold remove the fat from the surface. Spoon the daube into a rigid container, removing the bouquet garni, seal, label and freeze. Use within 2 months.

TO USE: thaw the daube overnight in the fridge. Turn into a deep pan and reheat, stirring occasionally until the daube is bubbling hot.

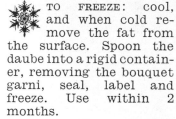

To make a bouquet garni, tie together the stem ends of the chosen herbs and a strip of orange peel

Sweet/Sour Cabbage with Sausage

Shredded red cabbage, braised with onion, apples and vinegar, is served hot with smoked sausage. It's a good dish, too, with game

2½lb (1.25kg) red cabbage
1 medium-sized onion
2 cooking apples
2 tablesp. (30ml) demerara sugar
3 tablesp. (45ml) wine vinegar
salt and pepper

Grease a large earthenware casserole.

Quarter the cabbage, remove the core and shred the leaves into a colander. Rinse under the cold tap and leave to drain. Peel and chop the onion. Peel, core and chop the apples.

Layer the shredded cabbage, onion and apples into the casserole, sprinkling the layers with the sugar, wine vinegar, salt and pepper. Cover with the lid and cook (325 deg. F, 170 deg. C, Gas No. 3) for 3 hours. ✳ Check the seasoning and serve with hot smoked sausage, frankfurters or a boiling ring, and jacket potatoes. Serves 4.

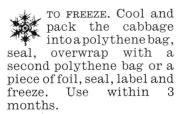 TO FREEZE. Cool and pack the cabbage into a polythene bag, seal, overwrap with a second polythene bag or a piece of foil, seal, label and freeze. Use within 3 months.

TO USE. Thaw the cabbage slightly, then tip it into a pan and heat through, stirring from time to time. Complete as from ✳ in recipe.

Pepper-stuffed Pork

The rice-filled peppers make an unusual stuffing for a loin of pork roasted and served cold. It looks attractive enough when sliced to make a good buffet party dish

Bone the pork or ask your butcher to do it for you. Lay the meat between 2 sheets of wetted greaseproof paper and, using a rolling pin or mallet, bat out the thick centre of the meat until the same thickness as the ends.

Put the 2 prepared stuffed peppers end to end down the centre and wrap the meat around them. Either sew up the join with thread or secure with string at 2-in. (5-cm) intervals.

Place the stuffed pork in a roasting pan and roast (350 deg. F, 180 deg. C, Gas no. 4) for about 2 hours or until cooked through. Set aside until cold. ✳ Remove thread or string. Slice and serve with salad. Serves 6-8.

3lb (1.35kg) loin of pork
2 small stuffed peppers
**   (see page 45)**

✳ TO FREEZE: cool the pork, then wrap in foil, seal, label and freeze. Use within 1 month.

TO USE: thaw 12 hours in fridge. Continue as from ✳ in recipe.

Osso Buco

This lovely dish of veal cooked with wine and tomatoes is to be found all over Italy. Just before serving a *gremolata* – a handful of chopped parsley, grated peel of half a lemon and a chopped clove or garlic mixed together – is sprinkled over the meat. Serve it with saffron rice

Peel and chop the onion and carrots. Heat the oil in a pan large enough to take the meat upright in one layer. Add the vegetables to the pan and brown lightly. Now brown the slices of veal all over. Keep the bones upright so that the marrow in the bone doesn't fall out during the cooking.

Pour the wine over the meat, add either the skinned and chopped tomatoes, purée and the stock, or the canned tomatoes with their juice.

Tie the strip of lemon peel, bay leaf and sprig of parsley together to make a bouquet garni and add to the pan; season with salt and pepper. Bring to the boil, cover the pan, lower the heat and cook 1½-2 hours or until the meat is tender. ❄ Discard the bouquet garni.

Arrange the veal on a heated serving dish. Sieve the contents of the pan, check the seasoning and pour over the veal. Sprinkle with chopped parsley or top with the traditional Milanese garnish of chopped parsley, mixed with the grated rind of half a lemon and finely chopped clove of garlic (see below).

Serve osso buco with a dish of saffron rice made by dissolving a little saffron powder in 2 tablespoons (30ml) stock and stirring this into the rice at end of cooking. Serves 4.

1 onion
2 carrots
2 tablesp. (30ml) oil
2 lb (900g) shin of veal, sawn into
   2-in. (5-cm) pieces
¼ pint (150ml) dry white wine
12 oz (350g) tomatoes plus 2
   teasp. (10ml) tomato purée and
   ¼ pint (150ml) chicken stock,
   or 1 x 15 oz (425g) can tomatoes
strip lemon peel
1 bay leaf
sprig parsley
salt and pepper
TO FINISH:
finely chopped parsley
grated rind ½ lemon (optional)
1 finely chopped clove garlic
   (optional)

❄ TO FREEZE: cool the stew, then place the pieces of veal in a large rigid container and pour over the cooking juices; seal, label and freeze. Use in 2 months.

TO USE: thaw the stew overnight in the fridge. Put the meat and juices in a pan, keeping the bones upright, and heat through for 45 minutes. Complete as from ❄ in receipe.

For osso buco's traditional garnish, chop parsley speedily in hachinette (herb cutter), then mix with grated lemon rind and chopped garlic

Jellied Beef

Long slow cooking in brandy, wine and vegetables makes the beef meltingly tender. Sliced and covered in jellied stock it is moist and full of flavour

3-3½lb (1.35-1.50kg) beef topside, top rump or silverside
2 onions
2 tablesp. (30ml) oil
salt and pepper
2 tablesp. (30ml) brandy
½ pint (300ml) red wine
2 carrots
1 clove garlic
1 bouquet garni (parsley, bay leaf and thyme)
1 calf's foot or 2 pig's trotters
½ pint (300ml) beef stock
TO SERVE:
cooked carrots

The meat should be tied in a compact sausage-shape, and larded (this means introducing fat into an otherwise lean piece of meat with strips of back pork fat). Larding won't be necessary if you use silverside. Ask your butcher to do it for you; otherwise, if you don't have a special larding needle, make deep incisions in the meat with a knife and push in the pieces of fat.

Peel and slice the onions. Heat the oil in a deep flameproof casserole, add the onions and colour them lightly.

Season the beef, put it into the pan and brown all over. Pour over the warmed brandy and set light to it. When the flames have died down, pour on the red wine, let it bubble for a minute or two, then add the raw carrots, peeled and roughly cut, the clove of garlic, peeled and crushed and the bouquet garni.

Tuck the split and washed calf's foot or pig's trotters down into the pan and pour on the stock; there should be sufficient just to cover the meat. Cover with foil and the lid and cook (275 deg. F, 140 deg. C, Gas no. 1) for 3-4 hours or until the meat is tender. It may take longer depending on the cut of meat used.

Set the meat aside to cool. Strain the liquid through a sieve into a bowl and leave to set to a firm, clear jelly. ✳

Slice the meat and arrange down the centre of a deep serving dish. Surround with whole cooked carrots. Remove the fat from the surface of the jelly, then melt the jelly over a gentle heat. Pour it carefully over the meat and carrots so they stay in position and leave in a cool place to re-set. Serve with a salad. Serves 6-8.

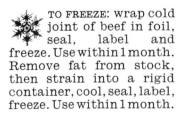 **TO FREEZE:** wrap cold joint of beef in foil, seal, label and freeze. Use within 1 month. Remove fat from stock, then strain into a rigid container, cool, seal, label, freeze. Use within 1 month. **TO USE:** thaw meat in fridge for 24 hours. Tip stock into a pan; complete as from ✳ in recipe.

Pork Escalopes

Thin slices of pork are dipped in egg and breadcrumbs and fried until golden and crisp. Cold they make good picnic fare; hot they can be served with vegetables or pasta and a sauce

Trim any fat and membrane from the fillet. Cut it almost through lengthways so that it can be opened up to double its width. Place on a piece of wetted greaseproof paper, cover with another piece and beat it out flat with a rolling pin or mallet.

Remove greaseproof paper and cut the flattened fillet into four escalopes.

Have the seasoned flour on a plate, the egg, beaten, in a flat dish and the breadcrumbs on a board or plate. Dip each escalope in turn in seasoned flour, then egg, then breadcrumbs.

Heat the butter, together with the oil, in a large frying pan. The oil helps to prevent the butter burning during frying. Put in the escalopes and fry for about 10 minutes, turning once. ❋Serve hot with vegetables of your choice or cold with salad. Serves 4.

12oz (350g) pork fillet
1oz (25g) seasoned flour
1 egg
4oz (100g) white breadcrumbs
2oz (50g) butter
4 tablesp. (60ml) oil

TO FREEZE: drain escalopes on absorbent kitchen paper. Cool rapidly, then wrap each one in foil or freezer paper, seal, label and freeze. Use within 2 months.

TO USE: thaw escalopes in fridge and serve cold or loosen foil wrappings and heat in preheated oven (350 deg. F, 180 deg. C, Gas no. 4) for 15 minutes. Complete as from ❋ in recipe.

Spicy Pork Chops

Although pork chops are a natural partner for a spicy tomato sauce, it's good with other meats as well. Make up double the quantity of sauce and freeze it away to serve with chicken or turkey portions or veal chops. Serve with noodles to mop up the sauce

4 pork chops
1 oz (25g) butter
1 tablesp. (15ml) oil
SAUCE:
1 small onion
1 tablesp. (15ml) oil
2 tablesp. (30ml) demerara sugar
1 tablesp. (15ml) lemon juice
6 fl. oz (180ml) tomato ketchup
1 tablesp. (15ml) Worcestershire sauce
½ pint (300ml) water

First make the sauce. Peel and finely chop the onion. Heat the oil in a pan, add the chopped onion and sauté until turning golden. Add the sugar, lemon juice, tomato ketchup and the Worcestershire sauce, then, stirring, pour in the water, bring to the boil, lower the heat and simmer for 30 minutes.

Trim the pork chops of surplus fat (see right), then fry them in the butter and oil in a frying pan until they are golden. Transfer them to an oven-proof dish.

Pour the sauce over the chops and bake (375 deg. F, 190 deg. C, Gas no. 5) for 30 minutes.
❇ Serves 4.

❄️ TO FREEZE: cool the chops in the sauce, pack in a foil dish or other rigid container, seal, label and freeze. Use within 3 months.

TO USE: thaw the chops overnight in the fridge. Reheat (375 deg. F, 190 deg. C, Gas no. 5) for 45 minutes.

Before frying the pork chops, cut off surplus fat with a sharp knife

Moussaka

There are many versions of this Greek speciality. Here, minced lamb, tomatoes and courgettes are layered into a dish and topped with potatoes and a cheese sauce. A good salad to accompany it would be tiny cubes of cucumber and a little chopped mint stirred into natural yogurt

2lb (900g) cooked breast or shoulder lamb
2 onions
4 tablesp. (60ml) oil
salt and pepper
2 teasp. (10ml) dried or fresh mint
2 eggs
1lb (450g) courgettes
12oz (350g) tomatoes
1lb (450g) potatoes
SAUCE:
1 pint (550ml) milk
1 carrot
1 onion
1 bay leaf
1 blade mace
6 peppercorns
1 egg
2oz (50g) butter
2oz (50g) flour
4oz (100g) strong Cheddar cheese

Mince the lamb. Peel and chop 2 onions. Heat 2 tablespoons (30ml) oil in a pan, add onion and fry gently for 2 minutes or until transparent. Stir in the lamb, salt, pepper and mint. Remove from the heat and stir in the beaten eggs.

Wipe the courgettes, cut into slices and put into a colander. Salt slightly and leave to drain for about 1 hour. Dry them and fry gently, turning, in the remaining 2 tablespoons (30ml) of oil until tender – about 5 minutes. Skin and slice the tomatoes. Peel the potatoes and cook in boiling salted water until tender. Drain and slice.

Layer the meat mixture, tomatoes and courgettes, finishing with the sliced potatoes, in a 4-pint (2.3-litre) capacity casserole.

To make the sauce, pour the milk into a saucepan with the carrot, peeled and sliced, the onion, peeled and cut in half, the bay leaf, mace and peppercorns. Put over a gentle heat to infuse for about 20 minutes. Strain and reserve. Separate the egg.

Melt the butter in a clean pan, add the flour and cook this roux for about 1 minute. Gradually stir in the flavoured milk and heat, stirring, until it boils. Boil for about 1 minute. Remove the pan from the heat and add 3oz (75g) of the grated cheese and egg yolk. Beat the egg white until forming peaks, then fold into the sauce. Adjust the seasoning.

Pour the sauce over the meat mixture in the casserole and top with the remaining grated cheese. ❄ Bake in preheated oven (350 deg. F, 180 deg. C, Gas no. 4) about 45 minutes. Serves 6.

❄ TO FREEZE: cool the moussaka, then cover with foil, seal, label and freeze. Use within 2 months.

TO USE: thaw moussaka in fridge overnight. Complete as from ❄ in recipe.

Beef Carbonnade

This is one of the national dishes of Belgium. Beef is stewed until tender in beer then topped with slices of bread spread with French mustard. The dish is then returned to the oven until the bread has crisped and browned

Cut the meat into large squares. Peel and slice the onion.

Heat the oil or melt the dripping in a pan. Put the meat in, a few pieces at a time, and brown well on all sides over a high heat. Remove and place in a casserole. When all the meat is browned lower the heat and put the onions into the pan, sprinkle with the sugar and brown lightly. Add the flour, stirring it into the juices. Pour on the ale, stock and add the bouquet garni and season with salt and pepper. Bring to the boil and pour over the meat.

Cover and cook about 1½ hours in preheated oven (325 deg. F, 170 deg. C, Gas no. 3) until the meat is tender. Remove bouquet garni. ✳ Turn the oven up to 400 deg. F, 200 deg. C, Gas no. 6.

Cut each slice of bread in two, spread with mustard and arrange over the meat, mustard side down. Press down gently so the bread can soak up some of the gravy. Dot the top of the bread with butter. Return to the oven and cook, uncovered, until the bread is crisp. Serves 4.

1½lb (675g) stewing beef
1 large onion
2 tablesp. (30ml) oil or 1½oz (40g) dripping
1 teasp. (5ml) sugar
1oz (25g) flour
½ pint (300ml) brown ale
¼ pint (150ml) beef stock
1 bouquet garni
salt and pepper
TO FINISH:
2 slices bread
French mustard
1oz (25g) butter

✳ TO FREEZE: cool the carbonnade, pack in a rigid container, cover, seal, label and freeze. Use within 3 months.

TO USE: thaw overnight in the fridge. Turn carbonnade into a casserole and reheat in oven (375 deg. F, 190 deg. C, Gas no. 5) for about 40 minutes. Complete as from ✳ in recipe.

Lambs'Tongues in Orange Sauce

After simmering in stock the tongues are coated in a well-flavoured brown sauce, enriched with red wine, fresh orange juice and redcurrant jelly

6 lambs' tongues
1 pint (550ml) stock

SAUCE:
1 tablesp. (15ml) oil
1 small onion
1 rasher bacon
1 tablesp. (15ml) flour
2 teasp. (10ml) tomato purée
1 pint (550ml) stock
1 bouquet garni
salt and pepper
1 orange, juice only
2 teasp. (10ml) redcurrant jelly
1 small glass red wine

TO FINISH:
creamed potatoes
1 orange
1oz (25g) butter
1 teasp. (5ml) granulated sugar

Wash the tongues and place in a pan. Pour over the stock, bring to the boil, lower the heat and simmer gently until tender, about 1½ hours. When cooked the skin should peel off easily.

While the tongues are cooking make the sauce. Heat the oil in a pan. Add the peeled and chopped onion, the bacon, cut into pieces, and cook until both are golden. Stir in the flour and cook for 1 minute. Add the tomato purée, stock and bouquet garni. If you haven't a well flavoured stock, use a small can of consommé made up to the pint with stock, made with a beef stock cube. Bring to the boil, stirring. Lower the heat and leave to simmer for 15 minutes, uncovered, then strain.

Return the sauce to a clean pan, add the orange juice, redcurrant jelly and wine, and simmer gently for about 20 minutes or until the sauce is shiny and slightly thickened. Check the seasoning.

Skin the tongues, trim the root and remove any bones. Halve them if liked. ❄ Spoon potato round the edge of a serving dish, arrange the tongues in the centre and coat with the sauce.

Cut the orange into thin slices and then into halves. Sauté them in the butter, sprinkling with the sugar as they cook. Use as a garnish. Serves 4.

❄ TO FREEZE. Place the tongues in a rigid container and pour over the sauce. When cold, seal, label and freeze. Use within 2 months.

TO USE. Thaw the tongues overnight in the fridge. Reheat them gently in a pan. Complete as from ❄ in recipe.

Kidneys Genièvre

Aromatic and spicy,
juniper berries (genièvre)
are used in casseroles,
marinades and sauces –
also in distilling gin. Here
they add a piquant flavour
to a dish of kidneys

1 medium-sized onion
2 teasp. (10ml) juniper berries
1 clove garlic
1oz (25g) butter
1 teasp. (5ml) oil
1½lb (675g) lambs' kidneys
1 tablesp. (15ml) flour
¼ pint (150ml) chicken stock
4 tablesp. (60ml) dry white wine
salt and pepper
TO FINISH:
2½floz (75ml) double cream

Peel and finely chop the onion. Crush the juniper berries in a pestle and mortar or on a wooden board with the end of the rolling pin. Remove papery coating from clove of garlic and crush.

Heat the butter and oil together in a sauté or deep frying pan. Add the onion, juniper berries and garlic and cook gently until the onion is softened but not coloured.

Skin and core the kidneys and cut into quarters or thick slices. Add to the onions and fry, turning until browned. Sprinkle over the flour, stir it into the juices and cook for 1 minute. Gradually add the stock and wine, stirring well to make a smooth sauce. Season with salt and pepper and cook for 10 minutes. ❋

Stir in the cream, reheat without boiling and check the seasoning before serving with rice. Serves 4.

❋ TO FREEZE: cool kidneys, pack into a rigid container, seal, label and freeze. Use within 1 month.

TO USE: thaw kidneys overnight in fridge and reheat gently in a thick pan. Complete as from ❋ in recipe.

Liver Stroganoff

Based on the famous
Russian dish, beef
Stroganoff, which has fillet
of beef as its main
ingredient – this is a
considerably less costly
version and tastes almost
as delicious

Cut the liver into finger-length strips. Wipe and trim the mushrooms; slice them if large. Peel and finely chop the onion.

Melt the butter in a large frying or sauté pan, put in the onion and cook gently until soft but not coloured. Add the mushrooms to the pan and stir them around for 1 minute. Add the lamb's liver and cook until it firms up and loses its raw look. Sprinkle in the flour and work it into the juices. Season with salt and pepper. Pour on the stock, raise the heat slightly and cook for 5 minutes. ❄ Stir in the soured cream, allow it just to heat through, then serve the liver on a bed of rice. Serves 4.

1lb (450g) lamb's liver
4oz (100g) mushrooms
1 small onion
2oz (50g) butter
1 tablesp. (15ml) flour
salt and pepper
¼ pint (150ml) stock
TO FINISH:
2 tablesp. (30ml) soured cream

❄ TO FREEZE: cool the liver and pack into a rigid container, seal, label and freeze. Use within 3 months.

TO USE: thaw the liver overnight in the fridge. Heat through gently in a frying pan and complete as from ❄ in recipe.

Sherried Kidneys with Pâté

Tender lambs' kidneys are cooked in a rich, smooth sauce, which is thickened and enriched with liver pâté

1 small onion
1 oz (25g) butter
1¼ lb (550g) lambs' kidneys
¼ pint (150ml) stock
1 teasp. (5ml) French mustard
2 tablesp. (30ml) sherry
2 level tablesp. (30ml) smooth
   liver pâté
salt and pepper

Peel and finely chop the onion, melt the butter in a pan, add the onion and cook until softened. Skin, halve and core the kidneys (see below). If they are large cut them into quarters. Add them to the pan and sauté quickly until they stiffen and brown. Pour in the stock, then stir in the mustard, sherry, and blend in the pâté. Season with salt and pepper to taste. Cook over a gentle heat for 10 minutes ❄ and serve with boiled rice or creamed potatoes. Serves 4.

❄ TO FREEZE: when cold, pack the kidneys in their sauce in a rigid container, seal, label and freeze. Use within 2 months.

TO USE: thaw the kidneys overnight in the fridge. Turn into a pan and re-heat for 10-15 minutes or until really hot. Check the seasoning. Complete as from ❄ in recipe.

Cut the skinned kidneys in half, lengthwise, and snip out the fatty core with a pair of scissors

Braised Oxtail

Trim excess fat off the joints before cooking so the sauce isn't too greasy. As a variation that gives a slightly piquant flavour try replacing half the water with cider

1–2oz (25–50g) dripping
1 oxtail, jointed
2 onions
2 carrots
2–3 sticks celery
2 leeks
1 tablesp. (15ml) flour
1 pint (550ml) water or beef stock
4 parsley stalks
1 bay leaf
salt and pepper

Heat the dripping in a flameproof casserole and fry the oxtail joints on all sides until well browned.

Peel and slice the onions, peel and quarter the carrots, cut the celery into chunks. Trim the root and most of the green part from the leeks and cut into chunks. Remove the oxtail joints and set aside.

Add the vegetables to the casserole and fry gently until just colouring. Sprinkle with the flour and stir it into the juices in the pan. Pour in the water or stock. Return the joints to the casserole. Add the parsley stalks and bay leaf, tied together, season and bring to the boil. Cover, reduce the heat and simmer for 2-3 hours or until the meat is tender and dropping from the bones. ❅ Remove the herbs and serve. Serves 4.

❅ TO FREEZE: leave the meat until cold, then remove any fat that may have settled on the surface. Pack in a rigid container, leaving ½in. (1cm) headspace, seal, label and freeze. Use within 3 months.

TO USE: thaw the meat overnight in the fridge, turn into a pan and bring to the boil; then reduce the heat and simmer about 30 minutes. Complete as from ❅ in recipe.

Kidneys Turbigo

Lambs' kidneys, sausages, mushrooms and baby onions are cooked in a sherry flavoured sauce

Peel the onions and blanch for 2 minutes in boiling water, drain and set aside. Skin the kidneys, cut in half lengthways and cut out the white core with scissors. Wipe and trim the mushrooms; halve them or leave whole if tiny.

Melt the butter in a deep frying pan or sauté pan and brown the kidneys and sausages in it. Then push them to one side of the pan and add the onions and mushrooms. Cook 2 minutes, then remove the sausages and slice each one into three diagonally. Return them to the pan.

Stir in the flour, then add the tomato purée, the sherry and stock. Bring to the boil, season and add the bay leaf. Cover, reduce the heat and simmer gently for 20 minutes. Remove the bay leaf. ❄ Turn the kidney mixture into a dish and keep warm while you prepare the croûtes. Cut 6 heart shapes out of the bread, using a biscuit cutter. Fry in hot oil until golden. Drain and arrange them round the edge of the dish. Serves 4.

8oz (225g) pickling onions
4 lambs' kidneys
4oz (100g) button mushrooms
2oz (50g) butter
8oz (225g) chipolata sausages
1 tablesp. (15ml) flour
1 teasp. (5ml) tomato purée
1 tablesp. (15ml) sherry
½ pint (300ml) beef stock
salt and pepper
1 bay leaf
TO FINISH:
3 or 4 slices stale white bread for croûtes
oil

❄ TO FREEZE: cool kidneys, then pack in a rigid container, seal, label and use within 2 months.

TO USE: thaw kidneys overnight in the fridge, then reheat gently in a sauté pan. Complete as from ❄ in recipe.

Chicken Bonne Femme

Tender sweet carrots and baby new potatoes are the traditional garnish for this simple but wholesome chicken dish

4 oz (100g) belly pork
1 roasting chicken – about 3 lb
  (1.35kg)
1 oz (25g) butter
1 tablesp. (15ml) oil
1 onion or 8 pickling onions
¾ pint (425ml) chicken stock
1 bouquet garni
TO FINISH:
1 teasp. (5ml) arrowroot
1 tablesp. (15ml) water
TO GARNISH:
baby carrots
new potatoes
finely chopped parsley

Remove the skin and bones from the pork and cut the meat into tiny cubes or strips. Divide the chicken into four or six joints.

Fry the pieces of pork until brown all over, push them aside, add the butter and oil to the pan, put in the chicken joints and brown them well on both sides. Add the onion, peeled and sliced, or the baby onions, peeled and left whole. Pour over the stock, tuck in the bouquet garni, bring to the boil, cover the pan, lower the heat and cook gently for 30 minutes. Remove the bouquet garni. ✳ Transfer the chicken joints and onions to a dish and keep warm. Strain the stock into a pan, bring to the boil and thicken with the arrowroot mixed to a paste with the water, and continue boiling until the sauce thickens. Check the seasoning. Pour the sauce over the chicken and garnish with freshly-cooked baby carrots and new potatoes; sprinkle with chopped parsley. Serves 4.

✳ TO FREEZE: pack the chicken in its sauce into a rigid container, seal, label and freeze. Use within 2 months.

TO USE: thaw the chicken overnight in the fridge, turn into an ovenproof dish and reheat (350 deg. F, 180 deg. C, Gas no. 4) for 35–40 minutes until piping hot. Complete as from ✳ in recipe.

Nasi Goreng

Mystifying its name may be, but this Indonesian delicacy means simply ''fried rice'' – but with a difference. To it are usually added chicken and prawns but ham, pork or other meats can be substituted. It is usually garnished with an omelet cut into strips, and served with a cucumber or tomato salad

8oz (225g) long grain rice
1 onion
1 clove garlic
2 tablesp. (30ml) oil
1 teasp. (5ml) chilli powder
8oz (225g) diced cooked chicken
1 tablesp. (15ml) soy sauce
salt and pepper
TO FINISH:
2 tablesp. (30ml) oil
6oz (150g) frozen prawns, thawed
2 eggs

Cook the rice in a large pan of boiling, salted water until tender, drain, rinse and dry.

Peel and finely chop the onion. Remove the papery coating from the garlic and crush the clove with the back of a knife. Heat the oil in a deep pan, then add onion and garlic. Cook gently until the onion has softened. Stir in the chilli powder and cook for 1 minute.

Add the chicken, rice and soy sauce to the pan and stir well together. Season with salt and pepper and continue to fry the mixture until the rice grains are coated with the oil, adding a little extra oil if necessary. ❋ Add the prawns and while they are heating make the omelet. Beat the eggs, season with salt and make a thin omelet with them. Cut it into ½-in. (1-cm) wide strips and lay them lattice-fashion over the rice. Serve with a tomato or cucumber salad. Serves 4.

❋ TO FREEZE: cool and pack the rice mixture into a rigid container, seal, label and freeze. Use within 1 month.

TO USE: thaw rice mixture in the fridge overnight. Heat oil in a pan, tip in the rice mixture and heat through, stirring. Complete as from ❋ in recipe.

Spanish Chicken

Tomatoes, green pepper
and stuffed olives make a
tasty and colourful mixture
in this chicken dish

Divide the chicken into 6 portions. Season each with salt and pepper.

Remove the rind from the bacon and cut into strips. Fry the bacon in a frying pan large enough to take the chicken joints for about 2 minutes until golden-brown; transfer to a dish. Add the oil to the pan. Put in the chicken joints and fry, turning, until golden-brown – about 10 minutes. Transfer them to the dish holding the bacon.

Peel the tomatoes and remove the seeds, cut the flesh into pieces. Wash the pepper, remove the core and white seeds; cut the flesh into strips. Wipe the mushrooms and slice them if large.

Add these vegetables to the pan in which the chicken was fried and cook gently for about 2 minutes. Pour in the wine and stir around to dislodge any sediment. Return the chicken joints and bacon to the pan. Season with salt and pepper. Bring to the boil, then lower the heat and simmer, uncovered, for about 30 minutes or until the chicken is tender. ❋ Add the olives and serve. Serves 6.

3½lb (1·50kg) roasting chicken
salt and pepper
2oz (50g) streaky bacon
2 tablesp. (30ml) olive oil
4 tomatoes
1 large green pepper
4oz (100g) button mushrooms
¼ pint (150ml) dry white wine
TO FINISH:
8 stuffed olives

❋ TO FREEZE: cool chicken, pack in large rigid container, seal, label and freeze. Use within 2 months.

TO USE: thaw chicken overnight in fridge, then reheat in oven at 350 deg. F, 180 deg. C, Gas no. 4, for about 40 minutes. Complete as from ❋ in recipe.

Turkey Fricassée

Turkey can now be bought portioned and made up into stewing packs as well as joints. Use stewing cuts for this fricassée of meat with mushrooms and chestnuts in a creamy sauce

Cut the turkey into cubes and put in a pan. Peel and halve the onion, peel and halve the carrot and add to the turkey. Cover with stock and add the bay leaf. Bring to the boil, lower the heat and simmer covered, until the turkey is tender, about 30 minutes – 1 hour, depending on the cut used.

Wipe and trim the mushrooms and sauté them briefly in a little butter.

Shell and skin the chestnuts. Put them in a pan, cover with water, bring to the boil and simmer until tender – about 30 minutes.

Remove the onion, carrot and bay leaf from the turkey. Add the mushrooms and chestnuts.

❋ Strain off the stock and reserve. Melt the butter in a pan, stir in the flour and cook gently for 1 minute. Gradually stir in the stock. Bring to the boil, stirring all the time to make a smooth sauce.

In a small basin, blend the egg yolk with the cream, add a little of the hot, but not boiling, sauce to the egg and cream liaison, then pour it slowly back into the pan. Add the sherry, check the seasoning, then stir in the turkey and vegetables. Serves 4.

❋ TO FREEZE. Cool the turkey and vegetables, pack into a rigid container, seal, label and freeze. Use within 2 months.

TO USE. Thaw the turkey mixture in the fridge overnight. Tip into a saucepan and heat through. Remove the pan from the heat and complete as from ❋ in recipe.

1¼ lb (550g) turkey for stewing
1 medium onion
1 carrot
¾ pint (425ml) stock
1 bay leaf
4 oz (100g) button mushrooms
a little butter
12 chestnuts

TO FINISH:
1 oz (25g) butter
1 oz (25g) flour
1 egg yolk
2 tablesp. (30ml) cream
2 tablesp. (30ml) sherry
salt and pepper

Chicken and Ham Pie

Traditional hot water crust is used for this pie but instead of the more usual minced meat the filling is layered chunks of ham and chicken

PASTRY:
12oz (350g) plain flour
½ teasp. (2.5ml) salt
4½oz (115g) lard
3½floz (105ml) water
FILLING:
3lb (1.35kg) chicken
8oz (225g) lean bacon or ham
4oz (100g) mushrooms
1 tablesp. (15ml) chopped parsley
salt and pepper
beaten egg
JELLIED STOCK:
reserved chicken carcass and giblets
1 pig's trotter
1 pint (550ml) water
1 carrot
1 onion
1 bay leaf

First make the pastry. Sieve the flour and salt into a bowl. Put the lard and water in a pan and bring to the boil. Pour into the flour and mix together with a wooden spoon. Cover and put to one side.

Using a sharp knife, skin the chicken, remove all the flesh, then cut into chunks. Reserve the carcass and giblets for the stock. Cut the rind from the bacon and cut into pieces or chop the ham roughly. Wipe and slice the mushrooms.

Cut off about one-third of the pastry and set aside for the pie lid. Use the rest to line a 1½-pint (825-ml) capacity game pie mould or a 6-in. (15-cm), 3-pint (1.70-litre) cake tin. This is best done by putting the pastry in the tin and moulding it up the sides with your hands.

Add the chicken, ham, mushrooms and parsley in layers, seasoning each layer with salt and pepper.

Roll out the remaining pastry for the pie lid. Damp the edges with water, lay over pie and pinch the edges to seal. Make a slit in the centre and use pastry trimmings to decorate. Glaze with beaten egg and bake in preheated oven (425 deg. F, 220 deg. C, Gas no. 7) for 15 minutes. Then reduce the oven temperature to 350 deg. F, 180 deg. C, Gas no. 4 and bake a further 1½ hours.

Remove the pie from the oven and cool for about 20 minutes. Carefully take it out of the tin and stand on a baking sheet. Brush the sides with beaten egg and return to the oven for a further 20 minutes. If the top is getting too brown, cover with greaseproof paper.

While the pie is cooking, make the jellied stock. Put the chicken carcass and giblets in a large saucepan with the trotter, water, peeled and sliced carrot, peeled and chopped onion, bay leaf and salt and pepper to taste. Bring to the boil and simmer for 2 hours. Strain and leave until just warm. Skim off any fat.

Remove the pie from the oven and cool slightly. Pour about ¼ pint (150ml) of the jellied stock through the hole in the top. Cool completely. ❋
Serves 6.

TO FREEZE: when cold, wrap pie in foil, seal, label and freeze. Use within 1 month. Rest of stock may be frozen in a rigid container for 3 months.

TO USE: thaw pie in fridge for 24 hours.

Crispy Chicken with Celery Sauce

Celery is an excellent flavouring vegetable. Here it is made into a creamy sauce to accompany crisp golden chicken portions

Divide the chicken into joints. Remove the skin and pat the flesh dry with kitchen paper. Season the breadcrumbs with salt and pepper.

Break the egg into a shallow dish and beat well with a fork. If using a small egg, add 1 tablespoon (15ml) oil and mix it in. It makes the egg go further and helps to moisten the meat. Dip the joints first in the beaten egg, then in the breadcrumbs. Then set aside while you make the sauce.

Separate the stalks of celery, remove the leaves and any rust marks, and chop up roughly. Put into a pan with the milk, season with salt and pepper, cover and cook until tender. Rub through a sieve or purée in a blender, then rub through a sieve. Even with a blender it is necessary to rub the purée through a sieve to make sure there are no stringy bits left.

Melt the butter in a clean saucepan, blend in the flour to form a roux, cook for 1 minute, then stir in the celery purée and stir constantly until boiling. Add a little cream to the sauce, check the seasoning and reheat if necessary. Keep warm whilst the chicken is being fried.

Heat the butter and oil in a frying pan and fry each chicken piece 6–8 minutes on both sides until cooked and golden. Serve at once, with the sauce separately. Serves 4.

2½lb (1.25kg) roasting chicken
4oz (100g) fine breadcrumbs
salt and pepper
1 egg
2-3 tablesp. (30-45ml) oil
2oz (50g) butter

SAUCE:
1 head celery – about 10oz (275g)
½ pint (300ml) milk
1oz (25g) butter
½oz (15g) flour
1-2 tablesp. single cream

TO FREEZE: drain the chicken pieces on absorbent kitchen paper and cool. Open freeze until hard, then pack them in polythene bags. Seal, label and return to the freezer. Use within 1 month. Cool the sauce, pack in rigid container, leaving ½in. (1cm) headspace for expansion, seal, label and freeze. Use within 2 months.

TO USE: unwrap and place the chicken pieces on a baking sheet; reheat from frozen (400 deg. F, 200 deg. C, Gas no. 6) for about 40 minutes. Tip the sauce into a pan and heat gently, stirring.

Chicken Korma

Korma is the Indian way of braising meat or vegetables. Here chicken is lightly spiced, then braised in yogurt. Turmeric is used to flavour the chicken and give it an attractive yellow colour

4 chicken portions or
1 x 2½lb (1.25kg) chicken, jointed
1 teasp. (5ml) ground coriander
½ teasp. (2.5ml) ground cardamom
½ teasp. (2.5ml) ground cumin
1 teasp. (5ml) ground turmeric
¼ teasp. (1.25ml) ground ginger
¼ pint (150ml) natural yogurt
2oz (50g) butter
1 medium onion
2 cloves garlic
¼ pint (150ml) water
1 tablesp. (15ml) ground almonds

Wipe and skin the chicken portions or joint and skin the whole chicken.

Make a paste of the spices and 1 tablespoon (15ml) of the yogurt. Make incisions with a sharp knife all over the chicken pieces and spread the spicy mixture over them. Leave for 2 hours.

Melt the butter in a pan. Peel and finely chop the onion and fry gently until transparent. Peel and crush the garlic and add to the onion. Put in the chicken joints and fry them all over until browned. Stir in the water and simmer, covered, for 30-40 minutes or until the chicken is tender. Remove the chicken joints.

ground almonds with the rest of the yogurt and stir it into the sauce. Cook, stirring, for 5 minutes. ✳ Replace the chicken joints in the pan, heat through, serve with rice. Serves 4.

❄ TO FREEZE. Pack the cooled chicken joints into a rigid container. Pour over the sauce, seal, label and freeze. Use within 1 month.

TO USE. Thaw the chicken overnight in the fridge and reheat (375 deg. F, 190 deg. C, Gas No. 5) for 1 hour. Complete as from ✳ in recipe.

Turkey Tetrazzini

A nourishing and filling lunch or supper dish. Take care not to overcook the spaghetti as it gets a second cooking in the sauce when the dish is completed

3oz (75g) butter
1½oz (40g) flour
½ pint (300ml) turkey or chicken stock
½ pint (300ml) creamy milk
2oz (50g) grated cheese
salt and pepper
2 tablesp. (30ml) sherry
8oz (225g) spaghetti
8oz (225g) button mushrooms
12oz (350g) cooked turkey

Melt half the butter in a pan, stir in the flour and cook for 1 minute. Gradually add the stock and milk, bring to the boil, then lower the heat and cook gently for 5 minutes, stirring continuously. Add 1½oz (40g) of the grated cheese. Season with salt and pepper and stir in the sherry. Set aside.

Cook the spaghetti in plenty of salted water but keep it slightly underdone. Drain.

Wipe and trim the mushrooms; leave whole if they are tiny, otherwise halve or quarter them. Melt the rest of the butter in a pan and sauté the mushrooms in it. Add these to the spaghetti.

Mix about a quarter of the sauce with the chopped turkey. Add the rest of the sauce to the mushrooms and spaghetti and mix together.

Spoon the spaghetti mixture into an oven-proof dish, 8¾in. (21.5cm) square. Top it with the turkey mixture. ❄ Reheat in the oven (350 deg. F, 180 deg. C, Gas no. 4) for about 30 minutes or until really hot. Sprinkle with the remaining ½oz (15g) cheese for the last 10 minutes of cooking time. Serves 4.

❄ TO FREEZE: cool the turkey and spaghetti mixture; if using a glass baking dish turn into a foil or other suitable freezer dish. Open freeze, and when hard cover with foil, seal, label and freeze. Use within 2 months.

TO USE: thaw the mixture overnight in the fridge, remove wrappings and complete as from ❄ in recipe.

Chicken in Lemon Sauce

The lemon gives a sharp, refreshing piquancy to the sauce. Serve the chicken with rice or fill the mixture into vol-au-vent cases and serve with vegetables

Put the chicken into a pan and just cover with cold water; bring to the boil, skim off any scum, then add the onion stuck with the cloves, the carrot peeled, bouquet garni, a little salt and the peppercorns. Lower the heat and simmer until the bird is tender — 45 minutes – 1 hour. Remove the bird from the stock and leave it to cool slightly while making the sauce. Strain and reserve the stock.

Put the milk in a pan, together with lemon rind, bay leaf and thyme, tied with a piece of cotton, and simmer for 15 minutes. Strain and reserve the flavoured milk.

Melt the margarine in a pan, stir in the flour and cook the roux over a gentle heat until golden. Remove from the heat and stir in the strained milk and stock. Return the pan to the heat and cook gently until the sauce is smooth and thickened. Add the juice of the lemon and cook the sauce a further minute.

Strip all the meat off the chicken and cut it into chunks or strips. Wipe the mushrooms and sauté them in the butter for 2 minutes. Add the chicken and mushrooms to the sauce. ❄ Reheat (but do not boil) and serve. Serves 4.

2½-3lb (1.25-1.35kg) chicken, giblets removed
1 onion
3 cloves
1 carrot
1 bouquet garni
salt
6 peppercorns

SAUCE:
½ pint (300ml) milk
piece lemon rind
1 bay leaf
sprig lemon thyme
1½oz (40g) margarine
1½oz (40g) flour
½ pint (300ml) stock
juice 1 lemon
4oz (100g) button mushrooms
1 oz (25g) butter

❄ TO FREEZE: cool chicken mixture and pack in rigid container, seal, label and freeze. Use within 4 months.

TO USE: thaw chicken mixture overnight in fridge, then tip into a pan and reheat, stirring from time to time, till hot.

Chicken Surprise

This is based on the classic recipe of chicken breasts wrapped round parsley butter, coated in breadcrumbs and fried. Here, cream cheese and garlic are blended with the butter for a delicious creamy stuffing

2 oz (50g) cream cheese
½ oz (15g) butter
½ clove garlic
1 teasp. (5ml) chopped parsley
salt and pepper
4 chicken breasts, about 6 oz (150g) each
1 oz (25 g) seasoned flour
1 large egg
3 oz (75g) fresh white breadcrumbs
oil for deep frying

Cream the cheese and butter together in a bowl until well blended. Remove papery coating from the garlic and crush to a pulp with a little salt with the back of a knife or crush in a garlic press. Mix with the chopped parsley and stir into the cheese mixture. Season with salt and pepper.

Form the cheese mixture into a pat and wrap in greaseproof paper; put in the fridge for about 20 minutes to firm.

Remove the bone from the breast joints with a sharp knife and take off the skin. Put each piece of breast between two sheets of greaseproof paper and beat out to about ½ in. (1 cm) thickness, using a rolling pin or mallet (see page 267)

Lay each breast out flat. Remove the cheese mixture from the fridge and divide it equally between the chicken breasts. Fold the edges of the breasts over, then roll up tightly. Secure each one with a cocktail stick.

Dip each chicken roll in flour seasoned with salt and pepper, then beaten egg, then roll in breadcrumbs ✳ (see right). Repeat the egging and crumbing. Heat the oil, to 350 deg. F, 180 deg. C (if you don't have a frying thermometer, the oil is at the correct temperature when a pinch of flour dropped in sizzles). Deep fry each breast for about 10 minutes or until crisp and golden. Lift out and drain on kitchen paper. Remove cocktail sticks and arrange the chicken rolls on a dish and serve with mangetout and new potatoes. Serves 4.

✳ TO FREEZE: open freeze the chicken rolls; when solid, wrap, seal, label and return to the freezer. Use within 1 month.

TO USE: thaw the chicken rolls overnight in the fridge. Remove wrappings and complete as from ✳ in recipe.

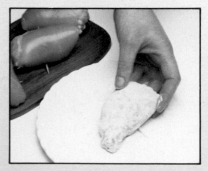

After stuffing and rolling up chicken breasts, roll in seasoned flour

Coat each floured chicken roll generously with beaten egg

Roll the 'egged' chicken pieces in breadcrumbs, shaking off excess

Put egged and crumbed chicken rolls on foil-covered tray to open freeze

Savannah Duckling

A splendid dinner party dish with its richly flavoured, mildly spiced sauce. Easier to serve if it is carved before dishing up – it's certainly better to do this if freezing, so that it takes up less freezer space and is quicker to thaw

1 duckling, about 4½lb (2kg), fresh or frozen and thawed
salt

SAUCE:
2 tablesp. duckling dripping, taken from roasting tin
2 shallots or 1 small onion
1 small green pepper
1 oz (25g) flour
½ teasp. (2.5ml) curry powder
¼ pint (300ml) natural unsweetened orange juice
¼ pint (150ml) duckling stock (made from giblets)
1 teasp. (5ml) caster sugar
1 tablesp. (15ml) orange-flavoured liqueur or brandy

GARNISH:
bunch watercress
fresh orange slices

Pat the duckling dry inside and out with absorbent kitchen paper. Prick the skin all over with a fork and sprinkle with salt. Preheat oven to 350 deg. F, 180 deg. C, Gas no. 4.

Place the duckling, breast uppermost, on a grill rack or trivet in a shallow roasting tin and roast on the centre shelf of the oven, allowing 25 minutes per lb (450g).

Meanwhile prepare the sauce. Peel and chop the shallots or onion. Halve the pepper, discard the core and seeds, and chop finely. Heat the duckling dripping in a saucepan. Add the onion and green pepper and fry gently for 2–3 minutes, turning as necessary.

Sprinkle in the flour and curry powder and stir over gentle heat for 1 minute. Remove the pan from the heat. Carefully blend in the orange juice and stock. Stir in the sugar.

Return the pan to the heat, bring to the boil and simmer the sauce gently for 2 minutes, stirring throughout. Stir in the liqueur or brandy and season to taste. ❄

Arrange the duckling on a hot serving dish, garnish with sprigs of watercress and fresh orange slices, and serve the sauce separately. Serves 4.

❄ TO FREEZE: quarter the duckling with a sharp knife or poultry shears or carve into portions. Arrange the portions in suitable foil containers and cover with cooled sauce. When cold cover with cling film, then seal the containers with lids or foil. Label and freeze. Use in 3 months.

TO USE: thaw the portions of duckling in fridge overnight, remove the lids and wrappings and reheat, uncovered, in a hot oven (425 deg. F, 220 deg. C, Gas no. 7) for 30 minutes. Complete as from ❄ in recipe.

Chicken in Fruit Sauce

By the time the chicken is cooked the orange juice and apricots have amalgamated into a thick, fruity sauce. Serve with boiled rice, preferably brown, which has a lovely nutty flavour

Soak the apricots in the orange juice overnight. Peel and chop the onion. Melt the butter in a large sauté or frying pan and cook the onion gently until soft. Put in the chicken portions, raise the heat and brown them well all over.

Drain the apricots, reserving the juice. Chop them into pieces and add to the chicken, stirring them round in the buttery pan juices. Pour over the reserved juice. Season with salt and pepper, lower the heat and simmer for about 45 minutes or until the chicken is tender and the juices reduced. ❄ Serve with rice and a green salad. Serves 4.

4oz (100g) dried apricots
½ pint (300ml) orange juice
1 medium-sized onion
2oz (50g) butter
4 chicken portions
salt and pepper

❄ TO FREEZE: cool the chicken mixture and pack into a rigid container, seal, label and freeze. Use within 3 months.

TO USE: thaw the chicken overnight in the fridge. Reheat in oven (350 deg. F, 180 deg. C, Gas no. 4) for about 40 minutes or until heated through. Complete as from ❄ in recipe.

Duckling with Apricot and Sherry Sauce

No last-minute carving here – the duckling is portioned before arranging on the serving dish. Apricots provide a sharp tang as contrast to the rich flesh of the duckling

Preheat the oven (350 deg. F, 180 deg. C, Gas no. 4). Pat the duckling dry inside and out with kitchen paper. Prick the skin all over with a fork and sprinkle with salt.

Place the duckling on a grill rack or trivet in a shallow roasting tin, the breast uppermost. Roast on centre shelf allowing 30 minutes to the pound. Remove the duckling from the oven 10-15 minutes before the end of the cooking time and brush apricot jam over the skin. Return the duckling to the oven to complete the cooking.

To prepare the sauce: if using fresh apricots, halve and discard the stones; make a syrup by dissolving the sugar in the water over gentle heat. Add the apricots to the pan and simmer gently until they are tender but still keeping their shape. If using canned apricots, use the syrup from the can.

Set 4 apricot halves aside and keep warm. Sieve the remaining apricots and syrup or liquidize in a blender. Make up to 1 pint (550ml) with the duckling stock.

Take 2 tablespoons (30ml) of the fat and juices from the roasting tin and place in a saucepan. Add the cornflour and stir until frothy. Remove the pan from the heat and gradually blend in the apricot and stock mixture, sherry and chopped parsley. Season well. Return the pan to the heat, bring to the boil, then simmer for 2 minutes, stirring throughout. Check the seasoning and if a slightly sharper sauce is preferred, add a little lemon juice.

Carve the duckling into four (see below) ❄ and arrange on a hot serving dish; garnish with the reserved hot apricots and sprigs of watercress. Serve the sauce separately. Serves 4.

4-5 lb (1.80-2.25kg) oven-ready duckling
salt
1 tablesp. (15ml) apricot jam
SAUCE:
8 oz (225g) fresh apricots, plus 4 oz (100g) sugar and ¼ pint (150ml) water, or 1 x 14½ oz (410g) can apricot halves
½ pint (300ml) stock, made from duck giblets
1 oz (25g) cornflour
4 tablesp. (60ml) dry sherry
1 tablesp. (15ml) finely chopped parsley
salt
freshly milled black pepper
lemon juice (optional)
TO GARNISH:
bunch watercress

❄ TO FREEZE: cool the duckling quarters as quickly as possible. Place them in a large foil container and put an apricot half on top of each portion. Cool the sauce and spoon over the duckling to cover. Seal, label and freeze. Use within 2 months.

TO USE: preheat the oven (350 deg. F, 180 deg. C, Gas no. 4). Remove the cover from the foil container and cook from frozen in preheated oven for 1 hour. Complete as from ❄ in recipe.

Split duckling in half by slicing through the centre breast bone and cutting completely through bird.

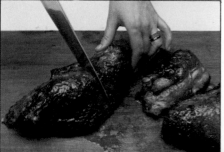

Divide each half in two by cutting as shown, to give 2 wing and 2 leg portions.

Pheasant with Apple

Pheasant are in season from October to February and when young are best plainly roasted or braised. This recipe is based on a dish originating in Normandy, hence the suggested use of Calvados – an apple brandy distilled in that part of France

1 x 2lb (900g) pheasant
2oz (50g) butter
2 tablesp. (30ml) Calvados or brandy
1 small onion
2-3 sticks celery
2 green apples
salt and pepper
pinch thyme
$\frac{1}{4}$ pint (150ml) cider
$\frac{1}{4}$ pint (150ml) double cream
TO FINISH:
triangles fried bread or apple rings sautéed in butter

Divide the pheasant into four – as for duckling, see page 136.

Melt the butter in a pan and sauté the pheasant until golden. Pour over the Calvados or brandy, set light to it and let it burn out. Remove the pheasant and keep warm.

Peel and chop the onion and add to the pan juices. Cut the celery sticks into small pieces; peel, core and chop the apples and add all to the pan. Cook gently until beginning to soften. Season with salt and pepper and the thyme. Pour on the cider and return the pheasant joints to the pan, cover and cook for about 40 minutes or until the pheasant is tender.

Place the pheasant joints on a serving dish and keep warm. Sieve or blend the vegetables and juices left in the pan. Stir in the cream, check the seasoning and reheat; pour over the pheasant.

✳ Garnish with triangles of fried bread or apple rings sautéed in butter. Serves 4.

✳ TO FREEZE: place pheasant joints in a rigid container. Sieve vegetables and juices, stir in the cream and check the seasoning. Pour the sauce over the pheasant. When cold, cover, seal, label and freeze. Use within 2 months.

TO USE: thaw pheasant overnight in the fridge; transfer to a casserole and reheat in oven (375 deg. F, 190 deg. C, Gas no. 5) for 40 minutes. Complete as from ✳ in recipe.

Game Pudding

Any mixture of game can be used to make this rich meaty pudding. If you can spare it, a glass of port would enrich and flavour it even further

First make the suet crust. Sift the flour and a good pinch of salt into a bowl and stir in the suet. Mix to a firm dough with cold water. Use three-quarters of the dough to line a 3-pint (1.7-litre) capacity boilable plastic or foil basin.

Toss the meat in seasoned flour: mix the flour with a little salt and pepper. Trim and wipe the mushrooms. Peel and finely chop the onion. Mix the meat, mushrooms, onion and herbs together. Spoon the mixture into the pastry-lined basin. Pour over the red wine and stock. Turn the edges of the suet pastry in a fraction over the meat.

Roll out the remaining quarter of suet pastry, dampen its edge and place in position on top of the meat in the basin, pinching the edges together. Cover the pudding with a piece of foil pleated across the middle to allow for expansion during boiling. Place the basin in a pan filled with enough hot water to reach half way up the side of the basin; boil for 3 hours, topping up the water from time to time. ✳ Serves 4–6.

TO FREEZE: remove the foil and, when the pudding is cold, re-cover it with clean foil. Overwrap in a polythene bag, seal, label and freeze. Use within 2 months.

TO USE: reheat the pudding in a pan of boiling water for 1½ hours.

2 tablesp. (30ml) seasoned flour
1½lb (675g) game (a mixture of boned venison, hare, pigeon, etc.)
4oz (100g) button mushrooms
1 small onion
½ teasp. (2.5ml) mixed herbs
¼ pint (150ml) red wine
2½fl oz (75ml) stock

SUET CRUST:
1lb (450g) flour
8oz (225g) shredded suet
about ½ pint (300ml) cold water

Pigeon, Sausage and Mushroom Pie

Pigeons may not have much flesh on them but what there is has a good gamey flavour. Here they're teamed with sausage and mushrooms to make a succulent puff pastry pie

1 carrot
1 onion
2 oz (50g) butter
3 pigeons
1¼ pints (700ml) beef stock
6 oz (150g) pork sausagemeat
1 tablesp. (15ml) oil
4 oz (100g) button mushrooms
1 oz (25g) flour
salt and pepper
7½ oz (212g) packet frozen puff
   pastry, thawed or home-made
   (see page 264)
beaten egg to glaze

Rest finger lightly on pie edge and, working upwards, knock up pastry edges with back of knife

Peel and slice the carrot and onion. Melt 1 oz (25g) butter in a large deep pan, add the carrot and onion, and cook until softened. Add the pigeons, halved, to the pan and brown them slowly. Pour on sufficient stock just to cover them. Put on the lid and simmer for 1 hour or until pigeons are just tender.

Cut the breast meat from the pigeons, return the carcasses to the pan and continue cooking to give flavour to the stock. Meanwhile, divide the sausagemeat into 12, and roll each piece into a ball. Heat the oil in a frying pan, add the sausage-meat balls and fry, turning them till brown and cooked through. Wipe the mushrooms and halve or quarter them if large. Mix the pigeon meat, sausagemeat balls and mushrooms together in a 2½-pint (1.4-litre) pie dish.

Melt the remaining butter in a pan and stir in the flour. Strain the stock, gradually add it to the pan and cook, stirring, till thickened. Adjust the seasoning and add this sauce to the meat in the dish.❄

Roll out the pastry, and cut a strip to line the edge of the pie dish, and use the rest of the pastry to cover the dish, trim the edges, knock up and flute (see left). Brush the pastry with beaten egg to glaze and bake in a preheated oven (425 deg. F, 220 deg. C, Gas no. 7) for 25 minutes or until the pastry is risen and golden-brown. Then turn the heat down to 350 deg. F, 180 deg. C, Gas no. 4 for 15-20 minutes. Serves 4-6.

 TO FREEZE: cool the meat mixture in its dish, wrap seal and label. Use within 2 months.

TO USE: thaw the cooked meat filling overnight in the fridge. Complete as from ❄ in recipe.

Venison Pasty

The meat needs long, slow cooking to tenderize it so this is done before covering it with the pastry. Port, stock and orange juice give it a really good flavour

1¼lb (550g) venison
1oz (25g) seasoned flour
1oz (25g) butter
6 tablesp. (90ml) port
6 tablesp. (90ml) beef stock
1 orange, grated rind and juice
½ teasp. (2.5ml) mixed herbs or
1 bouquet garni
7½oz (212g) puff pastry, frozen and thawed or homemade (see recipe on page 264)
beaten egg, to glaze

Cut the meat into cubes, then toss in the seasoned flour – made by mixing the flour with a little salt and pepper. Melt the butter in a pan and, when hot, fry the pieces of meat quickly to seal in the juices. Add the port, stock, rind and juice of the orange and sprinkle with herbs or add the bouquet garni. Bring to the boil, cover the pan, lower the heat and cook gently until the meat is tender – about 2 hours. Check the seasoning. ❄ Turn the meat into a 1½-pint (825-ml) capacity pie dish.

Roll out the pastry and cut a strip to line the edge of the pie dish. Use the rest of the pastry for a lid to cover the dish. Trim the pastry edges, knock up with the back of a knife and flute all round. Brush the pastry with beaten egg to glaze and bake in a preheated oven (425 deg. F, 220 deg. C, Gas no. 7) for 25 minutes or until the pastry is risen and golden-brown. Then turn the oven down to 350 deg. F, 180 deg. C, Gas no. 4 for 15 minutes. Serves 4.

❄ TO FREEZE: cool the meat mixture and turn into a rigid container, seal, label and freeze. Use within 2 months.

TO USE: thaw the meat filling overnight in the fridge. Complete as from ❄ in recipe.

Pigeon Casserole

Pigeons can be rather dry but cooked this way they're moist and delicious. It's difficult to give an exact cooking time as this will depend on the age of the birds. The older the birds obviously the longer the cooking time

Remove a small piece of peel from the orange; squeeze out the juice and remove any pips.

Heat the oil and butter in a pan. Put in the pigeons, split, and fry until well browned. Transfer them to a flameproof casserole. Sprinkle the flour into the fats remaining in the pan, stirring it in well, and cook for 1 minute. Gradually stir in the wine and stock, orange juice and redcurrant jelly. Bring to the boil and pour over the pigeons.

Peel the onions and add to the casserole, tuck in the piece of orange peel. Season with salt and pepper and cook (325 deg. F, 170 deg. C, Gas no. 3) for about 2-3 hours or until the pigeons are tender. The time depends on the age of the pigeons. Check seasoning. ❄ Serves 4.

1 orange
2 tablesp. (30ml) oil
1oz (25g) butter
2 pigeons
1oz (25g) flour
$\frac{1}{4}$ pint (150ml) red wine
$\frac{1}{2}$ pint (300ml) beef stock
1 teasp. (5ml) redcurrant jelly
8 pickling onions
salt and pepper

❄ TO FREEZE: cool, pack the pigeons into a rigid container, seal label and freeze. Use within 3 months.

TO USE: thaw the pigeons overnight in the fridge. Transfer to a casserole dish and reheat (350 deg. F, 180 deg. C, Gas no. 4) until bubbling hot – about 1 hour.

Rabbit with Mustard

Use a mild French mustard to coat the rabbit joints for this well-flavoured farmhouse stew

8 rabbit joints
2 tablesp. (30ml) French mustard
1 tablesp. (15ml) flour
1 medium onion
2 oz (50g) streaky bacon
2 oz (50g) butter
½ pint (300ml) chicken stock
salt and pepper
TO FINISH:
¼ pint (150ml) single cream

Wash and wipe the rabbit joints. Smear them all over with the mustard (see below), put them in a dish, sprinkle with flour and set aside for 2 hours.

Peel and chop the onion. Derind the bacon and cut it into strips. Melt the butter in a large pan, add the onion and bacon and fry gently until golden. Add the rabbit joints and brown lightly.

Pour in the stock, season with salt and pepper and bring to the boil. Cover the pan and simmer gently for 1 hour or until the rabbit is tender. ❄ Stir in the cream. Check the seasoning and serve. Serves 4.

❄ TO FREEZE: cool the rabbit, then pack into a large rigid container, seal, label and freeze. Use within 2 months.

TO USE: thaw the rabbit overnight in the fridge. Reheat in a pan until bubbling hot. Complete as from ❄ in recipe.

Use a pastry brush to smear rabbit joints with mustard

Covert Pie

Partridges have been used in this game pie but other game birds, pheasant for instance, would do just as well

1 brace partridges
1oz (25g) butter
8oz (225g) veal
4oz (100g) ham
4oz (100g) mushrooms
1 small onion
pinch thyme
salt and pepper
½ pint (300ml) thickened stock
5 tablesp. (75ml) sherry
TO FINISH:
7½oz (212g) puff pastry, frozen and thawed or homemade (see recipe on page 264)
beaten egg, to glaze

Halve the partridges. Melt the butter in a flame-proof casserole. Put in the partridges, brown them well all over, then take out and set aside.

Cut the veal and ham into small pieces. Clean and chop the mushrooms. Peel and chop the onion. Mix all these ingredients and the thyme together and put half of this mixture in the bottom of the casserole. Season, then arrange the partridge halves on top. Sprinkle the rest of the meat mixture in between and over the top of the patridges. Mix the stock and sherry together and pour it over the meat.

Cover with foil or a lid and cook (325 deg. F, 170 deg. C, Gas no. 3) for 1 hour or on top of the stove until the meat is tender.

❄Transfer the contents of the casserole to a 2-pint (1.1-litre) pie dish. Roll out the pastry and cut a strip to line the edge of the pie dish. Use the rest of the pastry to cover the dish. Trim the pastry edges, knock up with the back of a knife and flute all round. Brush the pastry with beaten egg to glaze and bake in a preheated oven (425 deg. F, 220 deg. C, Gas no. 7) for 25 minutes or until the pastry is risen and golden-brown. Then turn the temperature down (350 deg. F, 180 deg. C, Gas no. 4) for 15 minutes. Serves 4.

❄ TO FREEZE: cool the meat mixture and turn into a rigid container, seal, label and freeze. Use within 2 months.

TO USE: thaw the meat filling overnight in the fridge. Complete as from ❄ in recipe.

Civet of Venison

Venison is inclined to be dry as it has little natural fat so marinate it before cooking to give moisture and flavour. If you're using frozen venison just pour the marinade over and leave it to thaw. Any juices from the meat then leak into the marinade which is used to cook the venison

Put all the marinade ingredients into a basin. Cut the meat into largish cubes and add to the basin. Leave to marinate for 12–24 hours in a cool place or the refrigerator.

In a flameproof casserole fry the bacon, cut into strips, until the fat runs and it begins to brown. Add the oil to the pan. Drain and dry the meat, toss it in the seasoned flour (made by mixing a little salt and pepper with the flour) and add the pieces to the casserole. Raise the heat and brown the meat, turning it over and over.

Strain the marinade on to the meat. Add a little stock or red wine if necessary so that the meat is just covered. Tuck in the bouquet garni. Bring to the boil, cover and place in a preheated oven (325 deg. F, 170 deg. C, Gas no. 3) for about 2 hours or until the meat is tender.

Peel the onions and blanch in boiling water for 7 minutes; drain and place them in a pan with 1oz (25g) butter and the sugar. Cook gently, covered, shaking the pan from time to time until the onions are tender and well glazed. In a separate pan sauté the mushrooms in the remaining butter.

Remove the bouquet garni from the casserole.
✳ Check the seasoning, garnish the meat with the mushrooms and onions and serve. Serves 4–6.

2lb (900g) venison
2 rashers streaky bacon
3 tablesp. (45ml) oil
1oz (25g) seasoned flour
little stock or red wine, if necessary (see method)
1 bouquet garni
MARINADE:
2 carrots
1 onion
1 stick celery
8 peppercorns
1 bay leaf
few parsley stalks
½ pint (300ml) red wine
2 tablesp. (30ml) oil
1 tablesp. (15ml) red wine vinegar
TO FINISH:
4oz (100g) baby onions
4oz (100g) button mushrooms
2oz (50g) butter
1 teasp. (5ml) sugar

TO FREEZE: cool the civet. Pack into a rigid container, seal, label and freeze. Cool mushrooms and onions and pack together in a rigid container, seal, label and freeze. Use within 2 months.

TO USE: thaw meat overnight in the fridge. Reheat in the casserole (325 deg. F, 170 deg. C, Gas no. 3) for about 1 hour. Toss the mushrooms and onions in a little butter to thaw and reheat. Complete as from ✳ in recipe.

Hunter's Rabbit

An easy and tasty stew, with the rabbit
cooked in a well-seasoned
tomato sauce

1 rabbit, jointed
3 tablesp. (45ml) oil
1 onion
1oz (25g) flour
¾ pint (425ml) stock
1 small can tomatoes
1 tablesp. (15ml) tomato purée
1 clove garlic
1 bouquet garni
salt and pepper

TO FINISH:
8oz (225g) mushrooms

Rinse the rabbit portions in cold water and dry
them.

Heat the oil and gently fry the peeled and
chopped onion until soft but not coloured.
Transfer the onion to a casserole dish.

Dip the pieces of rabbit in the flour and fry
them in the oil, left over from frying the onion,
until golden on all sides. Transfer them to the
casserole. Tip any remaining flour into the pan
and stir it round to make a roux.

Gradually stir in the stock, tomatoes, tomato
purée and peeled and crushed garlic. Bring to the
boil and add the bouquet garni. Season with salt
and pepper. Pour over the rabbit; cover and cook
(325 deg. F, 170 deg. C, Gas No. 3) for 1½ hours or
until the rabbit is tender.

✳ Ten minutes before the end of cooking add
the sliced or quartered mushrooms. Check the
seasoning and serve with creamed potatoes and
carrots. Serves 4.

TO FREEZE. Remove
the bouquet garni
and cool. When cold
pack into a rigid container
seal, label and freeze. Use
within 1 month.

TO USE. Thaw the rabbit
overnight in the fridge and
reheat in a heavy-based
pan for about 30 minutes.
Complete as from ✳ in
recipe, adding the mush-
rooms 10 minutes before
the end of reheating.

Jugged Hare

One of the oldest of English dishes, it gets its name from the deep, lidded earthenware jug in which it used to be cooked. The gravy should be thickened with the hare's blood and not allowed to boil or it will curdle. If the blood isn't available or you can't face using it, then thicken the juices with flour as here

1 tablesp. (15ml) dripping
1 hare, jointed
2 onions
2 carrots
1 stick celery
1 bouquet garni
salt and pepper
1½ pints (825ml) stock
FORCEMEAT BALLS:
1 small onion
1oz (25g) butter
4oz (100g) fresh breadcrumbs
2oz (50g) shredded suet
1 tablesp. (15ml) chopped parsley
½ lemon, grated rind only
1 egg, beaten
TO FINISH:
1oz (25g) flour
1 small glass port
1 tablesp. (15ml) redcurrant jelly

Melt the dripping in a flameproof casserole. Fry the hare joints until they are browned all over. Peel and chop the onions and carrots and cut the celery into pieces. Add them to the hare together with the bouquet garni. Season with salt and pepper and cover with stock.

Put on the lid and place the casserole in the preheated oven (325 deg. F, 170 deg. C, Gas no. 3) for 2½–3 hours or until the hare is tender.

To make the forcemeat balls: peel and chop the onion. Melt the butter in a pan and soften the onion in it. Remove from the heat and stir in the breadcrumbs, suet, parsley and lemon rind. Season with salt and pepper and bind with beaten egg. Shape into small balls. ✳ Arrange the balls on a greased baking sheet and put in the oven with the hare for the last 20 minutes of the cooking time.

A few minutes before serving, blend the flour with a little cold water to a smooth cream and stir into the casserole with the port and jelly. Check the seasoning and when hot serve the casserole with forcemeat balls on top. Serves 6.

TO FREEZE: cool the hare and pack into a rigid container, seal, label and freeze. Use within 3 months. Open freeze the forcemeat balls and when hard pack into a polythene bag, seal, label and return to the freezer. Use within 1 month.

TO USE: thaw the hare overnight in the fridge. Transfer hare and gravy to a casserole and reheat (350 deg. F, 180 deg. C, Gas no. 4) for about 1 hour or until bubbling hot. Complete as from ✳ in recipe.

Rabbit and Pepper Pie

The filling in this plate pie
has good colour and
flavour contrast – pale
bland rabbit in creamy
sauce spiked with pieces
of aromatic red pepper

First make the pastry. Sieve the flour and salt into a mixing bowl. Cut the fats into small pieces and rub into the flour until the mixture resembles breadcrumbs. Add just enough cold water to mix to a firm but not sticky dough. Halve the dough and roll out one half large enough to line a deep pie plate, about 8in. (20cm) in diameter.

Peel and chop the onion. Cut the pepper in half lengthways, then remove the core and tiny white seeds inside and discard; chop the pepper into fairly small pieces. Melt the butter in a pan, add the onion and pepper and cook until soft. Stir in the flour and cook for 1 minute, then gradually add the stock and milk, stirring as you do so. Bring slowly to the boil, stirring all the time, and cook for 1 minute. Dice the cooked rabbit and stir in; check the seasoning. ❄

Fill the rabbit mixture into the pie plate. Roll out the remaining pastry to make a lid, dampen the pastry edges and place over the meat, pressing the pastry edges well together to seal them. ❄ ❄ Make 2–3 slits in the top of the pastry and bake in preheated oven (425 deg. F, 220 deg. C, Gas no. 7) for about 10 minutes, then reduce the heat to 375 deg. F, 190 deg. C, Gas no. 5 and bake for a further 15–20 minutes until the pastry is cooked and golden. Serve hot. Serves 4.

PASTRY:
10oz (275g) plain flour
pinch salt
2½oz (65g) lard
2½oz (65g) margarine
cold water to mix

1 small onion
1 red pepper
1½ oz (40g) butter
1oz (25g) flour
¼ pint (150ml) stock
¼ pint (150ml) milk
6oz (150g) cooked rabbit
salt and pepper

❄ TO FREEZE: cool the mixture before filling into the pie plate as from ❄ in recipe. Continue recipe until ❄ ❄ , then open freeze the pie until hard; slip into a polythene bag, seal, label and return to the freezer. Use within 2 months.

TO USE: unwrap the pie and cook from frozen as from ❄ ❄ in recipe, allowing an extra 10–15 minutes at the lower temperature.

French Apple Flan

This is the classic French apple tart. A crisp sweet pastry case is filled with thick apple sauce, topped with thinly sliced eating apples, then coated with apricot glaze to finish

6 oz (150g) plain flour
pinch salt
3½ oz (90 g) hard margarine or butter
1 oz (25 g) caster sugar
1 egg yolk

FILLING :
2 oz (50 g) butter
2 lb (900 g) cooking apples
4 oz (100 g) sugar
½ lemon, juice only
1 tablesp.(15 ml) apricot jam
2 red-skinned eating apples

Sieve the flour and salt into a basin, rub in the fat, then stir in the sugar and bind with the beaten egg yolk. Form the dough into a ball; wrap it in foil and chill in the fridge for 30 minutes.

To make the filling, melt the butter in a pan. Peel and core the cooking apples. Cut them up roughly and add to the butter, together with the sugar. Add 1 or 2 tablespoons water if the apples are rather dry. Cover the pan and cook until the apples are soft. Strain and reserve the juice, then sieve the apples and leave the purée to cool.

Roll out the pastry and line it into an 8-in. (20-cm) loose-bottomed flan tin. Spoon the apple purée into the flan case.

Put the reserved apple juices into a pan with the lemon juice and the apricot jam. Heat gently, stirring, bring to the boil and boil for 3 minutes to make a glaze.

Halve, core and cut the eating apples into thin slices. Arrange them neatly over the apple purée and brush with a little of the glaze. Bake the flan (400 deg F, 200 deg C, Gas No. 6) for 30 minutes. If the apple slices brown too quickly, cover with foil. Remove the flan from the oven and brush with remaining glaze. ❄Serve warm. Serves 4–6.

TO FREEZE. Cool the flan and either freeze in the flan tin or open freeze until hard, then remove from the tin and pack into a rigid container, seal, label and return to freezer. Use within 2 months.

TO USE. Remove wrappings, return the flan to the tin and reheat, loosely covered (375 deg F, 190 deg C, Gas No. 5), for 40 minutes. Serve warm.

Spicy Plum Pie

A truly ambrosial pie with the plums cooked in red wine and cinnamon. Serve it with chilled whipped cream or a baked egg custard

4oz (100g) sugar
½ teasp. (2.5ml) powdered cinnamon
¼ pint (150ml) red wine
2lb (900g) plums
6oz (150g) shortcrust pastry

Mix the sugar and cinnamon together and put into a pan with the red wine. Place over a gentle heat and stir until the sugar has dissolved.

Halve and stone the plums. Add to the pan. Turn up the heat and let the wine bubble up over the fruit. Turn the fruit and juices into a 1½-pint (825-ml) capacity pie dish, heaping the fruit in the centre, and leave until cold.

To make pastry, see recipe on page 170. Roll out pastry and cut a strip to fit round the edge of the dish; dampen the edge of pie dish with water and fit a strip of pastry on to it. Dampen the pastry edges and lift the pastry lid on to the dish; flute the edges. Use the pastry trimmings for decoration. ✽ Make slit in lid.

Bake pie in preheated oven (400 deg. F, 200 deg. C, Gas no. 6) for 30-40 minutes or until the pastry is crisp and golden and the plums are cooked. Serves 4-6.

✽ TO FREEZE: open freeze pie and when hard put into polythene bag, seal, label and freeze. Use within 1 month.

TO USE: thaw for 10 minutes whilst oven is heating; complete as from ✽ in recipe, allowing 40-50 minutes to bake.

Chocolate Pear Pudding

When baked the chocolate sponge should be slightly sticky under a crisp top. It then forms a delicious sauce mingling with the pears and walnuts

Put the water and sugar into a pan and dissolve over a gentle heat. Peel, halve and core the pears. Put each pear into the syrup as it's prepared so that it doesn't discolour. Poach the pears until tender – about 10 minutes.

Melt the butter, stir in the demerara sugar and walnuts. Pour into the bottom of an 8 × 2in. (20 × 5cm) baking dish or tin. Arrange the drained pears on top.

To make the sponge, cream the margarine and sugar together, then beat in the eggs. Sieve the flour and cocoa over the top and mix it in. Spoon over the pears. ❄ Bake in preheated oven (350 deg. F, 180 deg. C, Gas no. 4) for about 45 minutes. Serve with cream. Serves 4.

½ pint (300ml) water
4oz (100g) sugar
4 small pears
1oz (25g) butter
2oz (50g) demerara sugar
1oz (25g) chopped walnuts
SPONGE:
4½oz (115g) margarine
4½oz (115g) caster sugar
2 small eggs
4oz (100g) self-raising flour
1oz (25g) cocoa

❄ TO FREEZE: open freeze the pudding until hard, then cover, seal, label and return to freezer. Use within 2 months.

TO USE: bake the pudding from frozen in preheated oven (400 deg. F, 200 deg. C, Gas no. 6) for 30 minutes then reduce the temperature to 375 deg. F, 190 deg. C, Gas no. 5 for 20 minutes.

West Country Pancakes

We've used a Scotch pancake mixture for this pudding. The soft sponginess of these pancakes is particularly good with the apple filling. Keep the apples on the sharp side as the apricot glaze sweetens the dish

BATTER:
8oz (225g) self-raising flour
1 teasp. (5ml) caster sugar
pinch salt
1 egg
6–8 fl.oz (180–240ml) milk

FILLING:
1 lb (450g) cooking apples
¼ pint (150ml) cider
2oz (50g) granulated sugar

TO FINISH:
4 tablesp. (60ml) apricot jam
1 tablesp. (15ml) water
½oz (15g) toasted, flaked almonds

First make the batter. Sieve the flour, sugar and salt together into a large basin. Make a well in the centre and break in the egg. Gradually add the milk, working in the flour with a spoon until the mixture is the consistency of thick cream.

Heat a flat-bottomed frying pan or a griddle, lightly grease it and pour in sufficient mixture to make a 6-in. (15-cm) round. Cook the pancake 2 minutes or until bubbles rise, then turn over and cook a further 2 minutes. Continue until the batter is finished – you should have about 6 pancakes – and place each pancake between the folds of a clean cloth.

Peel, core and cut the apples into pieces. Cook with the cider and sugar until soft but not mushy. ❄To finish, make the glaze by heating the apricot jam and water together, bring to the boil and then sieve. Pile the pancakes on to a flat dish, layering them with the apple mixture. Pour the apricot glaze over the top and sprinkle with toasted almonds. Cut into wedges and serve with whipped cream. Serves 4.

❄ TO FREEZE. When the pancakes are cold stack with waxed or greaseproof paper between them, wrap in foil, seal, label and freeze. Use within 3 months. When the apple mixture is cold, pack into a rigid container, seal, label and freeze. Use within 3 months.

TO USE. Thaw the pancakes for 30 minutes at room temperature, then reheat in the oven (325 deg. F, 170 deg. C, Gas No. 3), loosely covered with foil, for about 10 minutes. Tip the apple mixture into a pan and heat gently. Complete as from ❄ in recipe.

Honey and Walnut Tart

A rich sticky flan filled
with a mixture of honey,
brown sugar, walnuts and
breadcrumbs. Best served
cold with, if you like,
stiffly whipped cream

8oz (225g) shortcrust pastry
2oz (50g) soft brown sugar
2oz (50g) butter
8oz (225g) honey
½ lemon
6oz (150g) chopped walnuts
3oz (75g) fresh white
breadcrumbs

Line an 8-in. (20-cm) diameter flan tin with pastry. Trim and set pastry trimmings aside to use for the lattice top.

Cream the sugar and butter together and stir in the honey. If it is thick and set, stand the jar of honey in a pan of hot water for a few minutes until the honey is liquid. Grate the rind of the half lemon and squeeze the juice (remove any pips) into the honey mixture. Fold in the walnuts and breadcrumbs. Spread the mixture over the pastry case.

Roll out the pastry trimmings and cut into narrow strips. Lattice those over the filling (see page 160), sealing the ends to the pastry edge.

Bake the tart in preheated oven (350 deg. F, 180 deg. C, Gas no. 4) for 30-40 minutes until golden and set. Check towards the end of the cooking time that the toffee-like filling isn't burning. ❄ Leave until the next day before cutting. Serves 6-8.

❄ TO FREEZE: when cold, open freeze tart, then slip it into a polythene bag, seal, label and return to the freezer. Use within 3 months.

TO USE: unwrap the tart and thaw at room temperature for about 4 hours.

Hungarian Apple Pie

Something a little different in apple pies. A rich short pastry encases a purée of apple. The unusual additions of apricot jam and ground almonds make a delicious pie of subtle flavours

First make the pastry. Sieve the flour and salt into a bowl, stir in the sugar, then rub in the margarine until the mixture resembles breadcrumbs. Beat the egg and use to bind the mixture to a paste. Wrap in foil and chill in the fridge for 30 minutes.

Peel, core and slice the apples into a pan, add the sugar and water, cover and cook over a gentle heat until the apples are soft. Beat them to a pulp, stir in the apricot jam and set aside.

Mix the caster sugar and ground almonds together and set aside.

Roll out two-thirds of the pastry and use it to line a 7-in. (17.5-cm) diameter flan tin. Bake blind at 375 deg. F, 190 deg. C, Gas no. 5 (line uncooked pastry case with foil or greaseproof paper, weight down with dried beans, pasta or crusts, and bake for 10-15 minutes. Remove the lining and return the flan case to the oven for a further 5 minutes until just coloured and dry). See step-by-step photo strip on page 260.

Spread half the sugar and almond mixture over the base of the flan, spoon in the apple, then spread the rest of the almond mixture over the top. Roll out the remaining pastry and cover the top with it, pressing the edges well together. Use the trimmings for decoration if liked. ❋ Bake in preheated oven (400 deg. F, 200 deg. C, Gas no. 6) until pastry is set and golden – about 15 minutes. Serves 4.

❋ TO FREEZE: open freeze pie and when hard slip it into a polythene bag, seal, label and return to the freezer. Use within 2 months.

TO USE: unwrap the pie and bake at 400 deg. F, 200 deg. C, Gas no. 6 for 40 minutes. If the pastry is getting too brown, cover with foil.

1¼lb (550g) cooking apples
4oz (100g) sugar
1 tablesp. (15ml) water
2 tablesp. (30ml) apricot jam
2oz (50g) caster sugar
2oz (50g) ground almonds
PASTRY:
8oz (225g) plain flour
pinch salt
1oz (25g) caster sugar
5oz (125g) margarine
1 egg

Rhubarb and Lemon Flan

A tangy lemon sauce covers the rhubarb
in a rich shortcrust flan case. A few cake
crumbs sprinkled over the pastry base help
to prevent the juices softening the pastry

*Space pastry strips across
flan; trim the pastry ends*

*Starting from centre, weave
pastry strips in and out*

*Continue until lattice is com-
plete; seal ends to flan edge*

Sift the flour and icing sugar into a basin, rub in the butter or hard margarine until the mixture resembles fine breadcrumbs. Mix to a firm dough with water – you'll need about 2 tablespoons (30ml). Roll out the pastry and line into an 8-in. (20-cm) diameter flan tin. Bake blind at 375 deg. F, 190 deg. C, Gas no. 5 (line uncooked pastry case with foil or greaseproof paper, weight down with dried beans, pasta or crusts, and bake as given in recipe for about 15 minutes; remove the lining and return the flan to the oven for a further 5 minutes until it is just coloured and dry).

Wipe the rhubarb, trim and cut into chunks. If you are using frozen fruit allow it to thaw slightly and drain it. Sprinkle the sponge cake crumbs over the base of the partly-cooked flan; these help to mop up juices so the pastry base doesn't soften. Arrange rhubarb chunks over the crumbs.

In a small pan blend together the sugar, cornflour, the egg, lightly beaten, and the grated rind of the lemon. Stir in 2 tablespoons (30ml) juice, squeezed from the lemon, and made up to ¼ pint (150ml) with water. Bring to the boil, stirring, and pour over the rhubarb.

Cut thin strips from the pastry trimmings and arrange them lattice-fashion over the filling (see left). Bake (400 deg. F, 200 deg. C, Gas no. 6) for 35 minutes or until golden. ❄ Serves 4.

6 oz (150g) plain flour
½ oz (15g) icing sugar
3 oz (75g) butter or hard margarine
2 tablesp. (30ml) water
FILLING:
12 oz (350g) rhubarb, fresh or frozen
2 tablesp. (30ml) sponge cake crumbs or crumbled boudoir biscuits
4 oz (100g) sugar
1 tablesp. (15ml) cornflour
1 egg
1 lemon

❄ TO FREEZE: cool the flan, then open freeze; slip it into a polythene bag or cover with foil, seal, label and return to the freezer. Use within 2 months.

TO USE: thaw the flan at room temperature for 2 hours. Then remove the wrappings and heat flan through in a preheated oven (350 deg. F, 180 deg. C, Gas no. 4) for 15-20 minutes.

Toffee Apple Pudding

A comforting cold weather pudding of apple and suet crust layers. The half and half mixture of flour and breadcrumbs produces a lighter dough than an all-flour one. Brown sugar and butter are used to coat the basin and form a toffee-like sauce when the pudding is cooked

4oz (100g) self-raising flour
4oz (100g) breadcrumbs
4oz (100g) shredded suet
cold water
1oz (25g) butter
3oz (75g) soft brown sugar
12oz (350g) cooking apples

Sieve the flour into a bowl, stir in the breadcrumbs, then the suet. Mix to a firm dough with cold water: you'll probably need about 6 tablespoons (90ml). Divide the dough into 2 small and 2 larger pieces. The pudding is going to be layered so you'll need the smaller quantities for the lower part of the basin.

Butter a 1½-pint (825-ml) capacity boilable plastic or foil basin and press the brown sugar on its base and sides.

Peel, halve, core and slice the apples and mix them with the remaining sugar.

Roll out the suet pastry into 4 rounds, increasing their diameters each time to fit the basin. Lay the smallest round on the bottom of the basin. Cover with some of the apple mixture. Continue layering, ending with the largest pastry round. Cover with foil, pleated across the middle. Tie or crimp it tightly round basin. Stand in a pan of water to come two-thirds up the side of the basin, cover and boil for 2 hours.

❊Turn out and serve with chilled whipped cream. Serves 4.

❊ TO FREEZE: leave the pudding until cold. Remove the foil and cover with a fresh piece, seal, label and freeze. Use within 3 months.

TO USE: thaw the pudding overnight in the fridge and reboil for 1 hour. Complete as from ❊ in recipe.

Gooseberry Charlotte

Slices of crustless buttered bread line out the dish which is then filled with cooked gooseberries. Don't add too much juice or the bread will be soggy rather than crisp. The surplus juice can be thickened with a little cornflour and served as a sauce

Top and tail the gooseberries and put them in a pan with the demerara sugar; use the smaller quantity of sugar first and towards the end of the cooking time taste and if necessary add the extra amount. Cook the fruit until it is soft and then set aside.

Grease a 1½-pint (825-ml) capacity soufflé dish or cake tin and sprinkle with half the caster sugar. Trim the crusts off the bread and cut into strips about 1in. (2.5cm) wide. Melt the butter and dip in the strips of bread; line the sides of the dish or tin with them. Cut a round of bread or trim strips to cover the bottom of the dish or tin completely, and dip in melted butter. Place in the dish or tin, then fill with the cooked gooseberries, drained of most of their juice; lay a final round or strips of bread, dipped in butter, to cover the fruit completely. ❋ Sprinkle with the remaining caster sugar, then bake in preheated oven (400 deg. F, 200 deg. C, Gas no. 6) for about 40 minutes. Serve hot with cream or custard. Serves 4.

1½lb (675g) gooseberries
6-8oz (100-150g) demerara sugar
1oz (25g) caster sugar
3oz (75g) butter
4-6 slices white bread from large sandwich loaf

❋ TO FREEZE: cool the charlotte, open freeze until hard, then slip into a polythene bag, seal, label and return to the freezer. Use within 3 months.

TO USE: uncover the charlotte and bake from frozen as from ❋ in recipe, and allow an extra 10 minutes cooking time.

Cherries Jubilee

If you haven't a chafing dish and burner for use on the table, flame the cherries in the kitchen and serve when the flames have died down. The dish won't look so impressive but will taste just as good. For a spicy flavour add a stick of cinnamon to the cherries when cooking them

VANILLA ICE CREAM:
½ pint (300ml) milk
½ pint (300ml) single cream
1 vanilla pod or vanilla essence
4 egg yolks
4 oz (100g) caster sugar
CHERRY SAUCE:
½ pint (300ml) water
4 oz (100g) sugar
8 oz (225g) cherries
TO FINISH:
1 tablesp. (15ml) brandy

To use a vanilla pod for flavouring, split in half, put in a pan of milk and bring almost to the boil. Remove pan from heat and leave milk to infuse for about 15 minutes

Pour the milk and cream into a milk pan; add the vanilla pod, split, if using, and heat the milk until it is almost boiling. Remove the pan from the heat and leave the milk to infuse (see left) for about 15 minutes. Take out the vanilla pod, rinse, dry and keep it for future use.

Tip the egg yolks into a large basin, add the sugar and beat until the mixture is thick and creamy. Gradually add the infused milk, stirring all the time. Stand the basin over a pan of simmering water or tip the mixture into the top of a double saucepan and stir until it thickens sufficiently to coat the back of a spoon. Remove the mixture from the heat. If using vanilla essence, add it at this stage, probably about 10 drops but taste as you go. Leave to cool. Pour the vanilla mixture into a rigid container, cover and freeze for about 30 minutes. Remove, turn ice cream into a bowl and beat well. Return it to the container and freeze until hard. The beating ensures a creamier texture in the finished ice. ✳

To make the cherry sauce: put the water and sugar into a pan. Heat gently until the sugar has dissolved completely, then bring to the boil and boil for 5 minutes. Reduce the heat. Stone the cherries and add them to the syrup. Cook them gently until they are tender – about 10 minutes. Transfer the cherries to a dish, using a perforated spoon, then boil the syrup until it is thick and reduced by about half. Return cherries to the pan.✳✳ Add brandy and flame it with a match.

To serve, put scoops of vanilla ice cream into sundae dishes and spoon over the hot cherries in their sauce. Serves 4.

✳ TO FREEZE: vanilla ice cream – seal and label the container and return to the freezer. Use within 1 month. Sauce – cool the cherries in their syrup. Pack into a rigid container, leaving about ½ in. (1cm) headspace for expansion, seal, label and freeze. Use within 1 year.

TO USE: transfer vanilla ice cream to the fridge to soften (this can take up to 1 hour, depending on the temperature of your freezer). Thaw the cherry sauce overnight in the fridge; tip into a pan and heat. Complete as from ✳ and ✳✳ in recipe.

Linzer Torte

A rich almond pastry flan is filled with raspberry jam or lightly cooked raspberries or even redcurrant jam to make this famous Austrian torte. Not perhaps what we think of as a torte (gâteau) but certainly something more than just a flan

7oz (175g) plain flour
pinch salt
4½oz (115g) butter
4½oz (115g) caster sugar
1 teasp. (5ml) powdered cinnamon
4oz (100g) ground almonds
2 egg yolks
12oz (350g) raspberry jam

Sieve the flour and salt into a mixing bowl. Rub in the butter. Add the sugar, cinnamon and ground almonds and work to a paste with the egg yolks. Gather into a ball and chill the dough for 1 hour. Cut off a piece of the pastry to use as lattice strips.

Roll out the pastry to fit an 8-in. (20-cm) diameter loose-bottomed flan tin. If you find the pastry breaks and crumbles – it is a very rich mixture – either patch it as you go or put the piece of pastry in the flan tin and press and mould it to the shape of the tin, making sure it is of even thickness. Spoon in the raspberry jam.

Roll out the remaining pastry and cut into 6 strips. Arrange these lattice-fashion (see page 160) over the jam. Turn the rim of the pastry over them. ✳ Bake in preheated oven (375 deg. F, 190 deg. C, Gas no. 5) for about 30 minutes. Cool slightly before pushing the base up out of the ring. Serves 4–6.

✳ TO FREEZE: open freeze the flan until hard, then slip into a polythene bag, seal, label and return to the freezer. Use within 3 months.

TO USE: unwrap flan and bake from frozen in preheated oven (425 deg. F, 220 deg. C, Gas no. 7) for 15 minutes, then reduce the heat to 350 deg. F, 180 deg. C, Gas no. 4 and bake for a further 30 minutes.

Spicy Pudding with Butterscotch Sauce

A lovely rich butterscotch sauce is served with a mildly spiced sponge pudding. If you're fond of mixed spice you can add about half as much again to the mixture, but it shouldn't be too dominant

Sift the flour, baking powder and salt into a bowl and stir in the sugar and mixed spice. Add the margarine, egg and milk and mix well until smooth.

Grease a 1–1½ pint (550–825ml) boilable basin and spoon the mixture into it. Cover with a piece of foil pleated across the middle to allow for expansion ❄. Stand in a pan of water to come half way up the sides of the basin and steam for 1–1½ hours. Don't forget to top up the water from time to time.

To make the butterscotch sauce, put the brown sugar, syrup and water into a pan, heat gently until the sugar has dissolved, then boil for 2 minutes or until the mixture begins to thicken. Stir in the cream or top of the milk and serve with the spicy pudding. Serves 4.

❄ TO FREEZE: seal the basin, label and freeze. Use within 2 months. Pour the sauce into a boiling bag, seal, label and freeze. Use within 2 months.

TO USE: cook the pudding from frozen as from ❄ in recipe allowing an extra 30 minutes steaming time. Reheat the sauce in a pan of boiling water.

6oz (150g) plain flour
1 teasp. (5ml) baking powder
pinch salt
4½oz (115g) soft brown sugar
1 teasp. (5ml) mixed spice
4oz (100g) soft margarine
1 large egg
2 tablesp. (30ml) milk

BUTTERSCOTCH SAUCE:
4oz (100g) soft brown sugar
2 tablesp. (30ml) golden syrup
2 tablesp. (30ml) water
2 tablesp. (30ml) cream or top
 of milk

These little gooseberry tarts were once made in a number of Gloucestershire villages, including Oldbury, for Whitsunday feasts. Their originality lies in the use of hot water crust for the pastry cases

Oldbury Tarts

Sift the flour and salt into a mixing bowl. Separate the egg. Put the lard and water in a saucepan, heat together until the fat has melted, then bring to the boil.

Make a well in the flour, add the egg yolk, cover with a little flour, then add the hot fat and water. Mix to a smooth dough.

Turn the dough out on to a floured surface and knead lightly. Shape it into a ball, cover and set aside in a warm place for 15 minutes to rest.

Cut off one-third of the dough and set aside for making the tart lids. Divide the rest of the dough into 6 pieces. Shape each piece round the base of a 3-in. (7.5-cm) diameter floured tumbler, to about 1½ in. (3.5cm) up the sides.

Cut 6 double thicknesses of greaseproof, the same depth as the pastry cases and long enough to wrap round them (see right). Wrap the strips round each pastry case, securing with string or a paper clip. Leave for 5 minutes, then carefully remove the glass from each case. Fill each case with the gooseberries, topped and tailed, and sprinkle with demerara sugar.

Roll out the remaining pastry and cut 6 lids, using the tumbler as a cutter. Wet the edges of the tarts, press the lids into position and seal.

Stand the tarts on a greased baking sheet, glaze the tops with beaten egg white and bake in preheated oven (400 deg. F, 200 deg. C, Gas no. 6) for about 30 minutes or until golden-brown. Remove the greaseproof paper strips. ❋ Serve hot or cold with cream. Makes 6.

12 oz (350g) plain flour
½ lev. teasp. (2.5ml) salt
1 egg
4 oz (100g) lard
¼ pint (150ml) water
1 lb (450g) gooseberries
6 oz (150g) demerara sugar

Wrap matching strips double thickness greaseproof paper round pastry on tumbler; secure with string or paper clip

❋ TO FREEZE: cool the tarts, pack them in a rigid container or polythene bag, seal, label and freeze. Use within 3 months.

TO USE: thaw the tarts for 3 hours at room temperature and serve cold, or re-heat the thawed tarts (350 deg. F, 180 deg. C, Gas no. 4) for about 15 minutes. Complete as from ❋ in recipe.

Cherry Frangipane

The frangipane topping to this cherry tart is a simplified version of the original which is a cream of milk, sugar, butter, eggs, flour and ground almonds

4oz (100g) shortcrust pastry (see below)
8oz (225g) black cherries
3oz (75g) ground almonds
4oz (100g) caster sugar
1 egg
½oz (15g) flaked almonds

Roll out the pastry and line into a 6-in. (15-cm) diameter flan tin. Stone the cherries and fill them into the pastry case. If they're very juicy, it's a good idea either to brush the base of the flan with egg white or sprinkle over a few cake crumbs before putting in the cherries to prevent the pastry base going soggy.

Mix the ground almonds and sugar together. Beat the egg and add a little at a time until you have a soft paste. Spoon this over the cherries and sprinkle with the flaked almonds. Bake in preheated oven (400 deg. F, 200 deg. C, Gas no. 6) for about 30 minutes or until the pastry is set and the top is golden-brown. Cool ❄ and serve. Serves 4.

TO FREEZE: when cold, pack the flan into a polythene bag, seal, label and freeze. Use within 2 months.

TO USE: thaw the flan at room temperature for about 3 hours, unwrap and serve.

SHORTCRUST PASTRY

4oz (100g) plain flour
pinch salt
2oz (50g) fat (butter, margarine, lard or mixtures of these)
cold water to mix

Sieve the flour and salt into a mixing bowl. Cut the fat into small pieces and rub into the flour until the mixture resembles breadcrumbs. Add just enough cold water to mix to a firm but not sticky dough. Wrap in foil or a polythene bag, ❄ and chill in fridge for about 30 minutes. Take out, unwrap and use according to chosen recipe. Makes enough to line 6-in. (15-cm) diameter *moule à manque* or flan tin.

TO FREEZE: seal, label and then freeze shortcrust pastry. Use within 3 months.

TO USE: thaw pastry at room temperature until it is soft enough to roll or shape as required.

Fruity Ginger Roll

A spicy ginger roll is filled
with a mixture of apples,
sultanas and nuts. Makes a
deliciously moist pudding
that is nicest served hot

Prepare the filling first. Melt the margarine in a
pan and add the peeled, cored and finely sliced
apples and all the other filling ingredients. Cook
over a very low heat until they are pulped.

To make the ginger roll, first grease a swiss roll
tin measuring 12½ × 8¾in. (31 × 21.5cm), line with
greaseproof paper and brush with melted fat.
Sieve all the dry ingredients into a mixing bowl.
In a pan, melt together, but do not overheat, the
margarine, treacle and syrup. Add the egg and
water to the syrup mixture and pour on to the
flour mixture. Mix well until blended, then turn
into the prepared tin.

Bake the roll in preheated oven (375 deg. F,
190 deg. C, Gas no. 5) for about 15 minutes or until
firm to the touch and springy. Turn out the roll
on to a lightly-floured paper and trim the edges
with a knife to neaten. Spread over the apple
filling, then roll up ❄ and serve with cream or
custard. Serves 4–6.

TO FREEZE: cool the
roll, then open
freeze until hard on
a foil-lined baking sheet.
Wrap the roll completely
in the foil, seal, label and
return to the freezer. Use
within 2 months.

TO USE: thaw the roll for
6–8 hours at room tem-
perature. Unwrap and
serve cold, or reheat the
thawed roll in preheated
oven (375 deg. F, 180 deg. C,
Gas no. 5) for about 20
minutes. Complete as
from ❄ in recipe.

4oz (100g) plain flour
1 teasp. (5ml) mixed spice
1 teasp. (5ml) ground ginger
1 teasp. (5ml) bicarbonate of
 soda
2½oz (65g) soft margarine
3 tablesp. (45ml) treacle
3 tablesp. (45ml) golden syrup
1 egg
2½ fl oz (75ml) warm water
FILLING:
½oz (15g) margarine
1lb (450g) cooking apples (after
 preparation)
4oz (100g) sultanas
1oz (25g) chopped nuts
1 tablesp. (15ml) sugar

Chocolate Brandy Roll

Chocolate, cream and brandy combine to make this a luxurious party pudding. It's very rich, so serve small portions

6oz (150g) margarine
3oz (75g) caster sugar
6oz (150g) flour
1oz (25g) cocoa
¼ pint (150ml) double cream
1 tablesp. (15ml) brandy

TO FINISH:
¼ pint (150ml) double cream
grated chocolate

Cream the margarine and sugar until light and fluffy. Sieve the flour and cocoa together and work into the creamed mixture. Form into balls about the size of a walnut and place well apart on a greased baking sheet. Flatten slightly with a fork or knife dipped in water. Bake in preheated oven (350 deg. F, 180 deg. C, Gas No. 4) for 10-15 minutes. Cool the biscuits on a wire rack.

Whip the cream lightly, flavour with brandy, then continue whipping until firm. Sandwich the biscuits together with the flavoured whipped cream, stacking them to make a roll; then turn roll on its side. ❄ Whip remaining ¼ pint (150ml) cream, and fork it all over the roll. Decorate with grated chocolate. Cut the roll into diagonal slices. Serves 6-8.

TO FREEZE. Wrap the chocolate roll in foil, seal and label. Use within 3 months.

TO USE. Loosen the foil and thaw the chocolate roll in the fridge for 4 hours. Unwrap and stand it on a serving dish. Complete as from ❄ in recipe.

Stack the biscuits, layered thickly with whipped cream, until quite high on a large sheet of foil. Then turn the roll on its side on the foil

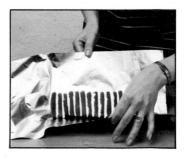

Continue layering the roll until all the cream is finished; then wrap round the foil to seal, and label and freeze

Pears in Cider

After long, slow cooking in cider and brown sugar, the hardest of pears will be tender, full of flavour and the colour of pale amber

1 pint (550ml) dry cider
4 oz (100g) soft brown sugar
4 hard pears
1 small lemon, thinly-pared
rind only

Pour the cider into a pan. Add the sugar and heat gently until the sugar has dissolved; then bring to the boil and boil for 2 minutes.

Peel the pears thinly, leaving the stalks on. Put the pears into a baking dish on their sides, add the thinly-pared lemon rind and pour over the syrup. Cover with a tight-fitting lid or piece of foil. Bake (325 deg. F, 170 deg. C, Gas no. 3) for about 1½ hours or until the pears are tender, turning them over once or twice during the cooking. ✳

Pour off the syrup into a pan and reduce by about half with fast boiling. Set aside to cool, then pour it over the pears arranged in a glass bowl or a china dish. Chill and serve with whipped cream. Serves 4.

✳ TO FREEZE. When cold pack the pears into a rigid container, cover with the syrup, seal, label and freeze. Use within 3 months.

TO USE. Thaw the pears overnight in the fridge. Complete as from ✳ in recipe.

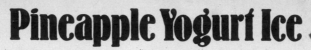

Pineapple Yogurt Ice

A sharp refreshing ice. The cream gives it a smoother, softer texture – though slimmers can omit it and get a perfectly acceptable, if slightly crunchier, ice

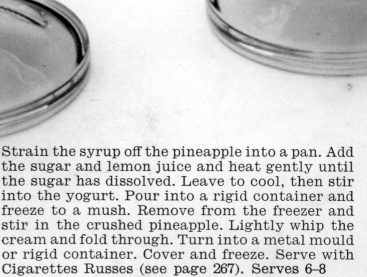

1 x 13¼oz (376g) can crushed pineapple
3oz (75g) caster sugar
1 tablesp. (15ml) lemon juice
½ pint (300ml) natural yogurt
¼ pint (150ml) double cream

Strain the syrup off the pineapple into a pan. Add the sugar and lemon juice and heat gently until the sugar has dissolved. Leave to cool, then stir into the yogurt. Pour into a rigid container and freeze to a mush. Remove from the freezer and stir in the crushed pineapple. Lightly whip the cream and fold through. Turn into a metal mould or rigid container. Cover and freeze. Serve with Cigarettes Russes (see page 267). Serves 6–8

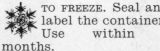 TO FREEZE. Seal and label the container. Use within 3 months.

TO USE. Transfer the ice to the fridge about 1 hour before serving.

Rice Cream with Oranges

A cool, refreshing compote of oranges provides colour contrast
to the rich creamy rice pudding

4½ oz (115 g) pudding rice
1½ pints (825 ml) milk
2 oz (150 g) sugar
6 fl oz (180 ml) double cream

ORANGE COMPOTE:
4 oz (100 g) sugar
¼ pint (150 ml) water
6 medium oranges

Put water into the base of a double boiler and the rice, milk and sugar into the top half. Cook gently, topping up the water as necessary and stirring the rice occasionally, until all the milk has been absorbed and the rice is thick and creamy. Leave the rice to cool, stirring frequently to prevent a skin forming.

Whip the cream and fold it into the cooled rice. Turn it into a mould and leave to set.

To make the compote, put the sugar and water into a pan with the finely grated rind of 2 of the oranges. Dissolve the sugar over a low heat, bring to the boil and boil for 1 minute. Remove the syrup from the heat and leave to cool.

Cut the ends off all the oranges then, using a small knife with a serrated edge, cut with a sawing motion round and round the orange to remove all pith and peel. Cut them into segments, slicing between the membrane, and remove any pips.❋To serve, turn the rice cream on to a dish, garnish with finely-pared orange rind or orange slices, if liked. Put the orange segments into a bowl, cover with cold syrup and serve with the rice cream. Serves 4–6.

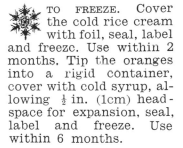 TO FREEZE. Cover the cold rice cream with foil, seal, label and freeze. Use within 2 months. Tip the oranges into a rigid container, cover with cold syrup, allowing $\frac{1}{2}$ in. (1cm) head-space for expansion, seal, label and freeze. Use within 6 months.

TO USE. Thaw the rice cream and oranges overnight in the fridge. Complete as from ❋ in recipe.

Slice ends off oranges

Using a sawing action cut round oranges removing all pith and peel

Cut into segments, slicing between the membranes

Honey and Brandy Ice Cream

Cream and eggs are sweetened with honey to make an exquisitely flavoured ice that's covered in brandy-flavoured whipped cream. The colourful bees on wire stems can be bought (see page 288) to give a special decorative touch

4 eggs
1 oz (25g) icing sugar
5 tablesp. (75ml) honey
7½ fl. oz (225ml) double cream
TO FINISH:
7½ fl. oz (225ml) double cream
1 tablesp. (15ml) brandy
1 tablesp. (15ml) caster sugar

Separate the eggs. Place yolks in a basin and beat with the icing sugar until well blended. Measure the honey into a pan and bring to the boil. Pour this on to the egg yolks, beating all the time. Continue beating until the mixture cools and thickens.

Lightly whip the first quantity of cream and stir it into the yolks and honey mixture. Whip the egg whites in a large bowl until they just hold soft peaks and fold lightly through the mixture. Turn it into a 1½-pint (825-ml) bombe mould or basin ❄ (not glass which can shatter during freezing), cover and freeze until hard.

Pour the remaining cream into a basin, add the brandy and sugar and whip until firm. Fill this cream mixture into a piping bag (see right), fitted with a ½-in.(1-cm) nozzle. Turn the ice out on to a plate, pipe cream round and round to cover, starting from the base. Return the ice to the freezer to harden for a few minutes, then Serve at once with Viennese Biscuits (see recipe on page 234). Serves 8.

❄ TO FREEZE: cover the ice, seal, label and freeze. Use within 1 month.

TO USE: complete as from ❄ in recipe.

Stand piping bag in jug, its sides folded down, for easy filling with cream or other mixtures

Rhubarb Ice with Ginger Crunch

The tart flavours of the rhubarb and orange in the ice blend well with the sweet gingery, crunchy base

1 lb (450g) fresh rhubarb to yield
   12 oz (350g) when prepared
1 orange
4 oz (100g) sugar
1-2 drops edible red food
   colouring, optional
¼ pint (150ml) double cream

GINGER CRUNCH:
2 oz (50g) margarine
1½ oz (40g) digestive biscuits
3 oz (75g) ginger nuts
1 oz (25g) demerara sugar

Wash and trim the rhubarb and cut into chunks. Place them in an ovenproof dish with the sugar and the grated rind and juice of the orange. Cover the dish loosely with foil and bake in a preheated oven (350 deg. F, 180 deg. C, Gas no. 4) for about 1 hour or until the rhubarb is tender.

Rub the rhubarb through a sieve or purée in a blender and, if liked, add a few drops of red food colouring. Lightly whip the cream and fold it through the purée. If you don't blend the fruit and cream too thoroughly together, you'll get an attractive marbled effect. ❄ Pour into a rigid container and freeze until firm.

To make the ginger crunch, first melt the margarine in a pan and remove from the heat. Using a rolling pin, crush the biscuits between two pieces of greaseproof paper or in a large polythene bag (see below). Stir the crumbs into the melted fat, together with the demerara sugar and when well blended, tip into a loose-bottomed 5½-in. (13.5-cm) diameter flan tin or ring, standing on a baking sheet. Press the crumb mixture round the sides and across the base to form a flan case. Leave to set. ❄❄ When firm, fill flan case with scoops of rhubarb ice and serve. Serves 4-6.

Biscuits crumble easily if put in a polythene bag and then crushed with a rolling pin

❄ TO FREEZE: pour the rhubarb ice into a rigid container, leaving ½ in. (1cm) headspace for expansion, seal, label and freeze. Use within 1 month. Open freeze ginger flan case, then carefully pack it into a rigid container, seal, label and return to the freezer. Use within 2 months.

TO USE: thaw the ginger flan case for 30 minutes at room temperature. Complete as from ❄ and ❄❄ in recipe.

Blackcurrant Sorbet

The sorbet is topped with fresh blackcurrants poached in sugar syrup. For a special occasion pour a measure of Cassis liqueur over each serving before topping with cream

Put the ½ pint (300ml) water and sugar into a pan and heat gently until the sugar has dissolved completely. Bring to the boil and boil for 5 minutes.

If using fresh fruit, strip currants off their stalks and rinse them in a colander. Reserve 4 oz (100g) blackcurrants for the sauce and put the rest into a pan with the 4 tablespoons (60ml) water and cook until soft. Sieve them and add the sugar syrup to the fruit purée. Make it up to ¾ pint (425ml) with water and turn the mixture into a shallow container; cool, then freeze until the mixture is nearly firm.

Whisk the egg whites until stiff. Turn the blackcurrant ice into a basin, break it down with a fork, then gently fold in the whisked egg whites to make the sorbet. Turn it into a rigid container, cover and freeze until firm. ❄

To make the sauce, put the remaining black-currants into a pan with 2 tablespoons (30ml) cold water and simmer until the fruit is tender. Add the sugar and simmer until it has dissolved. Blend the arrowroot with 1 tablespoon (15ml) water, stir it into the blackcurrants and boil, stirring, until the sauce thickens and clears — about 2 minutes. Cool. ✳✳

Scoop the sorbet into tall glasses and top with a spoonful of cold blackcurrant sauce and whipped cream. Serves 4.

✳ TO FREEZE: sorbet — seal and label the container. Use within 2 months. Sauce: when cool pack into a rigid container, leaving about ½ in. (1cm) headspace for expansion, seal, label and freeze. Use within 1 year.

TO USE: thaw the sauce overnight in the fridge. Complete as from ✳ and ✳✳ in recipe.

SORBET:
½ **pint (300ml) water**
4 **oz (100g) caster sugar**
8 **oz (225g) blackcurrants, fresh or frozen**
4 **tablesp. (60ml) water**
2 **egg whites**
SAUCE:
4 **oz (100g) fresh blackcurrants**
3 **tablesp. (45ml) water**
2 **oz (50g) sugar**
½ **teasp. (2.5ml) arrowroot**

Coupelles

These biscuit cups make delightful containers for fruit and cream or ice cream. Don't bake more than two or three at a time or you won't have time to mould them before they harden

2 egg whites
4 oz (100g) caster sugar
2 oz (50g) plain flour
2 oz (50g) butter

Grease a baking sheet and preheat the oven (400 deg. F, 200 deg. C, Gas no. 6).

Put the egg whites into a basin and beat in the sugar. Stir in the flour, then add the butter, cooled melted and mix gently together.

Drop tablespoons of the mixture, well apart, on to baking sheet. Don't bake more than three biscuits at a time or they'll harden before you can shape them. Spread the mixture out into thin rounds (see page 262) and bake for about 5 minutes in preheated oven until the biscuits are brown round the edges.

While baking, grease a clean apple, grapefruit or orange, or the inside of a small dish or cup, ready for shaping the cases.

Remove the baking sheet from the oven, and using a palette knife carefully lift off one biscuit and immediately press it firmly over the fruit or into the dish or cup. As soon as the biscuit is shaped, remove to a cooling rack. It's easier if you have 'moulds' ready because you must work quickly; the biscuits soon harden and then they won't shape without breaking. ❄

When biscuits are cold fill with ice cream and fruit or fruit and cream; serve at once. Makes 12.

❄ TO FREEZE: when cold, pack the biscuits into a rigid container, filling any spaces with crumpled paper so they can't slide about and break. Seal, label, and freeze for up to 6 months.

TO USE: thaw the biscuits on a wire rack for 10 minutes and complete as from ❄ in recipe.

Sherry Trifle

Layers of sherried sponge, apricots, custard and cream are topped with ratafias – little almond macaroon biscuits. The biscuits can be frozen – but not on the trifle or they'll soften. Freeze them, and the cream rosettes, separately; arrange decoratively on the trifle just before serving

6 trifle sponge cakes
apricot jam
1 x 15oz (425g) can apricot halves, drained and juice reserved
4 tablesp. (60ml) sherry
4 tablesp. (60ml) apricot juice
2 tablesp. (30ml) flaked, blanched almonds
1 x 14½oz (411g) can custard
½ pint (300ml) double cream

TO FINISH:
2oz (50g) ratafias

Split the sponge cakes, spread with apricot jam and sandwich them together. Cut them into pieces and arrange over the base of a ✳ glass serving dish. Pour the sherry and apricot juice over the sponge and arrange the apricot halves on top. Scatter the almonds over the fruit. Pour over the custard. Whisk the cream until it just holds its shape and spoon just over half of it over the custard.

Put the rest of the cream into a piping bag fitted with a star nozzle and pipe (see page 266) rosettes of cream ✳✳ on top of the trifle; finish decorating with ratafias. Serves 4–6.

✳ TO FREEZE: don't freeze trifle in a glass dish. Find a cake tin or polythene dish of similar size. Line it with foil (see page 260) and make trifle in this. Cover with foil and freeze until firm enough to lift out of the dish. Seal, label and return to the freezer. Pipe rosettes of cream on to a foil-lined tray, open freeze and when hard pack into a rigid container. If freezing ratafias put them in a polythene bag, seal, label and freeze. Use within 2 months.

TO USE: remove the wrappings, and if preformed, place the trifle in your serving dish and complete as from ✳✳ in recipe, arranging cream rosettes on top just before serving.

Christmas Pudding Snowball

Instead of traditional plum pudding, here's a spectacular presentation for a cool Christmas pudding: a rich, creamy ice, full of dried and candied fruits and nuts soaked in brandy, marsala or sherry

Put the raisins into a small basin. Chop the cherries and pineapple into small pieces and add them to the raisins, together with the wine. Leave to stand for 2 hours.

Separate the eggs. Beat the yolks with the sieved icing sugar until thick and creamy.

Lightly whip the first quantity of cream. Whisk the egg whites until stiff. Stir the yolks into the cream, then fold the egg whites lightly into the mixture. Tip this into a rigid container and freeze until beginning to harden, about 1 hour.

Tip the ice mixture into a basin and stir in the nuts, fruits and any remaining wine. Put into a mould or half fill two small basins, cover and freeze.❄

When firm turn out the ice. If you have used the two basins, put the two lots of frozen mixture together to form a ball.

Whip the remaining cream, and swirl over the ball of icecream. If liked, decorate with holly. Serves 4-6.

❄ TO FREEZE. Seal the mould or basins, label and return to the freezer. Use within 2 months.

TO USE. Turn out the ice and complete as from ❄ in recipe.

2oz (50g) raisins
2oz (50g) glace cherries
2oz (50g) candied pineapple
2 tablesp. (30ml) brandy, marsala or sherry
2 eggs
2oz (50g) icing sugar
¼ pint (150ml) double cream
1oz (25g) toasted hazelnuts or almonds
TO FINISH:
¼ pint (150ml) double cream

Summer Pudding

In the 18th century this most delicious of English puddings was known by the prosaic name of Hydropathic Pudding and was served to patients not allowed the then fashionable rich pastry desserts. Make sure there's plenty of juice in the soft fruit filling so the bread gets thoroughly impregnated with it

7 x ½ in. (6 x 1.5cm) slices day-old white sandwich loaf
1½ lb (675g) mixed soft fruit
strawberries, raspberries, redcurrants, blackcurrants and cherries
2 tablsp. (30ml) water
4 oz (100g) caster sugar
TO FINISH:
whipped cream

Trim the crusts off the bread. Line the bottom and sides of a 1½-pint (825-ml) pudding basin (see below) with the slices, cutting them to shape so that the bread fits closely together. Reserve a slice or two for the 'lid'.

Prepare the fruit, discarding any leaves and stalks. Wash the currants and cherries, but not the soft berries unless absolutely necessary. Stone the cherries.

Put the cherries and currants into a pan with the water and the sugar. Bring slowly to the boil and cook until the sugar melts and the fruit is just tender. Add the strawberries and raspberries and cook a further minute or two until their juices run but they retain their shape.

Spoon the fruit and juices into the bread-lined basin, reserving a little of the juice. Cover the surface with the rest of bread. Put a saucer or plate that just fits inside the dish on the bread and weight it down. Leave overnight in the fridge. Remove the weight and saucer. ❄ Invert a serving plate over the basin and turn upside down to unmould the pudding. Spoon reserved juices over any unsoaked bread. Serve with whipped cream. Serves 4-6.

❄ TO FREEZE: cover the basin with foil, seal, label and freeze. Pack the reserved juice in a small rigid container. Use within 2 months.

TO USE: thaw the pudding overnight in the fridge. Complete as from ❄ in recipe.

Trim slices of bread to a triangular wedge-shape so they fit snugly together in the basin

Tipsy Cake

So called because of the amount of liquor the sponge imbibes before being smothered in cream and decorated with angelica and glacé cherries

12oz (350g) stale sponge cake
6 tablesp. (90ml) seedless
raspberry jam
6 tablesp. (90ml) sherry
2 tablesp. (30ml) brandy
TO FINISH:
¼ pint (150ml) double cream
2½fl oz (75ml) single cream
angelica
glace cherries

Break up the sponge cake into pieces and put them into a basin large enough to take all the ingredients for mixing. Gently heat the raspberry jam in a pan and when it is melted pour it over the sponge. Mix together, then add the sherry and the brandy and mix well.

Spoon the sponge cake mixture into a 1-pint (550-ml) pudding basin. Put a small plate or saucer on top of the mixture; it needs to fit inside the basin and rest on the mixture. Place a weight on top and leave in a cold place overnight. The weighting presses the mixture together so that it's firmer for turning out and serving. ✳Whip the two creams together until thick, then spread over with a knife or pipe on to the cake. Decorate the tipsy cake with angelica and glacé cherries. Serves 4–6.

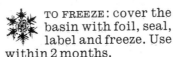 TO FREEZE: cover the basin with foil, seal, label and freeze. Use within 2 months.

TO USE: thaw the cake mixture at room temperature for 3 hours, then turn out on to your chosen serving dish. Complete as from ✳ in recipe.

Fruit Savarin

A rich yeast cake that's soaked in liqueur-flavoured syrup. Serve it with fruit salad and whipped cream for a sumptuous party pudding

Sieve the flour and salt into a bowl, rub in the butter until the mixture resembles fine crumbs. If using fresh yeast mix with the milk, beaten eggs and sugar or if using dried yeast add it to the milk only. Leave about 15 minutes until the yeast is dissolved and frothy; then add dried yeast liquid, if using, to sugar and eggs. Pour into flour mixture and beat to a smooth dough.

Half fill a 2-pint (1.1-litre) greased ring mould with the mixture, cover with oiled polythene and leave in a warm place to rise until almost to the top of the mould. Remove the polythene.

Stand the savarin on a baking sheet and bake in preheated oven (400 deg. F, 200 deg. C, Gas no. 6) for about 30 minutes or until golden-brown. Turn out of mould and cool.

For the fruit salad: put the sugar and water in a pan and heat gently, stirring, until the sugar is dissolved. Boil for 5 minutes, then cool. Slice the peach (remove skin if liked). Halve the grapes and remove the pips. Drain the pineapple and hull the strawberries.

❇ Stir the kirsch, if using, into the syrup. Place the savarin in a serving dish, then prick all over with a fork and spoon over the syrup until the savarin is well soaked. Brush with apricot glaze. Heap fruit salad in the middle and moisten it with any remaining syrup. Serves 4-6.

8oz (225g) strong white flour
1 teasp. (5ml) salt
4oz (100g) butter
**1 oz (25g) fresh yeast
  or ½oz (15g) dried yeast**
6 tablesp. (90ml) warm milk
4 eggs
1oz (25g) caster sugar

FRUIT SALAD:
8oz (225g) sugar
½ pint (300ml) water
1 peach
4oz (100g) grapes
**1 x 8oz (225g) can pineapple
  pieces**
2oz (50g) fresh strawberries
TO FINISH:
3 tablesp. (45ml) kirsch, optional
4 tablesp. (60ml) apricot glaze

❇ TO FREEZE: wrap the cooled savarin in foil, seal, label and freeze. Use within 2 months. Pack fruit salad and syrup into large rigid container, seal, label and freeze. Use within 2 months.

TO USE: thaw savarin for 2-3 hours at room temperature, then reheat in preheated oven (400 deg. F, 200 deg. C, Gas no. 6) for 10 minutes. Thaw fruit salad in fridge; then strain off the syrup and boil to thicken – about 3 minutes. Continue as from ❇ in recipe.

Blackberry and Apple Cream

Two favourite autumn fruits combine to make this creamy mould. Use well-flavoured apples and add grated lemon rind for extra zest

FIRST LAYER:
1 lb (450g) blackberries
4oz (100g) sugar
3 tablesp. (45ml) water
½oz (15g) powdered gelatine

SECOND LAYER:
1 lb (450g) cooking apples
3oz (75g) sugar
¼ pint (150ml) water
½ lemon, grated rind only
½oz (15g) powdered gelatine
¼ pint (150ml) single cream

Put the hulled blackberries, sugar and water into a pan and cook until the fruit is soft. Put 2 tablespoons (30ml) water into a small basin and sprinkle the gelatine over it. Stir, then stand the basin in a pan of hot water and leave until the gelatine has dissolved.

Sieve the cooked blackberries, stir in the dissolved gelatine and pour into a 2-pint (1.1 litre) mould. Leave to set.

When the blackberry mixture has set prepare the apple layer. Peel and core the apples and put into a pan with the sugar, water and lemon rind and cook until soft. Prepare the gelatine as above.

Sieve the cooked apples, stir in the dissolved gelatine and leave to cool slightly. Then stir in the cream and pour on top of the set blackberry purée. Leave to it set. ❄ Turn out of the mould and serve with cream. Serves 4.

❄ TO FREEZE. When set cover the mould with foil, seal, label and freeze. Use within 2 months.

TO USE. Thaw the mould overnight in the fridge, then complete as from ❄ in recipe.

Fresh Apricot Suèdoise

Suèdoise is a fruit purée, usually made from stone fruit, set with gelatine. This version uses apricots and is then coated with cream and decorated with ratafias – tiny almond biscuits

1½lb (675g) fresh or 1¼lb (550g) frozen apricots
6oz (150g) caster sugar
¼ pint (150ml) plus 5 tablesp. (75ml) water
rind of 1 lemon
½oz (15g) gelatine
TO FINISH:
¼ pint (150ml) double cream
2oz (50g) ratafia biscuits

If using fresh apricots, cut in half and remove the stones.

Put the sugar and ¼ pint (150ml) water in a pan and heat gently until the sugar is dissolved completely. Add the fresh or frozen apricots and lemon rind, and cook gently for about 8 minutes or until the apricots are soft. Strain, reserving the syrup.

Rub the apricots through a sieve or purée in a blender and make the purée up to 1 pint (550ml) with the reserved syrup. Put the remaining water into a bowl. Sprinkle over the gelatine and stand the bowl in a pan of hot water until the gelatine is dissolved completely. Stir the gelatine liquid into the apricot purée.

Pour the apricot mixture into a 6-in. (15-cm) diameter cake tin and leave to cool; then cover with foil ❄ and put in the fridge to set.

Pour the cream into a basin and whisk until thick. Turn the suèdoise out of the tin on to a serving dish and spread cream over the top and sides. Cover the top and sides with ratafia biscuits. Serves 4-6.

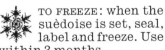 TO FREEZE: when the suèdoise is set, seal, label and freeze. Use within 3 months.

TO USE: thaw the suèdoise overnight in the fridge and complete as from ❄ in recipe.

Granita

Italian water ice simply made by freezing sweetened fruit juice or strong black coffee until set but not solid. Marvellously refreshing on a hot day

Put the coffee and sugar into a basin. Pour on ½ pint (300ml) boiling water and stir until the sugar is dissolved. Top up with ½ pint (300ml) cold water and set aside until cold. Pour into freezer tray, cover and freeze. When nearly set, stir lightly with a fork and return to the freezer. ✳When firm but not rock hard, spoon into glasses and if liked serve with whipped cream. Serves 4.

Put the sugar and water into a pan, heat gently, stirring until the sugar is dissolved. Bring to the boil and boil for 5 minutes; cool.

If using fresh raspberries, hull and pick over. Sieve the raspberries and stir in the cooled sugar syrup. Pour the mixture into a freezer tray, cover and freeze; when nearly set stir lightly with a fork and return to the freezer. ✳When firm but not rock hard, spoon into glasses and serve. Serves 4.

If using fresh melon, remove peel and seeds. Prepare, freeze and use as for Raspberry Granita, stirring in the lemon juice just before the first freezing. Serves 4.

✳ TO FREEZE: seal, label and return granita to freezer. Use within 2 months.

TO USE: remove granita from freezer, stand for a few moments, then complete as from ✳ in recipe.

COFFEE GRANITA
4 tablesp. (60ml) instant coffee
3oz (75g) sugar
1 pint (550ml) water

RASPBERRY GRANITA
6oz (150g) sugar
½ pint (300ml) water
1lb (450g) raspberries, fresh or frozen and thawed

MELON GRANITA
6oz (150g) sugar
½ pint (300ml) water
1lb (450g) fresh melon or frozen melon balls
2 tablesp. (30ml) lemon juice

Lemon Cream Pie

A crisp sweet meringue complements the pie's sharp lemon filling: a blend of eggs, sugar and lemon swirled through with thick cream

4 egg whites
8 oz (225g) caster sugar
¾ teasp. (3.75ml) cream of tartar
FILLING:
4 egg yolks
2 lemons, rind only of one, juice of both
5 oz (125g) caster sugar
¼ pint (150ml) double cream
TO FINISH:
¼ pint (150ml) double cream

Lightly pencil a circle 9 in. (23cm) in diameter on the underside of a sheet of non-stick paper, and line a baking sheet with it.

Whisk the egg whites until they are fairly stiff. Add half the sugar and the cream of tartar and whisk until the mixture is smooth, close-textured and holds up in stiff peaks when you lift out the whisk. Fold in the remaining sugar with a metal spoon, lightly but thoroughly. Spoon the meringue on to the prepared baking sheet and spread out to a circle the size of the pencilled guideline. Raise the edges of the meringue a little or put some of the meringue mixture into a piping bag fitted with a rose nozzle and pipe it round the edge of the circle, to form a "nest".

Bake (250 deg. F, 130 deg. C, Gas no. $\frac{1}{2}$) for about 2 hours or until the meringue is dried out and crisp. Transfer it to a wire rack to cool.

For the filling, beat the egg yolks with the lemon juice, rind and 4 oz (100g) sugar until blended. Cook in the top of a double saucepan or bowl over a pan of hot water, stirring until it begins to thicken. This will take about 10 minutes and it will thicken more as it cools. Whisk the first $\frac{1}{4}$ pint (150ml) cream until thick and fold into the lemon custard. ❊ Pile the lemon cream into the meringue nest. Whip the remaining cream, fill into a piping bag (an easy way to do this is show on page 181), fitted with a rosette nozzle and pipe it on to the lemon mixture. Serves 4.

❊ TO FREEZE: pack the lemon cream into a rigid container, and the meringue into another one; seal, label and freeze. Use within 1 month.

TO USE: thaw the lemon cream and meringue for 2$\frac{1}{2}$ hours at room temperature. Complete as from ❊ in recipe.

Biscuit Tortoni

A frozen cream pudding flavoured with sherry and crushed almond macaroons. 'Biscuit' is used in French to describe an ice cut in portions to look like biscuits. Tortoni was the owner of a Paris cafe who popularized cream ices in the 18th century

2oz (50g) macaroons (recipe on page 236 but omit nut topping)
½ pint (300ml) double cream
3 tablesp. (45ml) sherry
1 egg white
2oz (50g) icing sugar
TO FINISH:
2oz (50g) macaroons

The macaroons need to be hard and dry so they can be crushed, either with a rolling pin or in a blender. If they are soft, crisp them in the oven for 10-15 minutes and leave to cool before crushing.

Pour the cream into a basin and whisk until thick. Stir in the sherry and 2oz (50g) crushed macaroons.

Put the egg white in another basin and whisk it until stiff, gradually add icing sugar, beating until thick and glossy. Fold this into the cream mixture and turn into a 1-pint (550-ml) capacity loaf tin, cover with foil and freeze. ❄ When firm, turn out of tin and cover with remaining crushed macaroons, pressing them round the top and sides with a knife. Serve at once. Serves 6.

❄ TO FREEZE: seal, and label the container and return to freezer. Use within 2 months.

TO USE: turn out of container and complete as from ❄ in recipe.

Coffee Gâteau

The sponge fingers in this rich coffee butter cream gâteau can be replaced by a sponge cake cut into layers. Although it takes a little time to assemble, this is compensated for by not having to watch the oven – no cooking is involved

Cream the butter and icing sugar in a bowl until soft and smooth. Beat in the egg yolks, followed by the 2 teaspoons (10ml) instant coffee dissolved in 1 tablespoon (15ml) hot water.

Put the remaining black coffee in a shallow dish. Dip the sponge fingers one by one in the coffee and arrange 8 of them on a large sheet of foil. Cover with one-third of the coffee butter icing and arrange another layer of coffee-dipped sponge fingers on top. Repeat with the rest of the sponge fingers and butter icing, finishing with sponge fingers. Fold the foil over loosely, and leave to set firm. ❄

Unwrap gâteau. Whip the cream until stiff, then spread over the gâteau and sprinkle with toasted, flaked almonds to finish. Serves 4-6.

4oz (100g) unsalted butter
4oz (100g) icing sugar
2 egg yolks
2 teasp. (10ml) instant coffee
1 tablesp. (15ml) hot water
black coffee made with
 2½floz (75ml) water and
 1 teasp. (5ml) instant coffee
2 packets sponge fingers (32 biscuits in all)
TO FINISH:
¼ pint (150ml) double cream
2oz (50g) toasted flaked almonds

❄ TO FREEZE: freeze gâteau until hard, then wrap tightly in foil, seal, label and return to freezer. Use within 2 months.

TO USE: thaw gâteau overnight in fridge, unwrap and place on serving dish. Complete as from ❄ in recipe.

Choux Pastries

Choux pastry is really just a panada – a thick binding sauce – to which eggs are added. When baked the mixture puffs up into a crisp light pastry

PARIS BREST

1 quantity choux pastry as in
recipe on page 262
beaten egg or apricot glaze
1 oz (25g) flaked almonds,
toasted
TO FINISH:
¼ pint (150ml) double cream
2 teasp. caster sugar
1-2 drops vanilla essence
icing sugar

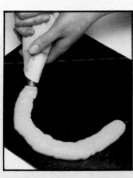

*Shape Paris
Brest by piping
a thin ring of
dough on a
greased baking
sheet*

CHOUX BUNS

1 quantity choux pastry as in
recipe on page 262
¼ pint (150ml) double cream
CHOCOLATE SAUCE:
6 oz (150g) plain chocolate
2 oz (50g) butter
4 tablesp. (60ml) water
2 oz (50g) caster sugar

Spoon the choux pastry into a piping bag fitted with a ¾-in. (2.5-cm) diameter nozzle. Pipe a ring about 8 in. (20cm) in diameter and 1½ in. (3.5cm) wide on to a greased baking tray.

Bake in a preheated oven (425 deg. F, 220 deg. C, Gas no. 7) for about 30 minutes until the choux ring is risen and golden. Ten minutes before end of cooking brush with beaten egg or apricot glaze and scatter with flaked almonds. Transfer it to a cooling rack. Slit it carefully around the middle and cool.

Put the cream into a basin and whip until beginning to thicken. Add the caster sugar and a drop or two of vanilla essence and continue whipping until thick. Fill into lower half of the choux ring. Cover with other half and dust with sieved icing sugar. Serves 4-6.

TO FREEZE: when cool, open freeze the unfilled choux ring, wrap, seal, label and return to the freezer. Use within 2 months.

TO USE: remove wrappings, and reheat choux ring from frozen (375 deg. F, 190 deg. C, Gas no. 5) for about 10 minutes until 'crisped'. Complete as from ❄ in recipe.

Grease a baking tray and, using a teaspoon, spoon the choux mixture into small mounds, keeping them spaced well apart so they have room to spread during baking. Bake in preheated oven (425 deg. F, 220 deg. C, Gas no. 7) for 15 minutes or until the buns are crisp and golden. Remove them from the oven. Make a slit in each bun to allow steam to escape and transfer to a cooling rack. Leave the buns until cold.

Whip the cream and fill into a piping bag, fitted with a plain nozzle, and pipe cream into each bun through the slits already made.

Make the chocolate sauce by putting all the ingredients into a small pan and heating gently, stirring from time to time. ❄ Leave the sauce to cool completely and start to thicken, then pile buns on to a dish and pour over the chocolate sauce. Makes 20.

TO FREEZE: open freeze the buns on a tray, then pack into a polythene bag, seal, label and return to the freezer. Use within 2 months. When cool, pour the sauce into a rigid container or boiling bag, seal, label and freeze. Use within 2 months.

TO USE: thaw the sauce. Remove wrappings and thaw the buns for 1 hour at room temperature. Complete as from ❄ in recipe.

Hazelnut Meringue with Peaches

Rounds of crisp nutty meringue are layered together with whipped cream and sliced peaches. Use fresh or home frozen peaches when available as their flavour is more pronounced

3 egg whites
6oz (150g) caster sugar
3oz (75g) ground hazelnuts
FILLING:
1 x 14½oz (410g) can sliced peaches or 2-3 fresh peaches
½ pint sugar syrup, made with 4oz (100g) sugar to ½ pint (300ml) water
½ pint (300ml) double cream
1 teasp. (5ml) caster sugar
TO FINISH:
¼ pint (150ml) double cream
8 roasted hazelnuts

Line 2 baking sheets with non-stick baking paper (available from stationers) or foil.

Whisk egg whites until stiff. Add 1 tablespoon (15ml) of the sugar and beat again for 30 seconds. Sprinkle over the rest of the sugar and fold in gently but thoroughly with a metal spoon, together with the ground hazelnuts.

Pipe or spread the mixture in 2×7in. (2× 17.5cm) rounds on to the prepared baking sheets and bake in preheated oven (275 deg. F, 140 deg. C, Gas no. 1) for 1-1½ hours or until the meringues are crisp and dry. Remove from the baking sheets and cool on a wire rack. ✳

Drain the can of peaches or peel and slice the fresh peaches and poach them in sugar syrup for about 5 minutes, then drain, and cool.

Whip together the ½ pint (300ml) double cream and sugar until thick. Spoon on to one of the meringue rounds. Arrange drained peach slices on top and cover with the second meringue round.

Whip the remaining cream until fairly stiff, then fill into a piping bag fitted with a rose nozzle and pipe 8 rosettes round the edge of the meringue. Top each rosette of cream with a toasted hazelnut. Serves 6-8.

✳ TO FREEZE: pack the meringue rounds in a rigid container, seal, label and freeze. Use within 2 months.

TO USE: thaw meringues overnight in fridge and complete as from ✳ in recipe.

Caramel and Hazelnut Ice Cream

Extravagant but luscious, the ice will be richer and smoother if you use all cream. Take care when making the caramel not to let it get too dark or the flavour will be spoilt

Place the shelled hazelnuts on a baking sheet and bake for 5-10 minutes at 350 deg. F, 180 deg. C, Gas no. 4 until well browned. Tip them on to a rough cloth, rub them briskly in the cloth and the skins will flake off. Chop the nuts and set aside.

Beat the egg yolks together with the teaspoon (5ml) sugar.

Put the rest of the sugar into a heavy-bottomed aluminium or stainless steel pan, together with the water, and set over a gentle heat, stirring from time to time, until the sugar has dissolved. Then turn up the heat, bring to the boil and boil rapidly without stirring until a good caramel colour. You won't be able to judge the colour so easily if the mixture is in a dark-lined pan.

Remove from the heat and pour in the cream, or cream and milk mixture, stirring. The caramel will harden into a mass so return the pan to the heat and heat gently, stirring until the caramel dissolves. Pour the caramel cream on to the egg yolks, stirring. Return the mixture to the pan, then stand the pan in a roasting tin of hot water (or use a double boiler) and cook, stirring until the caramel custard thickens enough to coat the back of the spoon. Don't let it get too hot or it will curdle.

Pour the mixture into a basin and leave to cool, stirring from time to time so a skin doesn't form. When cold pour into a freezer tray and freeze until it begins to thicken. Stir in the chopped nuts ❄ and return to the freezer until firm. Serves 4-6.

1½oz (40g) hazelnuts
3 egg yolks
3oz (75g) plus 1 teasp. (5ml) granulated sugar
1 pint (550ml) single cream or a mixture of single cream and top of the milk
2 tablesp. (30ml) water

❄ TO FREEZE: cover the ice cream, seal and label the container. Use within 3 months.

TO USE: transfer the ice from the freezer to the fridge about 30 minutes before serving.

Strawberry Charlotte

A lovely creamy mousse that's equally good with fresh or frozen strawberries. Home-made sponge fingers (see recipe on page 226) complete the charlotte

1 lb (450g) strawberries, fresh or frozen
7 oz (175g) caster sugar
juice of ½ lemon
juice of ½ orange
½ oz (15g) powdered gelatine
3 eggs
¼ pint (150ml) double cream
TO FINISH:
¼ pint (150ml) double cream
langue de chat biscuits or sponge fingers
(see recipe on page 226)
few strawberries

If using fresh fruit, hull and wipe the strawberries. Thaw frozen fruit. Rub fruit through a sieve: stir in 3 oz (75g) of the sugar until dissolved. This should give you about ¾ pint (425ml) of purée.

Pour the lemon and orange juices into a small basin, sprinkle over the gelatine and dissolve it over a pan of hot water. Put the remaining sugar into a basin with the eggs and stand over a pan of hot water. Whisk until thick. Remove the basin from the heat and continue whisking until the mixture is cold. If using an electric mixer heat isn't necessary but beat the egg mixture until it is thick enough for the whisk to leave a trail when it is lifted out. Lightly whip the first ¼ pint (150ml) cream.

Stir the strawberry purée and gelatine liquid into the egg mixture. Fold in the whipped cream and turn into a 6-7 in. (15-17.5cm) diameter soufflé dish or cake tin. Cover with foil and leave to set. ✳

When firm turn out the charlotte. Lightly whip the remaining cream. Spread the biscuits or sponge fingers with some of the cream (see below) and arrange them, overlapping, all round the charlotte (see below). Fill the remaining whipped cream into a piping bag, fitted with a rose nozzle, and pipe cream round the outer edge. Decorate with sliced strawberries. Serves 6.

 TO FREEZE: when the charlotte is set, seal label and freeze. Use within 3 months.

TO USE: thaw the charlotte overnight in the fridge and complete as from ✳ in recipe.

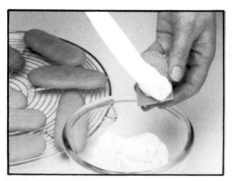

Trim sponge fingers so they stand just above top of charlotte. Spread whipped cream on underside of each

Press sponge fingers, cream side inwards, on to charlotte all round, overlapping them if liked

Continental Cheesecake

A rich, creamy topping containing lemon and raisins is baked on a sponge paste base and served chilled

1 lemon
1 large egg
8oz (225g) stale sponge cake
2oz (50g) butter
2 teasp. (10ml) custard powder
¼ pint (150ml) double cream
1½oz (40g) caster sugar
1lb (450g) cream cheese
1oz (25g) raisins

Grate the lemon rind into a basin and squeeze the juice on to it. Beat the egg.

Crumble the sponge cake in a blender or with your hands. Rub in the butter to make a rich paste. Knead it until the mixture is rather like marzipan, then press it into the base of an 8-in. (20-cm) diameter loose-bottomed sandwich tin.

Measure the custard powder into a large basin and blend in the cream, then the beaten egg and sugar, the lemon rind and juice and finally the cream cheese. Do all this in an electric mixer if you like but only long enough just to blend the ingredients. If you overbeat it, it will separate. Stir in the raisins.

Pour the mixture on to the base and bake in preheated oven (375 deg. F, 190 deg. C, Gas no. 5) for about 35 minutes. If not golden-brown and firm to the touch, reduce the heat to 325 deg. F, 170 deg. C, Gas no. 3 and bake until it is.

Cool the cheesecake in the tin. ❄ Refrigerate for 1 hour before turning out. Serves 8.

TO FREEZE: when cold open freeze cheese-cake; when hard pack into a polythene bag, seal, label and return to the freezer. Use within 2 months.

TO USE: thaw the cheese-cake overnight in fridge, then turn out.

St. Clement's Soufflé

The centre of this light,
frothy, lemony soufflé is
filled just before serving
with orange segments
poached in sugar syrup

Prepare a 6-in. (15-cm) diameter soufflé dish by tying a collar of double thickness foil round the dish so that it comes about 2in. (5cm) above the rim. Oil a small polythene tumbler and stand in the centre of the dish. Put a weight in it so it won't tip as you pour in the soufflé mixture.

Into a large basin grate the rind of the lemons. Separate the eggs. Squeeze out the lemon juice and add this, together with the yolks and sugar. Stand the bowl over a pan of hot water and whisk until the mixture is thick and the whisk leaves a trail as you lift it out. Remove from the heat.

Put the 2 tablespoons (30ml) water into a small basin. Sprinkle in the gelatine, let it stand a few minutes, then put the basin in a pan of hot water until the gelatine has dissolved. Cool slightly and pour it into the whisked egg mixture, stirring as you do so. Whip the cream until it begins to thicken and fold it into the lemon mixture. Stiffly whisk the egg whites until they stand up in peaks and fold them gently through the mixture. Pour it into the prepared soufflé dish, round the tumbler, and leave to set in the fridge. ❄

Put the sugar and water into a pan and heat gently until the sugar is dissolved, stirring from time to time. Boil for 2 minutes and set aside to cool. Cut the ends off the oranges then, using a small serrated-edged knife cut with a sawing motion round the oranges to remove all peel and pith. Cut them into segments slicing between the membrane. Remove any pips. Put orange segments into the sugar syrup, cover and put in the fridge to chill. ❄ ❄

When the soufflé has set carefully ease out the tumbler, then fill the centre with the drained orange segments. Moisten them with a little of the syrup. Whip the cream, if using, and pipe (see page 266) rosettes round the edge of the soufflé. Serves 4.

3 lemons
4 eggs
6oz (150g) caster sugar
2 teasp. (10ml) gelatine
2 tablesp. (30ml) water
¼ pint (150ml) double cream
ORANGE FILLING:
2oz (50g) sugar
¼ pint (150ml) water
2–3 oranges
TO FINISH:
¼ pint (150ml) double cream,
  optional

❄ TO FREEZE: open freeze the soufflé leaving the collar in position. When hard remove the weight from the tumbler, slip the soufflé in its dish into a polythene bag, seal, label and freeze. Use within 2 months. Tip the oranges with their syrup into a rigid container, leaving ½in. (1cm) headspace, seal, label and freeze. Use within 2 months.

TO USE: thaw both soufflé and oranges in fridge overnight and complete as from ❄ and ❄ ❄ in recipe.

Traditional Teabreads

Sometimes called Quick Breads, for that's just what they are to make. Richer than ordinary bread, plainer than cake – you'll find them good sliced and buttered

8oz (225g) self–raising flour
4oz (100g) margarine
4oz (100g) caster sugar
4oz (100g) chopped dates
4oz (100g) chopped walnuts
1 egg
milk

DATE AND WALNUT LOAF

Sift the flour into a basin. Rub in the margarine until the mixture resembles fine breadcrumbs. Stir in the sugar, dates and nuts. Add the beaten egg and enough milk (about 5 tablespoons (75ml)) to mix to a stiff dropping consistency.

Put the mixture into a greased $8\frac{1}{2}$- x $4\frac{1}{2}$- x $2\frac{1}{2}$-in. (21- x 11- x 6.5-cm) loaf tin. Bake in the centre of the oven (350 deg. F, 180. deg C, Gas No. 4) for about $1\frac{1}{4}$ hours or until risen and firm to the touch. Turn out on to a wire rack to cool. Makes 12 slices.

TO FREEZE. When cold wrap the loaf in foil, seal, label and freeze. Use within 3 months.

TO USE. Thaw the loaf at room temperature for 3-4 hours.

BANANA AND RAISIN LOAF

4oz (100g) margarine
8oz (225g) self-raising flour
2oz (50g) granulated sugar
4oz (100g) raisins
2 medium bananas
1 egg
2 tablesp. (15ml) milk

Melt the margarine in a small pan. Place the flour, sugar and raisins in a basin and mix together. Add the bananas, mashed, the egg beaten with the milk and the melted margarine and beat until the ingredients are well mixed.

Place the mixture in a greased 8½- x 4½- x 2½-in. (21-x11-x6.5-cm) loaf tin. Bake in the centre of the oven (350 deg. F, 180 deg. C, Gas No. 4) for 1¼ hours or until risen and firm to the touch. Turn the loaf out on to a wire rack to cool. Makes 12 slices.

Nut-topped Sponge

For a special teatime treat
try this light buttery sponge
with its crunchy nut and
toffee topping

2oz (50g) butter
2 eggs
3oz (75g) caster sugar
3oz (75g) plain flour
1½ teasp. (7.5ml) baking
powder
TOPPING:
2oz (50g) flaked almonds
2oz (50g) butter
2oz (50g) caster sugar
1 tablesp. (15ml) flour
1 tablesp. (15ml) cream or
top of milk

Grease 7-in. (17.5-cm) diameter cake tin.

Put the butter in a small pan and melt over a gentle heat. Break the eggs into a basin, add the sugar and whisk together until the mixture is a thick pale cream. Sieve the plain flour and baking powder over the top and fold in gently. Pour the melted butter on to the mixture and fold in gently with a metal spoon, being careful not to over-mix and flatten the mixture. Pour into the prepared tin and bake in preheated oven (350 deg. F, 180 deg. C, Gas no. 4) for 25 minutes.

While the cake is baking, make up the topping. Put all the topping ingredients into a pan and heat gently, stirring, until the fat and sugar have melted and the ingredients are well mixed.

Check the cake is cooked: press in the centre slightly with your finger and the cake should spring back and not retain an impression; if it docs, bake a few more minutes.

Pour the topping over the cake, return to the oven for 5 minutes, then put under a hot grill to brown the top. ✳ Makes 8-10 slices.

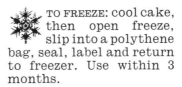 TO FREEZE: cool cake, then open freeze, slip into a polythene bag, seal, label and return to freezer. Use within 3 months.

TO USE: unwrap cake, stand on a wire cooling rack and thaw at room temperature for 4 hours.

Rum Babas

Based on the savarin mixture, but baked in individual moulds, babas are named after the liqueur with which they are flavoured. They should be really well soaked so that they're oozing with the boozy syrup

Use half the Fruit Savarin mixture as follows: pour the yeast batter into 8 greased baba moulds or castle pudding tins until half full. Cover with greased polythene and leave in a warm place for about 45 minutes until the mixture has risen to the top of the moulds. Remove polythene.

Stand the moulds or tins on a baking sheet and bake in preheated oven (400 deg. F, 200 deg. C, Gas no. 6) for about 15 minutes or until risen and golden. Cool babas slightly in the tins, then remove to a cooling tray.

Put the sugar and water for the syrup in a pan and heat gently, stirring, until the sugar is dissolved. Bring to the boil and boil for 5 minutes. Add the lemon juice and cool.

Stand the cooled babas on a plate or dish, prick them with a fork and spoon over the syrup until completely impregnated; then pour about 1 teaspoon (5ml) rum over each.

Whip the cream until forming peaks, fill into a piping bag, fitted with a rose nozzle, and pipe a little cream into the centre of each baba. If using castle pudding tins, pipe the cream on top of each pudding. ❄ Serves 8.

½ **quantity Savarin mixture (see page 193)**
SYRUP:
4oz (100g) granulated sugar
½ pint (300ml) water
1 tablesp. (15ml) lemon juice
about 2 tablesp. (30ml) rum
TO FINISH:
¼ pint (150ml) double cream

❄ TO FREEZE: open freeze completed babas until solid, then wrap, seal, label and return to freezer. Use within 2 months

TO USE: thaw babas for 5 hours in fridge and serve.

Kirsch Cake

This Swiss cake consists of nutty meringue layers sandwiching a light sponge soaked in a kirsch syrup. Kirsch is a spirit distilled from fermented ripe wild cherries, and its superb bouquet imparts a marvellous flavour to the cake

SPONGE:
4 egg yolks
3 tablesp. (45ml) hot water
3 oz (75g) caster sugar
4 oz (100g) self-raising flour
1 egg white

MERINGUE:
3 egg whites
6 oz (150g) caster sugar
3 oz (75g) ground almonds

FILLING:
1 oz (25g) cornflour
9 fl. oz (270ml) milk
5 oz (125g) unsalted butter
2 oz (50g) caster sugar
2 tablesp. (30ml) sieved red jam

KIRSCH SYRUP:
3 tablesp. (45ml) water
2 oz (50g) sugar
6 tablesp. (90ml) kirsch

TO FINISH:
sieved icing sugar
2 oz (50g) chopped roasted almonds

TO FREEZE. Open freeze the cake, then wrap completely in foil, seal, label and return to the freezer. Use within 1 month.

TO USE. Unwrap the cake and thaw at room temperature for 4 hours. Complete as from ❄ in recipe.

To make the sponge, beat the egg yolks, water and sugar together until thick and creamy. It takes several minutes to get a thick, creamy consistency. Sieve the flour over the mixture and fold in gently, taking care not to flatten out the air beaten into the eggs. Whisk the egg white until it forms peaks, then fold it lightly but thoroughly into the sponge mixture.

Spread the sponge batter in a greased 9-in. (23-cm) sponge tin and bake (375 deg. F, 190 deg. C, Gas No. 5) for about 25 minutes or until risen, golden and firm to the touch. Turn the sponge on to a wire rack to cool.

Make the meringue rounds by whisking the egg whites until they form soft peaks. Whisk in 1 tablespoon (15 ml) of the sugar. Sift together remaining sugar and ground almonds. Sprinkle this over the egg whites and fold in lightly but thoroughly.

Line two baking trays with foil or non-stick silicone paper and spread the meringue mixture on them in two 9-in. (23-cm) rounds. Bake at (275 deg. F, 140 deg. C, Gas No. 1) for 1-1¼ hours or until crisp and dry. Peel off the paper and set the meringue rounds aside.

Prepare the cream filling by making a paste with the cornflour and 4 tablespoons (60 ml) cold milk. Bring remaining milk to the boil, pour on to the paste, stirring. Return to the pan and bring to the boil, stirring all the time. Cream the butter and sugar together and when the cornflour mixture has cooled, add this a little at a time, beating well. Beat in the jam.

To make the syrup, put the water and sugar in a pan and heat gently until the sugar has dissolved, then bring to the boil. Remove from the heat and cool. When cold stir in the kirsch.

Assemble the cake in layers, starting with a layer of meringue. Spread a little of the cream filling over this, then position the sponge. Carefully spoon the kirsch syrup over the sponge. Spread with a little more cream filling. Top with the second meringue round and spread the remaining cream filling over the top and sides of the cake. Pat the chopped nuts round the sides. Place the cake on a cake board. ❄ Sieve icing sugar over the top and make a diamond pattern over the surface with the point of a knife. Serves 8-10.

Fancy Bread Rolls

Try out some of these fancy shapes when you're next making a batch of rolls. They look most tempting piled up in a basket

1lb (450g) strong plain flour, white or wheatmeal
1 level teasp. (5ml) salt
1oz (25g) margarine
1oz (25g) fresh yeast or ½oz (12.5g) dried yeast and 1 level teasp. (5ml) sugar
½ pint (300ml) lukewarm water

Sieve the flour and salt into a basin. Rub the margarine into the flour. Blend the fresh yeast in the water or dissolve the teaspoon (5ml) sugar in the water, sprinkle the dried yeast on top and leave until it goes spongy and frothy on top – about 10 minutes.

Pour the yeast liquid into the dry ingredients and mix well until the dough is firm and leaves the side of the bowl clean. Turn on to a floured board and knead well until the dough is firm and has a silky feel – this will take 5-10 minutes.

Place the dough in a clean warm bowl, cover with greased polythene and leave for about 45 minutes in a warm place or until the dough has doubled in size.

Knock it back, then cut into 12-16 pieces and shape into rolls or any of the following shapes:

Coburg: form a piece of dough into a roll, then cut a deep cross on the top with a sharp knife.

Cottage: cut a quarter off one of the pieces of dough. Shape both pieces into balls. Place the small one on top of the large one. Push the handle of a wooden spoon down through the middle of both, then pull it out sharply.

Knot: shape a piece of dough into a long sausage-shape and tie it loosely in a knot.

Plait: shape a piece of dough into a long, thin sausage, then cut into three strips, leaving one end joined. Form a plait and press the ends firmly together.

Place the shapes on a greased tray, cover with greased polythene and leave 20 minutes to double in size. Brush with milk or beaten egg for a brown, crisp crust or with flour for a soft one. Bake in preheated oven (450 deg. F, 230 deg. C, Gas no. 8) for about 15 minutes. Cool on a wire rack. Wrap in a teacloth for a soft roll.

TO FREEZE: pack the cooled rolls in poly-thene bags, seal, label and freeze. Use within 1 week for crispy rolls, or 3 months for soft rolls.

TO USE: thaw the rolls at room temperature for 1½ hours or wrap frozen rolls in foil and reheat in pre-heated oven (450 deg. F, 230 deg. 3, Gas no. 8) for about 10 minutes.

Yorkshire Teacakes

Just right for tea on a cold, grey winter's day. Split and toast both sides of the teacake, spread thickly with butter, sandwich together and serve cut in quarters while still hot

Sieve the flour and salt into a bowl. Rub in the butter, stir in the currants and the 1oz (25g) caster sugar. Warm the milk until just tepid, pour it into a small basin, add the remaining sugar and the yeast, give it a stir and let it stand for about 10 minutes until frothy.

Beat the egg and add, with the yeast mixture, to the dry ingredients. Mix to a firm dough, adding a sprinkling of extra flour if necessary.

Turn the dough on to a lightly-floured board and knead until smooth. Place the dough in a warm, greased basin. Cover the bowl with a piece of oiled polythene or a cloth and leave about 45 minutes in a warm place for the dough to double in size.

Knock back and knead the dough again until firm. Divide it into 6 equal pieces. Roll each into a ball, then roll each to a flattened round about 5in. (12.5cm) across. Place on a greased baking sheet, brush with milk and leave for about 15 minutes to rise again. Bake in preheated oven (400 deg. F, 200 deg. C, Gas no. 6) for 15–20 minutes. Cool the teacakes on a wire rack, covered with a tea towel to keep them soft. ❋ Split and toast to serve. Makes 6.

1lb (450g) strong white flour
1 teasp. (5ml) salt
2oz (50g) butter
2oz (50g) currants
1oz (25g) plus 1 teasp. (5ml) caster sugar
½ pint (300ml) warm milk
½oz (15g) fresh yeast or 2 teasp. dried yeast
1 egg

TO FREEZE: when cold pack the teacakes into polythene bags, seal, label and freeze. Use within 1 month.

TO USE: thaw the teacakes at room temperature for about 30 minutes, then complete as from ❋ in recipe.

A rich mixture of chocolate, ground almonds, butter and sugar make a cake luxurious enough to serve with coffee after dinner. And it would look equally attractive if made in a fluted ring mould or fancy cake tin

4 oz (100g) plain chocolate
2 tablesp. (30ml) water
4 oz (100g) butter
1 egg yolk
4 oz (100g) icing sugar
4 oz (100g) ground almonds
4 oz (100g) plain semi-sweet
 biscuits (Rich Tea or Petit
 Beurre)

Break up the chocolate and put the pieces in a pan with the water. Melt it over a gentle heat. Cut the butter into tiny pieces or flakes. Remove the pan from the heat and add the butter to the chocolate, a few pieces at a time, stirring to blend it in before adding more. Stir in the egg yolk, the icing sugar, which should be sieved, then the ground almonds.

   Break the biscuits into small pieces – it doesn't matter about their shape (see below). Fold them gently into the chocolate mixture. Turn into a 1-pint (550-ml) mould or loaf tin. ❄ Serves 8-10.

❄ TO FREEZE: cover the cake, seal, label and freeze. Use within 2 months.

TO USE: thaw the cake at room temperature for about 4 hours, then slice and serve.

Break the biscuits into small pieces about the size of your thumbnail – their shape doesn't matter – before folding them into the chocolate almond mixture

Chocolate Almond Cake

Little Madeleines

These plain but very good
small French cakes are
made from butter, sugar,
eggs and flour and baked
in special moulds with a
shell-like bottom. Some
versions have grated
lemon rind in the mixture

2oz (50g) plain flour
2oz (50g) butter
2 eggs
2oz (50g) caster sugar

If you don't have any specially-designed
madeleine pans, use ordinary bun pans. Grease
and flour them.

Sieve the flour and set it aside. Melt the butter
and leave it to cool slightly.

Put the eggs and sugar into a bowl and whisk
until the mixture is thick and mousse-like so
that the whisk leaves a trail in the mixture when
you lift it out.

Sieve the flour over the mixture and fold it in
very lightly with a metal spoon, then stir in the
cooled butter as rapidly as possible. Don't stir
longer than is necessary but just sufficient to
incorporate the butter or the mixture will
collapse. Spoon into the prepared pans filling
them about three-quarters full. Bake in preheated oven (400 deg. F, 200 deg. C, Gas no. 6) for
10 minutes. Turn out and cool on a wire rack.
Makes 14.

TO FREEZE: when cold
pack the madeleines
into polythene bags,
seal, label and freeze. Use
within 4 months.

TO USE: thaw the cakes at
room temperature on a
wire rack for 1 hour.

Ginger Slices

Dry sponge cakes tend to be used for trifles. Here's a rather more unusual way of using them to make spicy moist ginger slices with sultanas

Crumb the sponge cake in a blender or rub through a coarse sieve. Tip the crumbs into a bowl large enough to hold all the ingredients. Sieve the flour, baking powder and ginger on to the crumbs. Add the sultanas and stir all the dry ingredients together.

Put the brown sugar, milk and golden syrup into a pan and heat gently, stirring occasionally, until the sugar has dissolved. Pour this on to the dry ingredients and mix well.

Turn the mixture into a greased 7-in. (17.5-cm) square tin and bake in preheated oven (375 deg. F, 190 deg. C, Gas no. 5) for about 45 minutes or until risen and set. Cool slightly, then turn out the cake on to a wire rack and leave until cold. ✳

Sieve the icing sugar into a small basin and mix to a thin paste with a little water. Spread over the top of the ginger cake and when set, cut into slices. Makes 10 slices.

8oz (225g) stale sponge cake or plain cake
6oz (150g) plain flour
½ teasp. (2.5ml) baking powder
1½ teasp. (7.5ml) ground ginger
4oz (100g) sultanas
3½oz (90g) soft brown sugar
6fl oz (180ml) milk
6oz (150g) golden syrup
TO FINISH:
2oz (50g) icing sugar
water

✳ TO FREEZE: pack the cake in a polythene bag, seal, label and freeze. Use within 2 months.

TO USE: unwrap the cake and thaw on a wire rack about 3-4 hours. Complete as from ✳ in recipe.

Pitta Bread

A delicious flat bread found all over the Middle East. It's baked in a hot oven on hot trays so it puffs up immediately. When cooked it is wrapped in foil or a teacloth so it collapses and softens, leaving a shallow pocket inside which can be filled with salad or kebabs. The bread is also good for dips (see recipe on page 262)

1 pint (550ml) warm water
½ oz (15g) dried yeast
2 lb (900g) strong plain flour
1½ teasp. (7.5 ml) salt
3 tablesp. (45ml) vegetable oil

Put about 4 tablespoons (60ml) of the water in a bowl and sprinkle on the yeast. Leave in a warm place until frothy – this takes about 10 minutes.

Sieve the flour and salt into a bowl, make a well in the centre and add the yeast liquid. Mix to a soft dough with the rest of the warm water. Place on a floured board and knead for about 5 minutes or until it is smooth and elastic. Rinse, dry and lightly grease the mixing bowl, Put in the dough, cover with oiled polythene and leave to prove in a warm place for about 40 minutes or until doubled in bulk.

Turn out the dough on to a floured surface, knead lightly and divide into 12 pieces. Knead each piece into a ball. Put these on a floured tray, spaced well apart. Cover with oiled polythene and leave in a warm place for 30 minutes.

Roll out each piece on a floured surface to about 6 in. (15cm) long and 3 in. (7.5cm) wide – they should be about ¼ in. (5mm) thick. Cover with oiled polythene and leave in a warm place for a further 30 minutes.

Set the oven (450 deg. F, 230 deg. C, Gas no. 8) and preheat the trays on which the bread is to be cooked. When they are hot, put on them the loaves, spaced well apart, and bake for about 10 minutes or until risen and golden. Take out top tray, move up middle and lower trays to complete cooking; or bake in relays one tray at a time. Wrap the loaves completely in a clean tea cloth to cool and flatten. Makes 12.

TO FREEZE: cool the loaves, pack in polythene bags, seal, label and freeze. Use within 2 months.

TO USE: remove wrappings and put loaves, covered, in a moderate oven (350 deg. F, 180 deg. C, Gas no. 4) for about 15 minutes or till thawed and warmed through.

Suffolk Rusks

These are good to eat with butter and cheese or to serve with soup. They can also be used as a cobbler topping on sweet or savoury dishes. If you're doing this add them, ready baked and crisp, towards the end of the cooking time, dotting them with butter

2 tablesp. (30ml) milk
2 tablesp. (30ml) water
1 teasp. (5ml) sugar
$\frac{1}{2}$oz (15g) fresh yeast or 2 teasp. (10ml) dried yeast
8oz (225g) plain flour
1 teasp. (5ml) salt
1oz (25g) lard or margarine
1 egg

Put the milk and water into a pan and heat until tepid. Pour into a small basin, add the sugar and yeast and leave until frothy – about 10 minutes.

Sieve the flour and salt into a bowl, rub in the fat. Beat the egg.

Pour the yeast mixture and egg into the flour and work together to form a dough. Turn out on to a floured surface and knead until smooth. Turn into a greased, warmed bowl, cover with oiled polythene or a cloth and leave in a warm place to rise until doubled in size.

Knock back the dough and knead lightly on a floured surface. Divide into 8 pieces and roll out to 3-in. (7.5-cm) lengths. Place them on a greased baking sheet and leave to rise again for about 15 minutes.

Bake in preheated oven (425 deg. F, 220 deg. C, Gas no. 7) for 10 minutes. Remove from the oven and pull each rusk in half lengthways. Return to the oven, torn side up and bake until brown – about 10 minutes. Cool on wire rack. Makes 8.

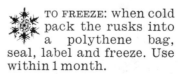 TO FREEZE: when cold pack the rusks into a polythene bag, seal, label and freeze. Use within 1 month.

TO USE: thaw the rusks at room temperature for $1\frac{1}{2}$ hours.

Cheese and Celery Loaf

Quick and easy to make, this savoury loaf is good on its own sliced and buttered or to accompany a thick mixed vegetable soup

Sieve the flour, salt and mustard into a basin. Rub in the margarine. Grate the cheese and stir it in. Wash, trim and finely chop or grate the celery and add to the mixture, stirring it in. Beat the eggs and add to the dry ingredients to form a firm dough. If the mixture is too dry, add a little milk. Grease 1 x 1lb (450g) loaf tin and put the dough into it.

Bake in preheated oven (375 deg. F, 190 deg. C, Gas no. 5) for about 45 minutes. Leave the loaf in the tin for a few minutes, then turn on to a wire rack to cool. ❄ Slice and serve with butter. Makes 14 slices.

8oz (225g) self-raising flour
1 teasp. (5ml) salt
½ teasp. (2.5ml) dry mustard
2oz (50g) margarine
3oz (75g) Cheddar cheese
2 sticks celery
2 eggs
little milk, optional

❄ TO FREEZE: when cold wrap the loaf in foil, seal, label and freeze. Use within 2 months.

TO USE: thaw the loaf at room temperature for 3–4 hours. Complete as from ❄ in recipe.

Old-fashioned Sponges

The cake with its firm texture and crusty top is ideal to serve with fruit compotes (see page 267). The sponge fingers can be used round a charlotte (see page 206) or sandwiched with cream and jam

OLD-FASHIONED SPONGE CAKE
5 eggs
10 oz (350g) caster sugar
6 oz (150g) plain flour, sieved

Sprinkle sugar in greased tin, tilt on side and turn to coat bottom and sides; tip out any surplus sugar

Separate the eggs. Put the yolks and 6 oz (150g) of the sugar in a mixing bowl, and whisk until pale and creamy.

In another bowl whisk the egg whites until stiff and forming peaks, then stir in the remaining sugar. Fold the whites into the egg mixture with the flour.

Grease an 8-in. (20-cm) diameter cake tin, sprinkle in a little sugar and turn the tin to coat the bottom and sides (see below); tip out any surplus sugar. Pour in the cake mixture and bake in preheated oven (350 deg. F, 180 deg. C, Gas no. 4) for about 1 hour or until the sponge is risen and golden-brown. Remove from the oven and turn the cake out on to a cooling rack. ❄ Serve with a fruit compote (see recipe on page 267). Serves 8.

❄ TO FREEZE: cool the cake, wrap in foil, seal, label and freeze. Use in 4 months.

TO USE: thaw the cake for 2 hours at room temperature. Complete as from ❄ in recipe.

SPONGE FINGERS
3 eggs
2½ oz (65g) caster sugar
few drops vanilla essence
2½ oz (65g) plain flour

Separate the eggs and put the yolks in a mixing bowl with the sugar. Whisk until pale and creamy. Add a few drops of vanilla essence.

In another bowl whisk the egg whites until stiff and forming peaks. Fold into the egg mixture with the sifted flour.

Spoon the mixture into a piping bag fitted with ½-in. (1-cm) diameter plain nozzle. Pipe 3-in. (7.5-cm) fingers on to a greased and floured baking sheet, keeping them spaced well apart. Bake in preheated oven (325 deg. F, 170 deg. C, Gas no. 3) for about 15 minutes or until golden-brown. Lift on to a wire cooling rack. ❄ When cold serve with a compote of fruit (see recipe on page 267), or ice cream. Makes 30.

❄ TO FREEZE: when cold, pack the sponge fingers in a rigid container, separating the layers with greaseproof paper. Seal, label and freeze. Use within 4 months.

TO USE: thaw the sponge fingers on a wire rack for 20 minutes at room temperature. Complete as from ❄ in recipe.

Chocolate and Coconut Cake

A plain cake with roughly chopped chocolate stirred into the mixture. If the family don't like coconut leave it out – it's only sprinkled over the chocolate icing

2oz (50g) chocolate chips
4oz (100g) margarine
4oz (100g) caster sugar
2 eggs
4oz (100g) self-raising flour
1oz (25g) ground almonds
½ teasp. (2.5ml) vanilla essence
ICING:
1oz (25g) cocoa
1 tablesp. (15ml) water
2oz (50g) icing sugar
1oz (25g) desiccated coconut

Roughly chop the chocolate chips. Cream the margarine and sugar in a bowl until light and fluffy. Beat the eggs and add to the creamed mixture. Stir in the flour, then the roughly chopped chocolate chips, ground almonds and vanilla essence. Turn the mixture into a greased 8-in. (20-cm) diameter cake tin and bake in pre-heated oven (350 deg. F, 180 deg. C, Gas no. 4), one shelf above the centre, for about 25 minutes. When cooked the cake should be golden and firm to the touch. Turn out and cool the cake on a wire rack.

While the cake is cooling make the icing: in a basin blend the cocoa and water together, then beat in the icing sugar. Spread this over the cake and sprinkle with the desiccated coconut. ❋ Makes 8 slices.

TO FREEZE: open freeze the cake until hard, then pack into a polythene bag, seal, label and return to the freezer. Use within 3 months.

TO USE: unwrap and thaw the cake on a wire rack at room temperature for 3–4 hours.

Coffee Nut Roll

This is a coffee-flavoured fatless sponge baked in a swiss roll tin. When cold it is filled with a rich coffee butter cream, rolled up, coated with more butter cream, then smothered with chopped toasted nuts

Break the eggs into a bowl, add the caster sugar and first quantity of coffee essence and whisk until the mixture is thick and fluffy. This will take several minutes by hand, but an electric mixer will speed up the process. When you lift the whisk out the mixture should retain an impression of it for a few seconds.

Sieve the flour over the mixture and fold it in gently with a metal spoon. Spread the mixture over a greased and lined $12\frac{1}{2} \times 8\frac{3}{4}$in. ($31 \times 21.5$cm) swiss roll tin (see Fruity Ginger Roll on page 171) and bake in a preheated oven (425 deg. F, 220 deg. C, Gas no. 7), one shelf above the centre, for 8 minutes.

Have ready a sheet of greaseproof paper, lightly dusted with caster sugar. Turn the baked sponge on to it. Remove the tin and carefully strip the baking paper off the sponge. Trim the edges with a sharp knife. Roll up the sponge with the sugar-dusted paper inside it, and leave to cool.

To make the icing: cream the fat in a bowl until soft and gradually work in the icing sugar. Combine well and flavour to taste with the remaining coffee essence.

Roughly chop the nuts.

When cold, unroll the swiss roll. Spread it with half the coffee icing. Roll up and spread over the rest of the icing, then roll it in the chopped nuts.
✻ Makes 10 slices.

3 eggs
3oz (75g) caster sugar
1½ teasp. (7.5ml) coffee essence
3oz (75g) self-raising flour
ICING:
4oz (100g) butter or margarine
8oz (225g) icing sugar
2 teasp. (10ml) coffee essence
2oz (50g) roughly chopped walnuts, toasted hazelnuts or roasted almonds

TO FREEZE: open freeze the roll on a foil-lined baking sheet. When hard wrap the roll completely in the foil, seal, label and return to the freezer. Use within 3 months.

TO USE: unwrap the roll and thaw at room temperature for 3–4 hours.

Frosted Layer Cakes

These light-textured cakes – one sharp-tasting pineapple, the other crunchy walnut – are filled and covered with a delicate American frosting; firm on the outside, soft and creamy inside

8 oz (225g) plain flour
2½ teasp. (12.5ml) baking powder
pinch salt
2 eggs
4 oz (100g) butter or soft margarine
8 oz (225g) caster sugar
3 oz (75g) walnuts
5 tablesp. (75ml) milk
FROSTING AND FILLING:
12 oz (350g) granulated sugar
4 tablesp. (60ml) water
2 egg whites
¼ teasp. (1.25ml) cream of tartar
1 oz (25g) walnuts
few walnut halves

TO FREEZE: pack the completed cake in a rigid container, seal, label and freeze. Use within 2 months.

TO USE: thaw the cake at room temperature for 3-4 hours.

WALNUT CAKE

Brush 7-in. (17.5-cm) diameter cake tin with melted fat and line the base with greased grease-proof paper. Sift the flour with the baking powder and salt into a bowl. Separate the egg yolks from the whites. Cream the butter and sugar together in a bowl until light and fluffy. Beat in the egg yolks, one at a time. Stir in the chopped walnuts. Fold the flour and milk alternately into the mixture.

Whip the egg whites until just stiff and fold them lightly through the mixture. Spoon into prepared tin and bake in preheated oven (375 deg. F, 190 deg. C, Gas no. 5) for 1 hour. Cool, then split into three layers. Chop the walnuts and put into a small basin.

Put the granulated sugar, water, egg whites and cream of tartar into a large basin and suspend over a pan of boiling water. Keep the water boiling slowly and dissolve the sugar while stirring; this will take about 10 minutes. Don't start whisking until the sugar has completely dissolved or you won't get a smooth icing.

Now, with the bowl still over the boiling water, start beating with a hand or rotary whisk. The icing will soon stiffen. Lift out the whisk from time to time and when it leaves a good trail over the surface, take it off the heat and continue whisking for a minute or two. Put just under half of the icing into the basin containing the walnuts, and mix. Use this to sandwich the cake layers.

Put the rest of the icing on to the cake and using a knife quickly swirl it over the top and round the sides. Decorate with walnut halves and leave to set. ❄ Makes 10-12 slices.

PINEAPPLE CAKE

Make as for Walnut Cake, using an 8 oz (227g) can of pineapple slices or pieces in place of the chopped walnuts. Add 4 oz (100g) of the pineapple, finely chopped, to the cake mixture and 3 tablespoons (45ml) of the juice instead of milk. Use the rest of the pineapple, finely chopped, mixed with half the icing for the filling. ❄ Makes 10-12 slices.

Iced Marmalade Bread

Not strictly a bread yet not a rich enough mixture to be termed a cake. It is moist and sweet with chunks of peel and sultanas. Could become a teatime favourite

12oz (350g) self-raising flour
3oz (75g) margarine
3oz (75g) soft brown sugar
2oz (50g) sultanas
1 egg
1 orange, juice only – about 3 tablesp. (45ml)
4oz (100g) thick-cut marmalade
2oz (50g) icing sugar
2–3 tablesp. (30–40ml) water

Sieve the flour into a bowl and rub in the fat until the mixture resembles fine breadcrumbs. Stir in the brown sugar and the sultanas. Beat the egg with the orange juice, add the marmalade and stir into the dry ingredients. Mix well to a soft, but not sticky, dough.

Shape the dough on a lightly-floured board, then place in a greased 8-in. (20-cm) diameter cake tin or savarin mould. Bake in preheated oven (375 deg. F, 190 deg. C, Gas no. 6) for 40 minutes. Cool on a wire rack.

Sieve the icing sugar into a small basin. Add the water, 1 teasp. (5ml) at a time, and beat until smooth. When the bread is cold drizzle the icing over the top and allow to set. ❋ Makes 10 slices.

TO FREEZE: open freeze the bread until hard, then pack into a polythene bag, seal, label and return to the freezer. Use within 3 months.

TO USE: unwrap the bread and thaw on a wire rack at room temperature for 3–4 hours.

Devonshire Splits

Traditional rolls made with an enriched dough. They are served split and filled with jam and cream – ideally the deep yellow clotted cream from Devonshire

If using fresh yeast, blend it with a little of the measured milk and the sugar. If using dried yeast, dissolve the sugar in half the warm milk, sprinkle the dried yeast on top and leave until spongy and frothy – about 15 minutes.

Sieve the flour and salt into a bowl. Melt the butter in the remaining milk and when at blood heat add, with the yeast liquid, to the flour.

Beat to an elastic dough, turn it on to a floured board and knead until smooth. Place the dough in a large greased polythene bag, tie lightly and leave in a warm place until it is doubled in size.

Turn the dough on to a floured board and divide into 8 pieces. Form each into a ball. Place them fairly closely together on a greased baking sheet. Prove (leave to rise again) until doubled in size, then bake in preheated oven (450 deg. F, 230 deg. C, Gas no. 8) for 15–20 minutes. ❄ Cool, then split them diagonally through the top almost to the base.

To serve, whip the cream. Divide the raspberry jam and whipped cream between the splits and fill into them. Makes 8.

½oz (15g) fresh, or 1½ teasp. (7.5ml) dried, yeast
¼ pint (150ml) warm milk
1 teasp. (5ml) sugar
8oz (225g) strong plain white flour
1 teasp. (5ml) salt
1oz (25g) butter
TO FINISH:
¼ pint (150ml) double cream
4 tablesp. (60ml) raspberry jam

❄ TO FREEZE: when cold, pack the rolls into polythene bags, seal, label and freeze. Use within 3 months.

TO USE: thaw the rolls at room temperature for 2 hours on a wire rack, then complete as from ❄ in recipe.

Viennese Biscuits

Melt-in-the-mouth biscuits that owe their soft crumbly texture to the addition of cornflour with the ordinary plain flour

6 oz (150g) butter or margarine
2 oz (50g) caster sugar
4 oz (100g) plain flour
2 oz (50g) cornflour
¼ teasp. (1.25ml) vanilla essence
TO FINISH:
icing sugar, sifted

Cream the butter or margarine and sugar together in a mixing bowl until light and fluffy. Sieve the flour and cornflour together and stir into the creamed mixture; add the vanilla essence.

Fit a piping bag with a large star nozzle. Spoon the mixture into the bag (an easy way to fill a piping bag is shown on page 181). Pipe the mixture on to a greased baking sheet into shapes as shown left. Bake in preheated oven (350 deg.F, 180 deg. C, Gas no. 4) for 15-20 minutes.

Slide the biscuits off on to a wire rack to cool ❄ Toss the biscuits in sifted icing sugar to serve. Makes 14.

❄ TO FREEZE: cool the biscuits, then pack them into a rigid container, seal, label and freeze. Use within 3 months.

TO USE: thaw the biscuits at room temperature for 30 minutes. Complete as from ❄ in recipe.

Fill biscuit mixture into icing bag and pipe into fancy shapes. Leave space for spreading in baking

Macaroons

These crisp, nutty biscuits are usually made with almonds. Try the ground hazelnut version for a change – they're really delicious

4oz (100g) ground almonds or hazelnuts
5oz (125g) caster sugar
2 egg whites
TO FINISH:
flaked almonds or whole hazelnuts

Mix together the ground nuts and sugar. Whisk the egg whites in a large mixing bowl until stiff and forming peaks. Using a metal spoon, fold in the nut and sugar mixture.

Line 2 baking sheets with rice paper.

Either fill the nut mixture into a piping bag fitted with a $\frac{1}{2}$-in. (1-cm) diameter plain nozzle and pipe or spoon the mixture on to the prepared baking sheets. Shape into 1-in. (2.5-cm) diameter circles or 3-in. (7.5-cm) long fingers.

Put an almond or hazelnut in the centre of each biscuit and bake in preheated oven (325 deg. F, 170 deg. C, Gas no. 3) for 20 minutes or until pale golden and firm to the touch. Cool slightly on the trays, then remove macaroons, breaking off the surplus rice paper around each one. Cool completely on a wire rack. ✳ Makes about 22 small or finger macaroons or 16 large ones.

✳ TO FREEZE: pack macaroons in polythene bags, seal, label and freeze. Use within 3 months.

TO USE: thaw macaroons about 30 minutes at room temperature.

Walnut Crescents

Deliciously short, sweet biscuits containing crunchy pieces of walnut. Try them with chopped hazelnuts or almonds for a change. Make sure they are cool – and dry if they've been frozen – before tossing in icing sugar or it will turn sticky

Cream together the margarine and butter, then work in the sugar until the mixture is light and fluffy. Stir in the hot water. Stir in the flour and finally the chopped walnuts. The mixture will be quite soft and sticky, so wrap it in waxed paper or foil and put in the fridge for 1–2 hours to firm up.

Take a small piece off the dough and roll it into a sausage shape about the thickness of a wooden spoon handle. Cut into 2–3in. (5–7.5cm) lengths, curve them into a crescent shape and arrange on a greased baking sheet, leaving space for them to spread slightly. Bake in preheated oven (325 deg. F, 170 deg. C, Gas no. 3) for 15 minutes. Lift the crescents on to a wire rack to cool. ❄ Toss them in sifted icing sugar. Makes about 48.

6oz (150g) margarine
2oz (50g) butter
3oz (75g) sugar
2 teasp. (10ml) hot water
8oz (225g) flour
2oz (50g) chopped walnuts
TO FINISH:
little icing sugar

❄ TO FREEZE: when cold pack the crescents into a rigid container with freezer paper or foil between the layers, seal, label and freeze. Use within 3 months.

TO USE: spread out the crescents on a wire rack and thaw at room temperature for 30 minutes. Complete as from ❄ in recipe.

Buttery Biscuits

These are the perfect complement to creamy ices and puddings. From France come Almond Tuiles and Cigarettes Russes. The "tuiles" are set over a rolling pin after baking to give them their characteristic "tile" shape – and name. The "cigarettes" are rolled round a pencil or wooden spoon handle. From Scotland comes rich, sandy – that's the ground rice – Shortbread. Shape it into rounds or fingers; add nuts for variety in taste and texture

2 egg whites
4oz (100g) caster sugar
2oz (50g) plain flour
½ teasp. (2.5ml) vanilla essence
2oz (50g) butter, melted
1oz (25g) blanched almonds, shredded or flaked

TO FREEZE. When cold pack the biscuits into rigid containers; crumpled paper can fill any gaps to prevent them sliding about and breaking. Seal, label and freeze for up to 3 months.

TO USE. Thaw the biscuits in the container for at least 30 minutes.

4oz (100g) plain flour
2oz (50g) ground rice
2oz (50g) caster sugar
4oz (100g) butter

TO FREEZE. When cold pack the biscuits into rigid containers; crumpled paper can fill any gaps to prevent them sliding about and breaking. Seal, label and freeze for up to 3 months.

TO USE. Thaw the biscuits in the container for 30 minutes. Sprinkle them with sugar.

ALMOND TUILES
Grease, or line with silicone paper, several baking sheets and preheat the oven (425 deg. F, 220 deg. C, Gas No. 7).

Put the egg whites into a basin, beat in the caster sugar, then stir in the flour and vanilla essence. Add the cooled, melted butter and stir gently. Drop teaspoons of the mixture, well spaced, on to the baking sheets. Spread them out into rounds with the back of the spoon. Sprinkle a few nuts on each. Bake until golden and browned round the outer edge, about 4 minutes. Lift the biscuits carefully off the baking sheets immediately and lay them over a rolling pin to cool. As soon as they have crisped, move them on to a wire rack to make room for the others. Makes 12.

CIGARETTES RUSSES
Make the mixture as for Almond Tuiles, spreading it into oblongs and omitting the nuts. Shape round a pencil or wooden spoon handle, holding them in position until set (see page 267). Slip off on to a wire rack to cool. Makes 12

SHORTBREAD
Mix the flour, ground rice and sugar together. Rub in the butter, gradually working the mixture to a stiff dough. Don't overwork it or the mixture will become oily. Pat out to a round about ½in. (1cm) thick and place on a baking sheet or in a sandwich tin. Prick all over with a fork. Crimp the edges and bake (325 deg. F, 170 deg. C, Gas No. 3) about 30 minutes or until firm and pale golden in colour. Cut into triangles and leave on baking sheet or in tin to cool. Makes 8 portions.

NUTTY FINGERS
Make the mixture as for Shortbread, and add 2oz (50g) chopped walnuts towards the end of the mixing. Shape into a shallow square tin, bake as above. Cut into fingers. Makes 12.

Fruity Flapjacks

Some kinds of flapjack are crisp, others sticky and chewy. This recipe produces a softish oaty biscuit which combines well with the fruit addition of sultanas

4oz (100g) margarine
1 tablesp. (15ml) light brown sugar
4 tablesp. (60ml) golden syrup
8oz (225g) rolled oats
2oz (50g) sultanas

Put the margarine, sugar and syrup into a pan large enough to hold all the ingredients. Heat the pan gently until the margarine has melted and the sugar dissolved. Remove from the heat and stir in the oats and sultanas.

Grease a baking tin $7 \times 7 \times 1\frac{1}{2}$in. ($17.5 \times 17.5 \times 3.5$cm); turn the mixture into it, spreading it level. Bake in preheated oven (375 deg. F, 190 deg. C, Gas no. 5) for 20 minutes until set and golden.

Cool slightly, then mark the mixture into squares or fingers and leave in the tin until cold. Makes 9.

TO FREEZE: pack the flapjacks into a polythene bag, seal, label and freeze. Use within 3 months.

TO USE: thaw the flapjacks at room temperature on a wire rack for 2 hours.

Butterscotch Biscuits

Little chips of butterscotch make a pleasant addition to this sweet biscuit mixture. Chopped nuts, chocolate or candied peel could also be used to make a selection of mixed biscuits

Crush the butterscotch in a blender or put in a polythene bag and, using a rolling pin or mallet, hammer it into tiny pieces. In a mixing bowl cream the margarine and soft brown sugar until light and fluffy. Beat the egg and stir in.

Sieve the flour and gradually beat into the mixture. Lastly stir in the butterscotch. Gather up the dough, which will be soft and sticky, wrap it in foil and chill it in the fridge for about 30 minutes.

Shape the mixture into a roll 2–3in. (5–7.5cm) wide. ❄ Cut into slices and bake in preheated oven (375 deg. F, 190 deg. C, Gas no. 5) for 10–15 minutes. Cool on a wire rack. Makes 20.

2oz (50g) butterscotch
4oz (100g) margarine
4oz (100g) soft brown sugar
1 egg
8oz (225g) self-raising flour

❄ TO FREEZE: wrap the roll in waxed paper, then foil, seal, label and freeze. Use within 4 months.

TO USE: remove the roll from the freezer and allow to soften slightly for 15-20 minutes, then complete as from ❄ in recipe.

Caramel Pastries

Palmiers ... Couques ... intriguing French names for crisp, caramelized biscuits which no one will guess are just puff pastry and sugar. See how they're made below and on page 266

PALMIERS
6 oz (150g) puff pastry or trimmings
granulated sugar
TO FINISH:
(optional)
whipped cream
jam

Spread a layer of sugar on your work surface and roll out the pastry on this to a rectangle about ¼ in. (5mm) thick. Sprinkle the dough with sugar as you roll. Fold in three, ends to centre, as you do when making puff pastry (see page 264), give a half turn and roll, fold and roll again. Fold and roll again. Fold in three as before and chill for 20 minutes.

Roll the dough out to an 8-in. (20-cm) square about ¼ in. (5mm) thick (see page 264). Fold the edge nearest you over twice to reach the centre (see page 264). Repeat this folding from the other side. Press lightly with the rolling pin, sprinkle with sugar, then close the two sides like a book. Press again lightly with a rolling pin and, with a sharp knife, cut the dough into crosswise pieces about ½ in. (1cm) thick. Place the shapes on a dampened baking sheet, well apart, and flatten them slightly. Bake in preheated oven (450 deg. F, 230 deg. C, Gas no. 8) for 5 minutes or until the palmiers are brown underneath, turn them over and bake for a further 5 minutes till the tops are caramelized. Cool on a wire rack. ❄ Sandwich the palmiers with whipped cream and jam, or leave plain and serve with fruit, ice cream or mousse. Makes about 12.

❄ TO FREEZE: pack the palmiers in a rigid container with waxed or freezer paper between the layers, seal, label and freeze. Use within 2 months.

TO USE: thaw the palmiers at room temperature on a wire rack for 10 minutes. Complete as from ❄ in recipe.

COUQUES
6 oz (150g) puff pastry or trimmings
granulated sugar

Roll out rounds to tongue shape on sugared surface so bottoms are sugar-coated

Roll out the pastry to about ⅒ in. (2.5mm) thick and with a 2-in. (5-cm) fluted cutter, cut into rounds. Put a thick layer of sugar in an oval on your work surface. Lay a 2-in. (5-cm) circle of pastry on it and roll to a tongue shape about 5 in. (12.5cm) long (see left), so the bottom is encrusted with sugar. Turn upside down on to a dampened baking sheet. Roll the rest of the pastry in the same way.

Bake in preheated oven (450 deg. F, 230 deg. C, Gas no. 8) for 5-8 minutes or until the sugar has caramelized. If some are ready before others remove them to a wire rack to cool as they burn easily. ❄ Makes about 18.

❄ TO FREEZE: pack the couques as for Palmiers above. Use within 2 months.

TO USE: remove the couques from their container and thaw them on a wire rack for 10 minutes.

Peanut Sticks

Nutty biscuits that are good
to serve with drinks or as
party nibbles. If you find
the dough difficult to
handle put it in the fridge
for about 30 minutes to firm
up slightly

3oz (75g) salted peanuts
6oz (150g) plain flour
3oz (75g) margarine
1 large egg
1 teasp. (5ml) Marmite
2 teasp. (10ml) water

Finely chop the peanuts. Mix the flour and nuts
together. Rub in the fat and mix to a dough with
the egg, adding a little water if necessary to bind
the mixture.

Break off pieces of the dough the size of a walnut and roll out to the thickness of a pencil,
about 4in. (10cm) long. If you like, they can be
shaped into pretzels by curling them round as if
to make a circle, but overlapping the ends.

Arrange the biscuits on a greased baking sheet.
Mix the Marmite with the water and brush over
the biscuits. Bake in preheated oven (375 deg. F,
190 deg. C, Gas no. 5) for about 15 minutes until
golden. Cool the biscuits on a wire rack ❋. Makes
about 25.

TO FREEZE: when cold
pack the biscuits in-
to a rigid container
with waxcd paper be-
tween the layers. Seal,
label and freeze. Use within 2 months.

TO USE: thaw the biscuits
at room temperature for
2 hours.

Oatcakes

Use oatmeal rather than flour when rolling out these biscuits. They're delicious with butter and cheese. According to their size and shape they may be called bannocks (round) or farles (quarters) in Scotland

Put the oatmeal in a bowl and sieve over it the flour, bicarbonate of soda and salt. Rub in the lard and mix to a stiff dough with the water. Knead lightly, then roll out thinly on a floured board. Cut into 3½-in. (8.5-cm) rounds. Or, if you prefer triangles, when the dough is rolled out cut into a round or rounds with a saucepan lid or plate, then cut into four or six triangles. Prick all over with a fork.

Put the oatcakes on a greased baking sheet and bake in preheated oven (400 deg. F, 200 deg. C, Gas no. 6) for 12 minutes or until the biscuits are pale brown. Spread them on a wire rack to cool.
❄ Makes 12.

4oz (100g) medium oatmeal
3oz (75g)plain flour
pinch bicarbonate of soda
½ teasp. (2.5ml) salt
1½oz (40g) lard
3 tablesp. (45ml) hot water

TO FREEZE: pack the oatcakes into a polythene bag, or rigid container, seal, label and freeze. Use within 3 months.

TO USE: thaw the biscuits at room temperature for 1 hour.

The Coffee Truffles are quick and simple to make . . . delicious to serve at the end of a meal. If you're feeling extravagant when making the Rum and Raisin Fudge, use 2 tablespoons (30 ml) rum instead of essence, and soak the raisins in it so they are plump and juicy.

Coffee Truffles

4oz (100g) plain chocolate
2oz (50g) butter
2 teasp. (10ml) instant coffee
1 tablesp. (15ml) water
2 egg yolks
2oz (50g) ground almonds
6oz (150g) icing sugar, sieved

TO FINISH:
drinking chocolate powder

Melt the chocolate and butter in a basin over a pan of hot water. Dissolve the coffee in the water and stir into the chocolate and butter mixture, together with the egg yolks. Remove from the heat and work in the ground almonds and icing sugar. Leave to chill for 1 hour or until firm.

Take pieces the size of a walnut and roll into balls. Put some chocolate powder into a polythene bag and drop the truffles into it, one by one, shaking to coat them. Spread them out on a plate to become firm. Makes 20.

TO FREEZE. Pack the truffles in a rigid container with waxed or freezer paper between the layers, seal, label and freeze. Use within 3 months.

TO USE. Thaw the truffles at room temperature for 30 minutes. Place them in paper sweet cases.

Rum and Raisin Fudge

1lb (450g) granulated sugar
$\frac{1}{4}$ pint (150ml) milk
2 tablesp. (30ml) cream
2oz (50g) butter
2oz (50g) raisins
few drops
rum essence

Grease a 7-in. (17.5-cm) square tin.

Place the sugar, milk and cream in a heavy-based pan and heat slowly, stirring occasionally, until the sugar has dissolved. Add the butter, bring to the boil and boil, stirring to prevent it sticking, until the mixture reaches the soft ball stage or 240 deg. F, 125 deg. C, on a sugar thermometer. If you have no sugar thermometer, test at intervals by dropping a teaspoon of the mixture into a cup of cold water. When it can be gathered up in the fingers to form a soft ball, remove the pan from the heat.

Stir in the raisins and rum essence and beat well until the fudge thickens creamily, but can still be poured.

Pour into prepared tin and when almost set mark into squares with a sharp knife. Makes about $1\frac{1}{2}$ lb (675g).

TO FREEZE. When cold divide fudge into squares and pack in a rigid container with waxed or freezer paper between the layers. Seal, label and freeze. Use within 3 months.

TO USE. Put the fudge on to a dish and thaw at room temperature for 20 minutes.

Colettes

Chocolate cases filled with a rich chocolate cream known as ganache. The cases are not too difficult to make – two coatings of chocolate are better than one. Leave in the fridge between each coating and be sure they are really hard before attempting to remove the paper cases

4oz (100g) plain chocolate small paper sweet cases

GANACHE CREAM:
4oz (100g) plain chocolate
¼ pint (150ml) double cream
1oz (25g) butter
2 teasp. (10ml) brandy, rum or kirsch

TO FINISH:
few shredded almonds

To make the chocolate cases, break the plain chocolate into a small basin and stand over a pan of hot water until melted. With a teaspoon, coat inside the paper cases with melted chocolate, making sure there are no holes. Put them in the fridge until firm, then give them a second coating. The sides need to be fairly thick or they will break when the paper cases are removed. Firm again in the fridge and when set carefully peel off the paper cases.

For the ganache cream, break the remaining chocolate into a small basin and stand over a pan of hot water until melted. Then bring the cream to the boil in another pan and pour over the chocolate, stirring well. Flake the butter into the mixture and stir it in until it is melted. Then stir in your chosen liqueur (add more if liked) and set the cream aside to cool and thicken.

Fill the cream into a piping bag, fitted with a rose nozzle, and pipe into the chocolate cases. Decorate with a few shredded almonds. Chill. Makes 12–15.

TO FREEZE: open freeze colettes till hard, then pack in a single layer in a rigid container. seal, label and return to the freezer. Use within 1 month.

TO USE: thaw the colettes 2-3 hours at room temperature.

Honey and Almond Fudge

The flavour of the fudge depends on the honey used, so you can try different honeys to discover which one will make a fudge to best suit your taste

Grease an 8×6in. (20×15cm) rectangular baking tin.

Place the sugar, milk, butter and honey in a large heavy-based saucepan. Stir over a low heat until the sugar has dissolved. Bring the mixture to the boil, stirring all the time to prevent it from sticking, and boil to 240 deg. F, 120 deg. C on a sugar thermometer when the mixture will form a soft ball if a little is dropped into a cup of cold water.

Remove the pan from the heat and stir in the chopped nuts. Place the pan on a cool surface and beat until the fudge is thick and creamy. Pour it into the prepared tin and when nearly cold mark into squares. When set cut with a sharp knife. ❄ Makes about 1½lb (675g).

❄ TO FREEZE: pack the fudge in layers in a rigid container, with a piece of foil or waxed paper between the layers. Use within 2 months.

TO USE: thaw the fudge at room temperature for about 30 minutes.

1lb (450g) granulated sugar
½ pint (300ml) evaporated milk
4oz (100g) butter
2 level tablesp. (30ml) honey
2oz (50g) chopped blanched
  almonds

DINNER PARTY DRINKS

... from the vital statistics of a Bloody Mary ... through the intricacies of vintages and vineyards ... to the choosing of your after-dinner port ... here's a bar-guide to entertaining at home

Choose either 10–12 fl oz (300–350ml) tumbler *or* large goblet for beer, cider, soft and mixed drinks

6–8 fl oz (180–230ml) stemmed wine glass for all wines, fruit juices and mixed drinks

5–6 fl oz (150–180ml) short tumbler holds spirits, mixed and soft drinks, vermouths and wine, if necessary

8–9 fl oz (230–280ml) champagne flute or tulip-shaped wine glass for sparkling wines, and mixed drinks

3–4 fl oz (80–100ml) sherry or small stemmed glass for sherry, madeira, port

3–4 fl oz (80–100ml) cocktail glass for these and other mixed drinks

Welcome your guests with an apéritif – sherry, white wine, champagne, mixed drinks or cocktails. If you serve snacks with the drinks you can count that as the first course and sit everyone down when the main course is ready on the table.

The snacks can be hot or cold (see pages 252 and 253) and preparing and freezing in advance will save time on the day.

Cocktails – there's a selection on the right – are making a comeback. They consist of one or more alcoholic drinks plus fruit juices, bitters, egg white or any other suitable ingredient to make an agreeable mixture.

For mixed drinks and cocktails you'll need an ice bucket or bowl, cutting board and knife, corkscrew and bottle opener, large jug, cocktail sticks, a long–handled spoon or glass rod for stirring, and a shaker – a screw topped jar will do.

A measure for spirits doesn't look very hospitable so practise beforehand, remembering that a small measure is 1 fl oz.

Garnishes will include maraschino cherries, lemon and orange slices and peel, olives, cucumber, mint, borage.

Mixed Drinks

Gin is a very pure spirit distilled from grain and then flavoured, principally with juniper berry. London Dry Gin, which used to be made only in London, is the type used for mixed drinks. Various firms have different recipes for flavouring which gives each of them a distinctive (though not over-stated) taste. Serve with mixers such as tonic or bitter lemon, and as a cocktail base.

Plymouth gin is unsweetened and is used as the base of 'pink gin'.

Dutch gin, known as Geneva (after the French for juniper: genièvre) or Hollands is highly flavoured. It should be chilled and served straight.

Vodka made in Britain has a neutral flavour which makes it ideal to use in mixed drinks in the same way as gin. Imported Russian and Polish vodkas have a more positive flavour and should be served straight and chilled.

Whisky is also of various types. Blended Scotch whisky combines the blandness of grain whisky with the character of barley malt whisky. Good makes contain a very high proportion of malt whiskies, and malt whiskies on their own are becoming increasingly popular. They should be served only neat or with water, while blended ones may be served neat, with water or soda water.

Irish Whiskey is a distinctive mellow spirit – mostly known as the basis for Irish coffee but good straight or with ice.

Bourbon from the U.S. is highly flavoured, distilled from grain which includes at least 51 per cent maize. Serve straight, on-the-rocks (over ice cubes) or with lemonade or ginger ale.

Rye Whisky is like Bourbon, but the chief grain used is rye.

Canadian Whisky is a fairly light-flavoured spirit of blended whiskies distilled from mixed grains with a high percentage of maize. Serve straight, with ice or with coke, lemonade or ginger ale.

Rum is a spirit made from a sugar-cane base. It varies from light-flavoured and pale to heavy and dark-coloured.

Jamaican rum is usually dark golden and pungent, although there are lighter ones available.

Barbados and Trinidad rums are light in colour and fragrant.

White rum is light in flavour and now widely produced, the best known being Bacardi, originally from Cuba.

Tequila is a dry white spirit which is served in the same way as gin with tonic, bitter lemon or orange juice.

Campari bitters is a deep pink aromatic bitters classified as a spirit. Serve it over ice with a slice of orange in a short tumbler. Add soda or lemonade to taste.

Pernod, Ricard (French term: **Pastis**), and the Greek **Ouzo** are aniseed–flavoured drinks with a hint of liquorice. Pour a measure into a tumbler and top up with iced water to taste (you'll find the water turns them milky white).

Manhattan Cocktail $\frac{2}{3}$ rye whiskey, $\frac{1}{3}$ sweet vermouth, dash Angostura aromatic bitters. Stir well and strain into cocktail glass. Decorate with a cocktail cherry.

Whisky Sour 1 fl oz (30ml) lemon juice, $\frac{1}{2}$ teasp. (2.5ml) icing sugar, 2 fl oz (60ml) whisky. Shake well and strain. Add soda water to taste, decorate with slice of lemon.

Bloody Mary $\frac{1}{3}$ vodka, $\frac{2}{3}$ tomato juice, juice of $\frac{1}{2}$ lemon, dash of Worcestershire sauce. Shake well and strain into tall glass. A stronger version gives 3 parts vodka to 4 parts tomato juice.

Gimlet Cocktail $\frac{2}{3}$ gin, $\frac{1}{3}$ lime juice cordial. Pour direct into small tumbler, stir, add ice and serve. May be topped up with soda water.

Tom Collins Cocktail Juice of $\frac{1}{2}$ lemon, 2 fl oz (60ml) dry gin, 1 teasp. (5ml) icing sugar, dash of Angostura aromatic bitters. Shake well and strain into tall tumbler. Add lump of ice, and top up with soda water.

Pink Gin Shake 3–4 dashes of Angostura bitters into chilled wine glass, swill round, then shake out surplus. Add a measure of Plymouth or London Dry Gin. Add soda water, or water or ice to personal taste.

Screwdriver Shake together $\frac{1}{3}$ vodka, $\frac{2}{3}$ orange juice. Strain into a glass, add ice and a slice of orange to serve.

Buck's Fizz Fill champagne glasses $\frac{1}{3}$–$\frac{1}{2}$ full with chilled fresh orange juice, then top up with chilled non-vintage Champagne or a sparkling hock.

Bronx Equal measures dry gin, Italian vermouth, and French vermouth, juice of $\frac{1}{4}$ orange per cocktail, crushed ice. Shake all ingredients with the ice in a shaker and strain into glasses.

Apéritifs

OVEN HOT DOGS

4 pieces thin-sliced bread; a little made mustard; 1oz (25g) butter, 2 rashers streaky bacon; 4 skinless pork sausages. TO FINISH: butter

Remove crusts from bread and with a rolling pin flatten and stretch bread slightly. Spread a little mustard across bottom edge of bread and a little butter across top edge. Derind and stretch rashers of bacon with back of knife and cut each one in two. Place half a rasher over the mustard top with a sausage and roll up. Repeat with rest of ingredients. Cut each roll in half. ✳ Spread a little butter on each and bake (400 deg. F, 200 deg. C, Gas no. 6) for about 15 minutes until crisp. Makes 8 rolls.

 TO FREEZE: place hot dogs in rigid container, seal, label and freeze. Use within 1 month.

TO USE: thaw at room temperature for 3–4 hours. Complete as from ✳ in recipe.

CREAMY CHEESE BITES

4oz (100g) butter; salt and pepper; pinch ground mace; 8oz (225g) grated cheese; 2 tablesp. (30ml) sherry.
TO FINISH: stuffed olives, crushed crisps, chopped nuts

Cream butter until soft, mix in seasonings, then work in cheese. Add sherry to make a smooth, creamy mixture.✳
Mould mixture round the olives and roll in crushed crisps or shape into small balls and roll in chopped nuts. Makes about 12.

 TO FREEZE: spoon cheese bites into a rigid container, seal, label and freeze.
Use within 2 months.
TO USE: thaw overnight in fridge. Complete as from ✳ in recipe.

The best way to prepare your palate and stimulate the appetite before a meal is with a wine-based drink, and the best of these is . . .

Sherry. True sherry is produced from the vineyards around Jerez de la Frontera in Spain, where the soil is said to be exactly right. It is really a strong wine made from white grapes which is then matured in casks, fortified with brandy and blended.

The longer the wine is matured, the darker, richer and more alcoholic it becomes, but in fact it is the pale, dry fino which is most enjoyed by connoisseurs. Another sherry of the fino type is Manzanilla, a very light and dry wine from Sanlucar, a village near the coast where the soil seems to give it a very special flavour.

Palo Cortado is a superb, expensive sherry, midway between a fino and an amontillado.

Amontillado, being a more mature wine, is darker in colour than fino, and is stronger and sweeter in taste. It may be medium dry or medium sweet.

Oloroso is golden-brown, richly flavoured and more alcoholic, usually medium sweet and may be preferred with the dessert, rather than as an apéritif. Cream sherries are oloroso types, though they may be pale or dark.

All the sherries should be served in glasses filled only to the halfway or two-thirds mark (so that the bouquet may be appreciated) and, in the case of fino, chilled. Fino does not keep well after it has been opened, but the other wines will improve in a decanter and keep several days.

Similar wines, though not with quite the same character, come from areas outside Jerez. The soil of the Montilla area is the same as the Jerez type and produces a similar wine – in fact, 'Amontillado' means 'to become like Montilla'. Sherries are also produced by other countries, notably South Africa, Cyprus and Australia, and the country of origin will always be marked on the label.

Port is normally thought of as being red but there is also a dry white port which is very suitable as an apéritif.

Dry white wines, still or sparkling, also make very acceptable apéritifs that many people like nowadays. The advantage is that you can continue to serve the wine throughout the meal if the food is suitable, or with the first course, and follow with red with the main course (see food and wine partners on page 258).

Try Vouvray, Muscadet or a white Burgundy like Mâcon-Villages (Chablis is right, but expensive). Or a Moselle or Hock, still or sekt – the German term for sparkling. For a special occasion, or special guests, offer . . .

Champagne. Vintage champagnes are very expensive, but the non-vintage, blended champagnes are of very high quality. Again, look for the shipper's name. The term 'brut' on the label means dry, 'sec' is usually medium and 'demi-sec' means medium sweet.

The sparkling wines produced in parts of France other than the Champagne district are less expensive but very enjoyable.

The Italian sparkling wine, Asti Spumante, is rather sweet for an apéritif and more suitable for parties.

Vermouth is a fortified wine from the Alps that is flavoured with herbs such as elder flower, gentian, coriander, clove and wormwood. In fact the name is a derivative of wormwood. Vermouth may be sweet or dry, dark golden or pale. The Italian ones, by Martini and Cinzano, are mainly sweet; the 'Rosso' (red) is dark and very sweet and 'Bianco' (white) is medium sweet. But their ranges also include dry white vermouth and a recently introduced rosé type, that is very popular. Punt-e-Mes is dark and bitter sweet.

Noilly Prat is the main dry French vermouth.

Chambéry is paler and drier than other French vermouths with a delicate fresh flavour.

Vermouth is served well chilled or over ice in a wine glass or tumbler with a twist of lemon peel. It may also be mixed with gin or vodka; with soda and a slice of lemon and ice. It makes a refreshing long summer drink.

There are other wine-based apéritifs, each with its own distinctive flavour.

Dubonnet is both red (sweet) and white (dry). It should be served well chilled or over ice in a wine glass or tumbler with a slice of lemon. Top up with soda, lemonade or tonic, if liked.

Lillet is a white wine fortified with Armagnac and served over ice with a twist of orange peel. Soda can be added if liked.

CHEESE CROISSANTS

PASTRY: 4oz (100g) flour; pinch salt; 4oz (100g) hard margarine; 4oz (100g) cream cheese. FILLING: 4oz (100g) cottage cheese with chives; 4oz (100g) grated mature Cheddar cheese; pepper; 1 egg. TO FINISH: beaten egg for glazing

Sieve flour and salt into a bowl, rub in the margarine and blend in the cream cheese until the mixture forms a soft dough. Wrap in foil and leave in fridge overnight. Blend all filling indredients together to form a thick cream. Check seasoning.
Roll pastry into a square 12 × 12in (30 × 30cm). Cut 9 × 4in (10cm) squares, then cut each square into two triangles. Place a little filling on the long edge, then roll over and over, seal and curve round into a crescent. Brush with beaten egg and bake in preheated oven (350 deg. F, 180 deg. C, Gas no. 4) for 15 minutes. ❄ Makes 18.

 TO FREEZE: cool croissants, pack in a polythene bag, seal, label and freeze. Use within 2 months.
TO USE: thaw croissants 2–3 hours at room temperature and serve cold or reheat from frozen (350 deg. F, 180 deg. C, Gas no. 4) for about 5 minutes.

Or you could serve . . .

Dips: serve any of the following with plain biscuits or fingers of toast:
Hummus (page 38)
Fish Pâtés (page 46)
Rillettes (page 52)
Potted Pigeon (page 60)

Savoury flans: cut into narrow wedges to serve:
Smoked Mackerel Quiche (page 30)
Spinach and Cottage Cheese Flan (page 32)
Tomato and Cheese Tart (page 44)
Pissaladière (page 56)
Asparagus Flan (page 58)

Wines

When you come to choose a wine to go with your meal, the best move is to find a wine merchant you can trust – and trust him. But it does help to have some idea of what he is talking about, and to know the qualities of the familiar names that are hovering at the back of your mind. Of course, many of those well-known château-bottled wines are rare and expensive, but it may be that a similar, lesser known one from the same area will appeal to you and to your pocket – or you may want to cherish your guests with one of the great names.

The major wine-producing countries control the quality of their wines by specifications marked on the label. Good French ones are labelled 'Appellation Contrôlée', or AC.

Some bottle labels now have the letters 'GL' followed by a number. That denotes the percentage of alcohol in the wine which may be anything between 8 and 16 per cent.

A helpful move on the part of supermarkets is to label bottles clearly so that you know whether the wine is sweet or dry, light or full-bodied, and you may even see recommendations about which type of food it partners best.

The subject of French wines is a fascinating but enormous one, so it takes some nerve to shut one's eyes and plunge in. You will instantly seem knowledgeable if you know that claret is a general description of red Bordeaux wine. The term derives from the French 'clairet' or clear, and distinguishes the light-bodied wine of Bordeaux from the heavier wines of Burgundy (Bourgogne is its French name). The bottle shape will tell you which is which – Burgundy is in a long-necked bottle; Bordeaux in a 'shouldered' type.

Bordeaux is the largest wine-producing area of France; it has many of the greatest names but you will also find good but less expensive wines – remember to look for 'Appellation Contrôlée' on the label.

This large region is divided into districts whose names you will recognize: Médoc and Haut Médoc (a district of many fine wines), St. Emilion, Pomerol, Graves and Sauternes (the latter is a sweet white dessert wine). Other districts are Côtes de Blaye, Côtes de Bourg, Côtes de Fronsac, Entre Deux Mers, Premières Côtes de Bordeaux.

Within these districts are further sub-divisions or communes. In the Haut Médoc there are Pauillac, Margaux, St Julien, St. Estèphe. And within these communes are the châteaux whose wines (such as Château Lafite) will be very expensive, but all wines from the Médoc area will be very reliable and often reasonable in price.

Burgundy is the home of full, red wines and includes the marvellous Côte d'Or region which is again sub-divided into Côte de Nuits and Côte de Beaune. 'Côte' actually means 'hillside' rather than coast, as one would have imagined, so the name Côte d'Or – golden hillside – conjures up a sunlit vision which accounts for the quality of the wines.

Beaujolais is another well-known part of the Burgundy region, although it is south of the area under the rule of the old dukes of Burgundy. Other districts are Mâconnais, Mercurey (or Côte Chalonnaise).

The vineyards here are very small and the wines from them are sold to a man called a négociant-éleveur who blends and matures the wine himself. This means that his name becomes important on the bottle – names such as Bouchard Père et Fils and Louis Latour.

From the Côte de Nuits, names you will know are Clos de Vougeot, Chambertin, Nuits St. Georges. From Côte de Beaune: Volnay and Pommard, or the less expensive Auxey-Duresses and Monthélie. Burgundy wines can be very expensive, especially those bottled by the grower, but ask your wine merchant for help in choosing a cheaper Bourgogne Rouge.

Beaujolais is grown from a different type of grape – the Gamay rather than the Burgundian Pinot Noir – and are lighter wines to be drunk when they are young. Beaujolais is the one red wine that can be drunk slightly chilled, or at any rate cool, as the French do. 1977 was not a good year for Beaujolais, but look for 1976, and the négociants Thorin, Piat and Duboeuf.

Beaujolais-Villages is stronger than the basic Beaujolais, and among the names of the villages are Moulin à Vent, Fleurie, Juliénas, Brouilly, St. Amour, Chénas and Morgon.

The area of Burgundy also produces famous white wines from the districts of Chablis (very expensive now), Meursault, Puligny-Montrachet, Santenay. From Mâcon, the most famous is Pouilly-Fuissé. All of these white Burgundies are dry but body and strength depend upon the

Wine: how much for how many

1 bottle (70cl)	6– 8 glasses
1 litre bottle	10–12 glasses
Magnum (2 bottles)	12–16 glasses
1½ litre bottle	15–18 glasses
½ gallon jar	18–24 glasses
1 gallon jar	36–48 glasses

vintage and this depends on the weather during the year in question.

Other white wines come from the region of the Loire – like Vouvray and Muscadet to be served with fish and white meat. A variety of wines come from the Middle Loire around Anjou and Saumur and two excellent ones from the eastern end of the valley- Sancerre and Pouilly Fumé, not to be confused with the Burgundian Pouilly Fuissé. Some of the wines are pétillant, or semi-sparkling.

Anjou is a name you will know for its rosé wine. Cabernet d'Anjou is a sweeter version made from the Cabernet grape.

Good but less expensive wine comes from the Rhône. There are great names here, too: Châteauneuf-du-Pape, Hermitage, Côte Rôtie. But Côte du Rhône on the bottle means you have a strong and very pleasant wine – not for keeping but to be drunk and enjoyed as you buy it. Also from this region another very pleasant, but dry and full-bodied rosé – Tavel.

Wines from the Côtes de Provence are not so high in quality, but some of them, white and rosé, are very good with shellfish. There is a wide variety of less expensive but pleasant wines from the Midi, and from the south west of France, in the Bergerac region, comes the sweet white Monbazillac, rather like Sauternes but less expensive.

A final, important wine-growing region of France produces white wines that are very high in quality and of a dry and fruity type. This is Alsace, where German grapes are used, though these wines are higher in alcoholic quantity than the German ones. You will find the names of the grapes – Sylvaner, Riesling, Muscat, and Tokay d'Alsace on the label. A very spicy, fragrant wine comes from the Gewürztraminer grape. The bottles are long-necked green ones in the Moselle style.

Which brings us on to German wines and you can again impress people if you can recognize a hock (which is a rich, flowery wine) in its brown bottle, and a Moselle (delicate, less alcoholic) in its green one.

Hock is an English term for the wines that are produced along the River Rhine, while Moselles come from the region around the river Moselle, which is a tributary of the Rhine.

The labels will mention the grapes: Sylvaner is mild and fruity, used for medium dry wines, Riesling produces top quality wines of a dry type

SERVING WINE

Champagne, white and dessert wines: serve chilled. Half an hour in the fridge – not the freezer – will be enough, or use a wine cooler. Don't put ice in the wine.

Full red wines: serve at room temperature. Stand upright in a warm room for at least a day before it's needed. Open at least an hour before it's to be drunk to give it a chance to 'breathe'. If there's a lot of sediment decant the wine.

Beaujolais: serve either at room temperature or chilled

with an excellent flavour, Müller-Thurgau is fruity and Ruländer is full-bodied.

You will also see on the label the producer's name, village, region – plus category as follows.

'Kabinett' shows it's a high-quality wine with mature grapes, no added sugar.

And for sweeter high-quality wines:

'Spätlese' means high-grade wine from grapes picked late in the season, when they have had extra maturing and sweetening time.

'Auslese' means it is wine made from selected bunches of late-picked grapes.

'Beerenauslese': very expensive, from selected very ripe berries.

'Trockenbeerenauslese'. Also very expensive, and rare, from grapes with 'noble rot' (see below).

'Eiswein', also rare, is made from grapes that have been left on the vine until the first winter frosts.

Noble rot, or 'pourriture noble' sounds bad, but in fact it produces the wonderful Trockenbeerenauslese of Germany and the great Sauternes of France.

Among the hock, good quality wines come from Rüdesheim, Ramenthal, Hochheim (from which the term 'hock' probably comes), Oppenheim, Nierstein, Deidesheim.

From the Moselle, principal villages are Piesport, Zell, Bernkastel, Wiltingen, Eitelsbach, Brauneberg, with Wiltingen, Eitelsbach on the tributaries Saar and Ruwer respectively.

The country producing the greatest amount of wine in Europe now is Italy. The wines are rich in flavour and not expensive – and indeed an appreciable quantity is exported to France. Among the red, big heavy ones (as they say in the wine trade) are Barolo and Barbaresco; very good and lighter ones are Valpolicella, Bardolino and Chianti. Soave is a very pleasant dry white, and white Orvieto is full-flavoured and may be dry to semi-sweet. Carafe wines of this type are becoming increasingly popular in this country in view of their reasonable prices. From Sicily comes Corvo, which is red or white.

Spain produces several wines of good quality, fairly high alcholic quantity and inexpensive to buy. Two of the most well-known are the light-bodied and fruity reds from Rioja and Panadès.

Another very rich, full-bodied and popular wine is Bull's Blood, or Egri Bikaver which comes from Hungary. Also from this country – Tokay (tock-eye), a sweet white dessert wine.

VINTAGE CHECK

Red Burgundy
Good years:
1962, 1964, 1969, 1971, 1972, 1976
Bad years:
1960, 1963, 1968, 1975

Bordeaux
Good years:
1961, 1962, 1966, 1970, 1971, 1975, 1976
Bad years:
1960, 1963, 1968

Loire
Good years:
1969, 1970, 1971, 1974, 1976
Bad year:
1968

Rhône
Good years:
1960, 1961, 1964, 1966, 1967, 1969, 1970, 1972, 1976
Bad years:
1963, 1965, 1968

White Burgundy
Good years:
1962, 1966, 1967, 1969, 1971, 1976
Bad years:
1960, 1963, 1965, 1968

Hock
Good years:
1971, 1976
Bad years:
1960, 1963, 1968

Moselle
Good years:
1971, 1976
Bad years:
1960, 1963, 1968

Port, vintage years
1945, 1947, 1948 (all very good), 1950, 1954, 1955 (very good), 1958, 1960, 1963, 1966, 1967, 1970, 1975 (the last four should be bought for 'laying down')
A vintage chart is only a general guide because there are always small areas that will produce a good (or bad) wine against the general trend. The weather particularly affects the more northern areas such as Germany and Alsace; plenty of sunshine there will sweeten and enrich the grapes (remember the summer of 1976?).

As Spain is known for its sherry but also produces table wine, so Portugal is known for its port but also has its own wine. Look for Vinho Verde (called green because the grapes are picked before they are fully ripe) which is an effervescent white.

In Yugoslavia an important wine-growing district for white wines is Lutomer; you will see bottles carrying this name and the name of the grapes – Riesling and Sylvaner.

Another country that one does not immediately connect with wines is South Africa. The equable climate of this country ensure an unchanging degree in quality which is also enforced by KWV, the growers' organisation. Look for Niedeberg and for labels with the KWV initials.

WINE AND FOOD PARTNERS

Oysters: dry Champagne or Chablis, also Guinness.

Fish: dry white wine.

White meat: rosé; white wine from Germany and Alsace; Champagne; light reds such as claret or Beaujolais.

Red meat: game, casseroles: full red wine such as red Burgundy.

Desserts (though not chocolate-based ones): chilled sweet white wine.

Cheese: full red wine or port.

WINE AND FOOD PARTNERS

Rules used to be very strict about which wine should go with certain foods, and are less so now; but since it would be unkind both to the food and the wine if you served, for instance, a sweet white with the red meat course, it is as well to have some idea of what is correct—see notes.

Of course nowadays very few people would actually produce a different wine or each course. They may start with a dry white with the first course, if it is suitable, change to a red wine at the main course stage and continue with red for the cheese stage. This is why desserts are often served to follow cheese.

You should be safe if you follow the rule that a light wine goes before a heavy one (dry white before red).

The sweet white dessert wines have been rather neglected (possibly because they were being drunk in the wrong circumstances) but they are becoming popular again now. Serve chilled to accompany a sweet course they are delicious.

Champagne can be served throughout the meal, but your guests may prefer a still wine.

Dry, light white wines, apart from being stimulating apéritifs, go with hors d'oeuvre starters and shellfish. This type includes Muscadet, Alsace Sylvaner, Piesporter, dry Orvieto, Soave, Vinho Verde, Lutomer Riesling.

Full-bodied white wines, dry to medium sweet, are good with fish, veal, chicken and include white Burgundies and white Bordeaux, hocks and Moselles.

Rosé wines and roast lamb and veal go well together, and light-bodied red wines also suit lamb and veal. The richer chicken dishes, such as coq au vin, require a more full-bodied red.

Full red wine of the Burgundy type is the classic accompaniment for red meat, game and casseroles and pastas. Try also the more robust clarets such as St. Emilion; or Bull's Blood, Chianti or Rioja.

Port

Rich, fruity, mellow, port is a fortified (with brandy) sweet wine that, with Roquefort or Stilton cheese, makes a perfect end to a good meal.

Port is a type of wine that is known by the name of the shipper, rather than the vineyard. If he decides that the harvest of a certain year is likely to produce particularly good port, he takes the risk of reserving the wine and it becomes 'vintage' port, and is matured – for years – in the bottle, and always requires decanting.

Tawny port is blended and matured in the cask. It is pale with a nutty fragrance and flavour.

Ruby port is fuller, doesn't improve in the bottle and is not of such a high standard as vintage. The Vintage Character Ports are the best in this category.

Look for the shippers' names of Cockburn, Croft, Dow, Sandemans, Taylor, Graham, Warre, and Fonseca.

Brandy

Cognac is double-distilled from wines of the Cognac area of France. The finest Cognacs are the Grandes Champagnes – nothing to do with the sparkling wine but an area of vineyards at the heart of Cognac. Brandy is matured in the cask, not in the bottle, and the labelling shows how long it has been allowed to mature before being bottled. 3-star is 5–10 years old to VSOP (20–30 years) to XO (up to 45 years).

Armagnac is a brandy that comes from the Armagnac district. It is fuller bodied and generally drier than Cognac and matures more quickly.

MENU

Consommé Madrilène

———

Suprême de Saumon Glamis

———

Selle d'Agneau Windsor
Haricots Verts au Beurre
Céleris au Jus
Pommes Nouvelles à la Menthe
Salade

———

Bombe Glacée Royale
Friandises

WINES

Fino La Ina

———

Ayler Kupp Spätlese 1971

———

Château Latour 1945

———

Krug 1964

———

Sandeman 1955

Menu for a grand occasion: the banquet given at Buckingham Palace for the President of France on the occasion of his State visit to Britain on 22nd June, 1976

CHEF'S TECHNIQUES

Boning and Stuffing a Shoulder of Lamb

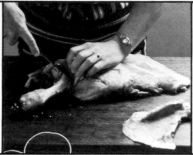

1 Using a boning knife, cut meat from blade bone; then remove bone by cutting at ball and socket joint

2 Loosen shin bone by cutting away meat round it but ensuring meat is left attached to shoulder

3 When cleaned of meat, remove the shin bone by breaking joint at elbow and cutting through

Preforming a Trifle

1 Instead of risking a glass dish, freeze trifle in a cake tin or same-sized polythene container

2 Line container with foil, allowing plenty of overlap. Smooth foil inside to ensure an even finish

3 Arrange sponge pieces over bottom of dish, then cover with your chosen fruit, custard and cream

Lining a Flan Tin for Baking 'Blind'

1 Roll out pastry to a round a little larger than the top of the flan tin

2 Lift up pastry by folding it back over rolling pin and unroll over tin. This helps prevent stretching

3 Carefully ease the pastry into the flan tin, gently pressing it into each flute with fingertips

4 To loosen remaining bone, tunnel round it with boning knife to free it of meat; then pull out

5 Tuck loose ends of shin meat into cavity; sew up this side with trussing needle and strings

6 Fill stuffing into cavity; fold over meat ends and roll joint into a uniform shape; tie with string

4 Open freeze trifle until hard. Wrap foil over top, turn out, seal, label and return to the freezer

5 When trifle is required, take out of the freezer and remove foil wrappings

6 Replace the trifle in your chosen glass dish to thaw. Decorate it just before serving

4 Run rolling pin across flan tin to cut off surplus pastry. Line with foil or greaseproof paper

5 Spread over dried pasta or beans to stop centre rising and sides collapsing when baked 'blind'

6 Bake (400 deg F, 200 deg C – Gas no 6) 15 mins. Remove foil, bake 5 mins. more till dry and just coloured

Making Choux Pastry

1 2½ oz (65g) plain flour
¼ pint (150ml) water
1½ oz (40g) margarine
2 eggs

2 Sieve the flour on to sheet of greaseproof paper. Put the water in pan with the margarine

3 Heat until the fat has melted. Bring to the boil. Tip in the flour all at once

Shaping Coupelles

1 2 egg whites
4 oz (100g) caster sugar
2 oz (50g) plain flour
2 oz (50g) butter

2 Put egg whites into a basin. Beat in sugar, then flour and mix in the melted butter gently

3 Spoon mixture into thin rounds, well apart on greased sheet; bake 5-6 mins. (400 deg. F, 200 deg. C, Gas no. 6)

Pitta Bread

1 1 pint (550ml)
warm water
½ oz (15g) dried yeast
2 lb (900g) strong plain flour
1½ teasp. (7.5ml) salt
3 tablesp. (45ml) vegetable oil

2 Put 4 tablespoons (60ml) water into a bowl; sprinkle dried yeast on. Leave to froth (about 10 mins.)

3 Sieve flour and salt. Make a well, add yeast and rest of water. Mix to a soft dough, then knead

4 Remove pan from heat and beat till the paste is smooth and forms a ball. Cool slightly

5 Beat eggs, mix in a little at a time; it goes lumpy at first so keep beating till thick and smooth

6 Add rest of egg mixture and beat till thick and smooth again. Set aside till cold before using

4 Have ready greased oranges, grapefruit, apples or small dishes. You have to work quickly when biscuits are cooked

5 Remove biscuits from oven. Carefully lift off one and press firmly over fruit or into dish. Repeat moulding with remainder

6 When firm – this only takes a few seconds – transfer shaped biscuits to wire rack to cool

4 Cover dough and prove. Knead lightly, divide it into 12. Roll into balls, place on floured tray and cover with oiled polythene.

5 Leave for 30 mins. Roll out balls of dough to 6 x 3-in. (15 x 7.5-cm) wide pieces. Cover, prove 30 mins.

6 Bake bread on pre-heated trays for about 10 mins. Wrap in foil or teacloth to cool and flatten

Making Puff Pastry

1 Sieve 1 lb (450g) plain flour and 1 teasp. (5ml) salt into a basin. Have ready 1 lb (450g) butter or hard margarine. Take 2 oz (50g) fat and rub in to flour. Add ½ pint (300ml) cold water all at once and mix to a firm dough

2 Flatten out the rest of the fat. Roll dough to an oblong long enough to enclose fat

3 Put fat in centre, wrap over dough top and bottom. Seal sides and centre join and give dough a half turn

Shaping a Vol-au-vent Case

1 Roll out dough to about ½ in. (1cm) thickness. Cut 2 rounds using 6-7 in. (15-17.5cm) plate or pan lid as a guide

2 Put 1 round on dampened baking sheet; paint 1½-in. (3.5cm) strip round edge with wet pastry brush

3 Using 5 in. (12.5cm) plate as guide, cut centre out of other round for lid; put on baking sheet

Boning a Best End to make Noisettes

1 If butcher hasn't done so strip off skin. Cut out flat piece of gristle to be found at one end

2 Start boning by cutting along the chine bone (another name for the spine), keeping knife as close to the bone as possible

3 Using short strokes, cut along the cutlets, again keeping the knife close to the bones

4 Roll again to an oblong, keeping corners square, with short, sharp strokes so as not to squeeze out the fat

5 Fold dough in three, seal, give it a half turn and roll out again. Fold and seal; rest it in fridge for 15 mins.

6 Indent shows dough has had one rolling; repeat rolling and folding twice more (6 in all); rest in fridge 30 mins. before use

4 Lift pastry ring on to dampened edge of first round, press together and knock up sides with knife

5 Brush top only with beaten egg; if it runs edges will seal and sides will not rise properly

6 Make criss-cross marks on lid; mark slanting cuts on ring. Bake as in recipe on page 65

4 Trim off excess fat if any at thin end, then roll up tightly, starting at thick chine end

5 Tie firmly with string all along the roll at 1 in. (2.5cm) intervals

6 Cut between each piece of string; the noisettes are then ready either for cooking or freezing

Shaping Palmiers

1 Roll out sugared pastry to 8 in. (20cm) square about ¼ in. (5mm) thick. Fold nearest edge twice to reach centre; repeat on other side

2 Sprinkle with sugar, press lightly with rolling pin, close sides like a book. Press lightly again

3 Cut in crosswise pieces about ½ in. (1cm) thick. Put on dampened baking sheet, flatten slightly and bake as in recipe.

Piping Cream

1 Fit pipe into bag; spoon whipped cream into bag till half full. Ease it down with one hand, and twist top round tightly

2 Pipe cream using one hand to apply pressure, the other as a guide. Release pressure, push into rosette, lift sharply

3 For shell border, hold the pipe at an angle to surface; press, then pull the pipe sharply away with the pressure off

Boning Trout

1 Scrape away scales with knife, cut off head just below gills; vandyke tail by snipping into a V; split belly open

2 Clean under running cold tap. Turn fish skin side up and press hard along the backbone with fist

3 When the backbone has been loosened, turn the fish over and carefully lift out the bones

Fruit Compote

1 Dissolve 4 oz (100g) sugar in ½ pint (300ml) water. Bring to boil and boil 5 mins.

2 Wash and halve 1 lb (450g) plums or apricots. Remove stones

3 Put fruit into syrup. Bring to boil so syrup rises over fruit. Reduce heat, simmer gently till fruit is tender. Cool

Shaping Chicken Rolls

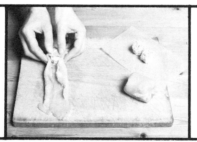

1 Place each chicken breast between two sheets grease-proof paper; beat out flat with a rolling pin or mallet

2 Put portion of savoury butter in the centre of flattened breast. Fold in the sides and roll up neatly

3 Secure each chicken roll with a cocktail stick before egging and crumbing (see page 132)

Shaping Cigarettes Russes

1 Spread the mixture into oblongs on a silicone-lined or well greased baking sheet. Space the oblongs well apart to allow for spreading during baking. When baked ease biscuits off with a palette knife

2 Roll the biscuits while they are still hot and pliable. Rest the handle of a wooden spoon along one edge of biscuit and then carefully roll up

3 Hold the biscuit for a moment or two until set, then gently slip it off the spoon handle and on to a wire rack to cool. Repeat rolling process until all the biscuits are shaped

PACKAGING FOR THE FREEZER

Your guide to what's what in wrapping and storing for the freezer

Probably the first thing that any novice freezer-owner learns is the need for good freezer packaging. The object of this packaging is to exclude the cold, dry air from your food, thus preventing it from becoming dried out ('freezer burn') or going rancid (the oxidisation effect caused by the combination of air with fat and salt).

There is no health hazard involved in this: it is simply that inadequately packaged food will certainly lack texture and will change flavour; and will not repay the time and effort you have expended in preparing a recipe or in carefully shopping for good quality ingredients. So it is surely worth thinking in detail about the best kind of packs for your own kind of freezer cookery.

The most frequently used packaging item is the **polythene bag.** And this is of course perfectly adequate for the storage of small 'ingredient' items – vegetables, meats, small fruits. Care should be taken to 'collapse' a bag properly around the food to force the air out. The neck of the bag must be tightly tied; most people find the paper-covered-wire form of tag-tie is the most efficient.

Polythene bags should be bought in moisture-and-vapour-proof weights. Medium thin bags, 120 gauge, can be used for short-term storage. If you have any doubts about the thickness of a bag, you would be wise to put one bag inside another. Thicker 200 gauge bags give extra strength where products are being moved frequently within the freezer. Polythene bags can, if you are careful, be washed and re-used, but it would be best to sterilise in the kind of solution used for baby's bottles.

While the polythene bag is perfectly suited to the storage of, say, a ready-prepared quantity of breadcrumbs or sliced onions or home-grown gooseberries, more thought needs to be given to the freezing of cooked dishes .

The experienced freezer cook generally finds that she collects and uses – and re-uses – more and more **rigid plastic containers** as the years go by. The cash outlay is greater but the main advantages go on for much longer – the best part being that rigid plastic is stackable, therefore saving freezer space, especially when you are using plastic boxes that are square or oblong.

Rigid plastic containers come in a wide range of shapes and sizes including fancy moulds

The firmer the plastic, the better the seal. If you buy the cheaper, flimsier plastic boxes (or use empty ice-cream containers, for instance) you should check the seal by squeezing the closed container to see if air puffs out around the lid – and be prepared to overseal with freezer tape if necessary.

Some containers can also be bought with coloured lids, useful if you are systematic enough to follow a colour-coding system. This is usually red for meat, green for vegetables, blue for fish, orange for fruit, yellow for pastries. There are also some plastic containers available in various fancy shapes – eg ring moulds, jelly moulds – and are worth considering if you make many savouries or cold desserts like those on pages 66, 178 and 193.

Plastic containers are quicker and easier to label than are polythene bags. You can use a waxy crayon or chinagraph pencil to write on the sides or lids of boxes, washing the writing away when you re-use.

A more recent advantage of the rigid plastic container is the fact that it can also, in many cases, be used in a microwave oven. If you possess a microwave and wish to defrost and reheat, say, a stew, you can do so from frozen, still in its plastic box, in a matter of minutes, then pour the stew into a prewarmed dish for taking to the table. But before using any plastic container in the microwave test it by putting it in, empty, on 'high' for 15–20 seconds. If the container feels warm or is distorted don't cook or heat in it.

Foil is another 'indispensible' in the freezer cook's packaging repertoire. In many instances you can heat frozen food through without even unwrapping (though *not* in the microwave). A frozen loaf, foil wrapped, thaws in a low oven in 45 minutes.

Some cooks like to use foil to 'line out' a china or glass dish in which a pudding is being prepared (see page 260). The dish is then frozen solid and the foil-plus-pudding is lifted out and over-wrapped as a frozen parcel which can be 'peeled' later, while still frozen, and slipped back into its original dish for thawing and serving. The same kind of lining-out method is sometimes recommended when a cooked recipe like a stew is being made in ovenware that you might not want to keep out-of-use in the freezer. We find that this can be tricky if at any stage it is necessary to stir the stew, for the foil can easily be torn, the

A frozen stew can be dipped in hot water to 'unmould', then wrapped in foil

liquid seeping between foil and dish so that it is hard to turn out even after freezing. Probably an easier method of 'foil wrapping' a casserole recipe is to allow the dish to cool, then place it in the freezer until solid. Remove from freezer and dip the dish into hot water just long enough to loosen; turn the frozen food out, like turning out a jelly, on to a sheet of foil large enough to allow you to wrap it round closely.

Another use for foil (which in our experience is best bought in freezer rather than household weight, and in the largest possible economy size) is that of making 'lids' for any dish without needing any further closures.

Some **foil dishes** are very handy to have. If you choose the kind with smooth rather than ridged sides they can even be re-used if handled with care. You can freeze them and cook straight from the freezer; they can also be very useful for batch baking. Foil dishes need to be covered in the freezer; some come with foil-lined lids or white card on which you can write. Others can be overwrapped with foil or popped into a polythene bag. Again, these dishes must not be used in a microwave oven. And it may be worth noting that some acidic fruits may cause a foil dish to 'pit' during freezing.

Clear film, now available in freezer-weight, usually comes in rolls like foil and has the advantage of being completely transparent. You cannot use it for cooking except in a microwave oven, unless it is the kind of film labelled 'roasting bag'. The best and handiest is the giant-size of freezer film in a cutter box with a serrated edge. Clear film is, we think, most useful for the close-wrapping of small items; eg, slices of cake for a picnic can be wrapped individually and transported still frozen to thaw safely en route. We also find crumpled clear film is useful for holding down fruits that might discolour if allowed to surface from a syrup in which they are being frozen. (For this purpose crumpled Cellophane is possibly better, because slightly bulkier, but we find that it is usually not to be found when you want it!).

For use in the wrapping of larger items – a joint of meat for instance – you may find that the edges of the film tend to 'lift' in the cold air of your freezer and may need to be secured with a small piece of freezer tape.

Boiling bags are like polythene bags but are specially heat-treated so that you can take them from the freezer and drop them (still twist-tied

Use crumpled clear film to keep fruits submerged in sugar syrup

at the neck) into boiling water to thaw and re-heat. More expensive than plain polythene, but they are ideal for soups, sauces, purées, curries, stews, provided the food doesn't contain sharp bones that might pierce the bag. Especially useful perhaps for milk-based sauces, where heating from frozen can be especially tricky, needing careful watching in the pan if it is not to 'catch'. What's more, no messy washing up of pans!

Boiling bags can be reheated in the microwave oven, but should be stood in a bowl and the bag pierced once or twice with scissors, as they have been known to 'explode' when the contents are rapidly heated.

Interleaving sheets are a form of packaging that should perhaps be more accurately described as 'inner wrapping'. They are small sheets of grease-and-moisture proof paper that are useful to stop foods sticking to one another when frozen – chops for instance – and can make packing and unpacking much easier. You can, of course, substitute cut-up polythene or foil or clear film if you want to avoid yet another packaging buy.

Toughened ceramic – eg Pyrosil – can go straight from freezer to oven or cooker top. Do not confuse this kind of toughening with the cheaper ovenproofing: it should be clearly stated on the label of the dish or plate. Generally these ceramics are too expensive (and heavy) for long-term storage in the freezer, but they can still be useful for a dinner party dish prepared, say, a week ahead to go from freezer to oven to table.

Glass containers can sometimes be used for freezing cold foods though we don't feel that it is really to be recommended. Test a glass container first by freezing overnight, empty, in a bag. We have found that they can shatter for no apparent reason, even if they have safely been frozen before – a kind of 'fatigue' affects them, so that it is always safest to enclose glass containers in a bag in case of accidents. Milk bottles have a high 'fatigue' record, incidentally.

Labels. We know some clever freezer owners manage to remember their frozen goods by shape alone and by where they're put in the freezer. But unless you're a very organised person in sole control of the freezer it's better to label.

Re-usable plastic labels are good for frequently used foods; wired-paper tags with attached 'flag' labels can work well for bags. Some polythene bags come with opaque panels on which you can

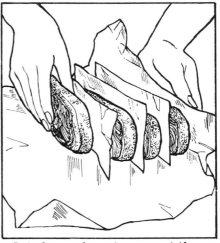

Interleave chops to prevent them sticking together when frozen

write: if you prefer these, remember to write on the bag before you fill it. Use waxy crayon or *oil*-based felt tip, because ordinary pencil or ink will run when it becomes even slightly frosted. Keep your label-writing tool, be it crayon or pen, firmly anchored somewhere near the freezer.

Freezer tape is useful in that the ordinary sticky tape will not usually stick at sub-zero temperatures. It can be bought in reels, also with one of the 'butcher's machines' that automatically tapes-and-seals the twisted necks of polythene bags. These machines do ensure a completely effective seal if you don't mind the fact that you cannot re-use the bags.

FREEZER EXTRAS

Freezer baskets are ideal for keeping a chest freezer in some semblance of order. If you group foods of one type together in each basket you won't need to scrabble through the whole freezer whenever you want something. They are available, made-to-measure, and supplied by mail order. Look for manufacturers' advertisements in cookery magazines.

Freezer trays. You can use baking sheets, roasting tins or tea trays. If you prefer to invest in special stacking trays (by mail order as above) you can choose from two types: the wire mesh kind or the less expensive lightweight toughened plastic.

Autosealers are electrically-operated heat sealers and come with a roll of seamless plastic to make your own bags. With some machines you can buy heat-resistant plastic sheeting to make your own boiling bags to whatever size you like. This is really rather in the 'kitchen equipment' range, especially in financial outlay and is mainly useful for those who wish to make their own well-sealed (but not re-usable) polythene bags. You'll need kitchen wallspace if you're thinking in terms of a wall-mounted version, plus storage space for the rolls of plastic.

Shape purées, soups and sauces into 'bricks'. Pour into a polythene bag standing in a box. When frozen remove from box, seal and stack in freezer

MENUS FROM THE FREEZER

Relax and enjoy your parties by planning and freezing the meal weeks ahead of the day.

On the following ten pages are over a hundred menus, all made with recipes that are in this book. (A quick check in the index will tell you exactly where; the only recipes you won't find are the obvious ones – like vegetables – or the simple ones, like salads.)

Some of the menus are planned to provide luxury meals (pp 274-275) and an equal number are designed for the times when the budget dictates something less expensive (pp 276-277). If you want a meal that is somewhere 'in between' take a look at our hot weather/cold weather range (p 283).

And when you've worked your way through these you can try your own combinations of courses. Just remember to keep a balance of rich and plain, spicy and bland. No one wants a thick soup followed by a richly sauced meat dish followed by a creamy mousse. Contrast and complement flavours and textures and try to include something fresh: a seasonal vegetable, a crisp green salad, a selection of fresh fruit.

There will probably be occasions when you want a meal of only two courses. Our selection (pp 282-283) provides a choice. You can have 'starter and main course only' perhaps following this with fresh fruit, cheese, coffee. Or pick a main-course-plus-pudding menu – particularly suitable when you are serving 'nibbles' with drinks before the meal.

When you want guests to serve themselves from a buffet – see our suggestions (pp 283) that are geared to either hot or cold weather.

When freezing away your menus, don't forget the garnishes you'll be needing. You can freeze croûtons for your soups, butter pats for bread rolls, chopped herbs or herb butters for the final touch to a dish of plainly cooked vegetables. Add a large bag of ice cubes, a container of lemon slices – for the extra drinks you'll be serving.

Almond Soup

Savannah Duckling
Petits Pois
Buttered Courgettes
New Potatoes

Coupelles
with raspberries and
whipped cream

Pisto
with Fancy Bread Rolls

Jellied Beef
Rice salad
Mangetout Peas

Honey and Walnut Tart

Melon and Grapes in
Port

Covert Pie
Creamed Potatoes
Brussels Sprouts *or*
Braised Red Cabbage

Rum Babas

Duck and Liver Terrine
with toast

Trout with Orange
New Potatoes
Mixed Green Salad

Kirsch Cake

Luxury Dinner Menus

Asparagus Flan

Prawn Creole
Brown Rice
Mixed Green Salad

Tipsy Cake

Smoked Mackerel
Quiche

Pheasant with Apple
Creamed Potatoes
Brussels Sprouts
Grilled Mushrooms

Honey and Brandy
Ice Cream
with Cigarettes Russes

Green Pea Soup
with Melba Toast

Salmon Kulibyaki
Cucumber Salad
Tomato Salad

Hazelnut Meringue
with Peaches

Leeks à la Grecque
with French bread

Seafood vol-au-vent
New Potatoes
Petits Pois

Fruit Savarin
with cream

Chicken Layer Pâté
with French bread

Burgundy Beef
Creamed Potatoes
Buttered Carrots

Sherry Trifle

Sprout and Hazelnut
Soup with croûtons

Duckling with Apricot
and Sherry Sauce
Croquette Potatoes
Broccoli Spears

Christmas Snowball

Broccoli Soup
with Parmesan cheese

Lamb Reform
Potatoes
Creamed or Leaf
Spinach

Honey and Brandy
Ice Cream
with Viennese Biscuits

Sorrel Soup

Plaice with Mushrooms
and Prawns
New Potatoes
Mangetout Peas

Linzer Torte

Individual Cheese
Soufflés

Pigeon, Sausage and
Mushroom Pie
Jacket Potatoes
Braised Celery

Hazelnut Meringue
with Peaches

Asparagus Flan

Veal Roll with Spinach
Cucumber Salad
Potato Salad

Cherries Jubilee

Ham and Tongue
Mousse

Pheasant with Apple
Creamed Potatoes
Braised Celery

Cherry Frangipane

Mushroom Broth
with Melba Toast

Game Pudding
Creamed Potatoes
Brussels Sprouts
Braised Celery

Biscuit Tortoni

Potted Pigeon
with toast

Apricot Stuffed Lamb
Roast Potatoes
Buttered Courgettes

Chocolate Brandy Roll

Taramasalata
with toast

Civet of Venison
Potatoes
Braised Red Cabbage
or
Cauliflower Florets

Coffee Nut Roll

Smoked Haddock Shells

Beef Carbonnade
Cauliflower
Pisto

Apricot Suèdoise

Goujons of Plaice
with Paprika Dip

Pepper Stuffed Pork
Dwarf French Beans
Buttered Carrots

Linzer Torte

Mushroom Broth
with Melba toast

Crab Mousse
New Potatoes
Petits Pois
Green Salad

Coupelles
with ice cream and
strawberries

Vichyssoise

Plaice Florentine
Minted New Potatoes
Tomato Salad
with French dressing
and chives

·French Apple Flan
with whipped cream

Leeks à la Grecque

Rosemary Lamb
Cobbler
Carrots
Buttered Cabbage

West Country Pancakes
with whipped cream

Spinach and
Cottage Cheese Flan

Kidneys Turbigo
Rice
Buttered Carrots
Minted Peas

Apricot Suèdoise

Chilled Vegetable
Soup

Hunter's Rabbit
Buttered Cabbage
Creamed Potatoes

West Country Pancakes
with whipped cream

Inexpensive Dinner Menus

Curried Parsnip Soup
with croûtons

Beef Carbonnade
Buttered Noodles
Brussels Sprouts

Spicy Plum Pie
with thick pouring
cream

Tomato and
Cheese Tart

Lamb Reform
Broad Beans
New Potatoes

Apricot Suèdoise

Carrot and Coriander
Soup with croûtons

Liver Stroganoff
Boiled Rice
Dwarf French Beans

Rhubarb Ice with
Ginger Crunch

Country Pâté
with French bread or
Melba toast

Savoury Baked Fish
Leaf Spinach
Buttered New Potatoes

Pears in Cider
with Shortbread

Leeks à la Grecque

Daube of Lamb
Jacket Potatoes
Green Salad
with French Dressing

Spicy Plum Pie
with thick pouring
cream

Individual Onion Flans

Pork Escallopes
Buttered Noodles
Creamed Spinach

Pineapple Yogurt Ice
with Cigarettes Russes

Taramasalata
with French bread

Chicken Bonne Femme
Cauliflower Florets

Coffee Gâteau

Devilled Sardine Pâté
with toast

Stuffed Beef Rolls
with Mushroom Sauce
Duchesse Potatoes
Broccoli Spears

Oldbury Tarts
with whipped cream

Sweetcorn Soup
with
croûtons

Turkey Fricasseé
Creamed Potatoes
Leaf or
Creamed Spinach

Pears in Cider

Rillettes
with French bread or
Fancy Bread Rolls

Sherried Kidneys
with Pâté
Rice
Tomato Salad

Lemon Cream Pie

Sweetcorn Soup

Ham and
Parsley Mould
Potatoes
Tomato Salad

Toffee Apple Pudding

Individual Onion Flans

Beef Goulash
Noodles
Green Salad

Pears in Cider

Kipper Pâté

Lambs' Tongues in
Orange Sauce
Creamed Potatoes
Leaf Spinach

Coffee Gâteau

Rillettes
with French bread

Crispy Chicken
with Celery Sauce
Croquette Potatoes
Runner Beans

Fruity Ginger Roll

Pisto
with hot Fancy Bread
Rolls

Lamb in Dill Sauce
Broad Beans
Duchesse Potatoes

Blackberry and Apple
Cream with Tuiles

Kipper Pâté
with toast

Chicken Surprise
Grilled Mushrooms
French Green Beans
New Potatoes

Fruit Compote
with Old-fashioned
Sponge

Broccoli Soup
with croûtons

Spicy Pork Chops
Noodles
Peas

Gooseberry Charlotte
with whipped cream

Summer Soup

Veal Roll with Spinach
Cucumber Salad
Potato Salad

Coffee Gâteau

Green Pea Soup
with Melba Toast

Plaice with Mushrooms
and Prawns
New Potatoes
Green Salad

Summer Pudding
with whipped cream

Crab Mousse
with brown bread and
butter

Osso Buco
Saffron Rice
Green Salad

Cherries Jubilee

Hummus
with Pitta Bread

Chicken Surprise
New Potatoes
Grilled Mushrooms
Dwarf French Beans

Apricot Suèdoise

Hot Weather Menus

Sorrel Soup
with Suffolk Rusks

Pepper Stuffed Pork
Tomato and
Onion Salad
Green Salad

Linzer Torte

Courgettes Ragoût

Ham and Parsley Mould
Rice Salad
Dwarf French Beans

Paris Brest
with raspberries

Pissaladière

Chicken in
Lemon Sauce
Rice
Baby Carrots
Peas

Fruit Compote
with nutty Shortbread

Vichyssoise

Lamb Cutlets en Croûte
Potatoes
Broccoli Spears
Buttered Carrots

Hazelnut Meringue
with Peaches

Mackerel with
Breton Sauce

Kidneys Genièvre
Duchesse Potatoes
Broad Beans

Summer Pudding
with whipped cream

Chilled Vegetable Soup

Plaice Florentine
Duchesse Potatoes
Baked Tomatoes

Gooseberry Charlotte
with thick pouring
cream

Chicken Layer Pâté
with toast or hot
Fancy Bread Rolls

Seafood Vol-au-vent
New Potatoes
Petits Pois

Rhubarb Ice with
Ginger Crunch

Vichyssoise

Jellied Beef
New Potatoes
Mixed Green Salad

Coupelles
with ice cream and
fresh peaches

Individual Cheese
Soufflés

Trout with Orange
Sauté Potatoes
Buttered Courgettes

Cherries Jubilee

Smoked Mackerel
Quiche

Lamb Reform
New Potatoes
Green Salad

Strawberry Charlotte

Cucumber and
Yogurt Soup

Liver Stroganoff
Rice
Petits Pois

Strawberry Charlotte

Pisto

Chicken and Ham Pie
New Potatoes
Tomato and Onion Salad

Blackcurrant Sorbet

Taramasalata
with Pitta Bread

Duckling with Apricot
and Sherry Sauce
New Potatoes
Buttered Courgettes

Coffee Granita

Plum Soup

Lamb Reform
Croquette Potatoes
Cauliflower Florets

Biscuit Tortoni

Spinach and
Cottage Cheese Flan

Sherried Kidneys
with Pâté
Rice
Tomato Salad

Caramel and Hazelnut
Ice Cream with Tuiles

Rillettes
with French bread

Chicken Bonne Femme
Mangetout Peas
Buttered Courgettes

Oldbury Tarts
with whipped cream

Mackerel with
Breton Sauce

Spanish Chicken
Rice
Dwarf French Beans

Blackcurrant Sorbet
Cigarettes Russes

Carrot and Coriander
Soup with Suffolk Rusks

Stuffed Beef Rolls
with Mushroom Sauce
Braised Leeks
Potatoes

Hungarian Apple Pie
with whipped cream

Hummus
with Pitta Bread

Chicken in Fruit Sauce
Rice
Brussels Sprouts

Choux Buns
with cream and
chocolate sauce

Curried Parsnip Soup
with croûtons

Rosemary Lamb
Cobbler
Potatoes
Braised Leeks

Blackberry and
Apple Cream
with shortbread

Individual Onion Flans

Braised Oxtail
Creamed Potatoes
Buttered Cabbage

Continental Cheesecake

Cold Weather Menus

Spinach and
Cottage Cheese Flan

Hunter's Rabbit
Jacket Potatoes
Cauliflower Florets

Tipsy Cake

Sprout and Hazelnut
Soup with croûtons

Venison Pasty
Creamed Potatoes
Carrots

Sherry Trifle

Watercress and
Chicken Soup
with Melba Toast

Lambs' Tongues in
Orange Sauce
Creamed Potatoes
Brussels Sprouts

Pears in Cider
with nutty Shortbread

Devilled Sardine Pâté
with toast

Beef Carbonnade
Potatoes
Cauliflower Florets

Rice Cream
with Oranges

Mushroom Broth
with Melba Toast

Jugged Hare
Jacket Potatoes
Braised Red Cabbage

Spicy Plum Pie
with thick pouring
cream

Stuffed Aubergines

Lamb in Dill Sauce
Potatoes
Buttered Carrots

Spicy Pudding with
Butterscotch Sauce

Stuffed Aubergines

Chicken Korma
Rice
Dwarf French Beans

Pineapple Yogurt Ice
with Tuiles

Broccoli Soup
with Parmesan cheese

Scalloped Fish
Creamed Potatoes
Leaf Spinach
Baked Tomatoes

West Country Pancakes
with whipped cream

Pisto
with Fancy Bread Rolls

Sherried Kidneys
with Pâté
Duchesse Potatoes
Braised Leeks

Toffee Apple Pudding

Sprout and Hazelnut
Soup with croûtons

Pigeon, Sausage and
Mushroom Pie
Duchesse Potatoes
Braised Red Cabbage

Chocolate Almond Cake

Leeks à la Grecque

Daube of Lamb
Jacket Potatoes
Brussels Sprouts

Chocolate Pear
Pudding

Gnocchi

Pigeon Casserole
Croquette Potatoes
Braised Celery

Fruity Ginger Roll

Potted Pigeon
with French bread

Savoury Baked Fish
Creamed Spinach
Potatoes

Spicy Pudding with
Butterscotch Sauce

Smoked Haddock Shells

Apricot Stuffed Lamb
Roast Potatoes
Roast Parsnips
Brussels Sprouts

Pears in Cider

Stuffed Peppers

Daube of Lamb
Potatoes
Cole Slaw Salad

Sherry Trifle

Mushroom Broth
with Melba Toast

Gammon with
Pineapple and
Green Pepper Sauce
Creamed Potatoes
Leaf Spinach

Spicy Pudding with
Butterscotch Sauce

Carrot and Coriander
Soup with croûtons

Beef Goulash
Noodles
Celery and
White Cabbage Salad

Hungarian Apple Pie
with whipped cream

Cod and Corn Pie
Creamed Potatoes
Leaf Spinach

Pineapple Yogurt Ice
with shortbread

Tomato and Cheese Tart

Pork Escallopes
Cucumber Salad
Sauté Potatoes

Ham and
Tongue Mousse
Fancy Bread Rolls
and butter
Green Salad

Rhubarb and
Lemon Flan

Gammon with
Green Pepper and
Pineapple Sauce
Croquette Potatoes
Broccoli Spears

Chocolate Almond Cake

Two-course Lunch Menus

Moussaka
Cucumber, yogurt and
mint salad

Melon Granita

Chicken and Ham Pie
Mixed Salad

Chocolate Pear Pudding

Sweet/Sour Cabbage
with Sausage
Jacket Potatoes

Caramel and Hazelnut
Ice Cream
with Shortbread

Beef Goulash
Noodles
Mixed Green Salad

Rhubarb Ice
with Ginger Crunch

Rabbit and Pepper Pie
Creamed Potatoes
Buttered Cabbage

Pears in Cider

Liver Stroganoff
Rice
Green Salad

Gooseberry Charlotte
with whipped cream

Sweetcorn Soup

Rabbit and Pepper Pie
Duchesse Potatoes
Cauliflower

Pork Fricassée
Noodles
Buttered Carrots

Chocolate Pear Pudding

Smoked Fish Pie
Carrot Salad

Raspberry Granita

Turkey Tetrazzini
Cole Slaw

Pears in Cider

Rabbit with Mustard
Broad Beans
New Potatoes

Continental Cheesecake

Cold Weather Buffets

Turkey Tetrazinni *or*
Smoked Fish Pie

Carrot Salad
Cole Slaw with Celery

Blackberry and
Apple Cream
Choux Buns with cream
and Chocolate Sauce

Nasi Goreng *or*
Prawn Creole

Red and White
Cabbage Salad
Chicory and
Watercress Salad

St. Clements Soufflé
Pears in Cider
Tuiles

Hot Weather Buffets

Asparagus Flan

Jellied Beef *or*
Cold Stuffed Veal Roll
Tomato Salad
Carrot and
Cucumber Salad
Pisto

Summer Pudding
Chocolate Brandy Roll

Ham and Parsley Mould
or
Chicken and Ham Pie

Mixed Green Salad
Cucumber and
Yogurt Salad

Strawberry Charlotte
Hazelnut Meringue
with Peaches

GLOSSARY OF FREEZING TERMS

The language of freezing includes some important words and phrases that are worth understanding

Ascorbic Acid This is Vitamin C, a synthetic form of which can be bought from the chemist. It is added to cold sugar syrup before pouring over 'pale' fruits such as apricots and peaches to help retain their colour. Add a $\frac{1}{4}$ teaspoon [1.25 ml] ascorbic acid to each pint (550 ml) sugar syrup. It can be bought in crystal or tablet form.

Blanching Vegetables, and some fruits are best if blanched before freezing. This is a process of immersing the food into rapidly boiling water. Blanching this way will stop enzyme action that would eventually cause loss of flavour, colour and nutritional value in storage. Bring a large pan of water to the boil – not less than 8 pints [4.5 l] water to 1 lb [450 g] vegetables – plunge the prepared vegetables in and time them from the moment the water returns to the boil, which shouldn't take more than 1 minute. Timing is important. If the vegetables are in the water too long they'll emerge mushy after their final cooking. When blanching time is up, plunge the vegetables immediately into ice cold water to stop them cooking and cool them. Drain and pack.

Blanching times: use a standard dictionary of freezing to find exact blanching times for all fruit and vegetables. As a general guide, the smaller and lighter-in-texture the produce, the shorter the blanching time; for instance peas, sliced green beans, sliced courgettes should be blanched for 1 minute only, broad beans take 2 minutes, thin stalks of broccoli 3 minutes and thicker stalks 4 minutes. Large corn on the cob may take as long as 8 minutes.

Cross flavouring If foods aren't carefully wrapped the flavour of one food can be picked up by another. The foods most likely to spread themselves are curries, smoked fish, onions, garlic. It is a good idea not only to wrap these foods closely but to overwrap them as well.

Dehydration This is the removal of moisture from food and occurs if it hasn't been properly wrapped. Meat particularly can become dry, tough and tasteless.

Drip loss The loss of food's natural juices, particularly from meat, during thawing. The drip loss is likely to be greater if the food was frozen slowly. Freezing quickly and thawing slowly minimises drip loss.

Dry pack This refers to the packing of fruit without either sugar or sugar syrup and is particularly suited to soft fruits such as strawberries and raspberries.

Dry Sugar pack This means to pack fruit in dry sugar. As it thaws the fruit and sugar combine to make a delicious syrup.

Enzymes These are naturally occurring substances present in all foodstuffs. They're not poisonous but they will, in the long run, bring about undesirable changes such as loss of flavour and colour. The blanching of vegetables (and some fruits) before freezing halts this action while the freezing process itself slows down the activity in other foods.

Fast Freezing The flavour and texture of food will be better if fast frozen, so about 2 hours before freezing fresh or freshly cooked foods, turn on the fast freeze switch. This will stop the thermostat coming into action and the freezer temperature will keep dropping to at least —28° C or whatever is the lowest temperature your particular freezer can achieve. When it reaches that temperature put in your cooled fresh food. Keep the fast freeze switch on until the food is frozen. For amounts under 1 lb (450g) the fast freeze switch is not necessary.

Freezer Burn If you've ever taken a piece of meat or poultry out of the freezer and discovered greyish white marks on the surface, that's freezer burn. You'll probably find the meat tough and dry when cooked. The marks are caused by dehydration and can be avoided by careful wrapping to exclude air.

Free flow If fruits and vegetables are spread out on a tray and frozen uncovered in large quantities, then packed into a polythene bag, they will remain separate and freeflowing. It is easy then just to tip out the amount you need, then return the remainder in the bag to the freezer.

Headspace When you are freezing soups, sauces, fruits in syrup, etc., you must leave a little space between the top of the contents and the lid. Liquid expands when frozen and if a carton is filled to the top the lid will be forced off in the freezer.

Interleaving The use of pieces of paper or foil between pieces of food to allow easy separation.

Oxidation This is the absorption of oxygen into the fat cells which occurs if food isn't wrapped correctly. It gives food an unpleasant flavour and smell.

Open freezing Fruit and vegetables are spread out on trays and put in the freezer, uncovered, until hard; they then become free flow. Open freezing can also be used for iced cakes and decorated desserts, so that the decoration isn't damaged when being wrapped.

Rancidity The effect of the absorption of oxygen into fat cells. All fatty meats and fish are particularly subject to rancidity, hence their short freezer life.

Syrup pack This is the packing of fruits in sugar syrup. To make a medium syrup dissolve 8 oz (225g) sugar in 1 pint [550 ml] water; for heavy syrup use 1lb [450 g] of sugar to 1 pint [550 ml] of water. Always add cold syrup to fruit and see that it covers it completely.

Temperature For the normal storage of frozen food the temperature inside your freezer should be about 0 deg. F (—18 deg. C). It is important that this temperature should not be raised because the quality of the food will suffer. (See 'fast freezing'.)

Thawing Not all foods need to be thawed before cooking. Vegetables are much tastier if they are cooked from frozen. Fruit and meat: thaw or cook from frozen. Poultry: thaw completely before cooking. The thawing of some foods can be speeded up if necessary but on the whole it is better to thaw slowly – in the wrappings – in the fridge.